Flats" — one of the happiest nights
in my life

Ben Welstin. Una Venning

Lilian Braithwaite

Arthur E. Sisson

?

George Byrne

S. Stewart-T.

Adrianne Allen.

Raymond Massey

Eddie Marsh

D1126135

IVOR

IVOR

SANDY WILSON

MICHAEL JOSEPH

First published in Great Britain by
Michael Joseph Ltd
52 Bedford Square
London WC1B 3EF
1975

ISBN 0 7181 1408 6

Designer: Crispin Fisher
Picture research: Mary Anne Norbury
Filmset in Photon Univers 10 on 12 pt by
Richard Clay (The Chaucer Press) Ltd, Bungay, Suffolk
and printed in Great Britain by
Fletcher and Son Ltd, Norwich

CONTENTS

The author wishes to thank the following for their help:

Robert Andrews
Maidie Andrews
Sir Felix Aylmer
Lady Aylmer
Jennifer Aylmer
Sir Michael Balcon
Dorothy Batley
Roma Beaumont
Joan Benham
Mrs Jane Brunel
Christopher Brunel
Joyce Carey
John Counsell
Dame Cicely Courtneidge
Joan Crawford
Zena Dare
Dorothy Dickson
Adrian Edwards
Gwen Ffrangcon-Davies
Olive Gilbert
Peter Graves
Binnie Hale
Irene Handl
Haro Hodson
Teddy Holmes
Isabel Jeans
Michael Kennedy
Collie Knox
Vanessa Lee
Raymond Mander and Joe Mitchenson
Betty Marsden
Murray MacDonald
Alan Melville

Phyllis Monkman
John Morley
Winifred Newman
Anthony Nicholls
Beverly Nichols
Maureen O'Sullivan
Anne Pinder
Mabel Poulton
Joan Rees
Cyril Ritchard
Alec Robertson
June Rose
Graham Samuel
Barry Sinclair
Heather Thatcher
Dame Sybil Thorndike
Geoffrey Toone
Roland Wade
Elisabeth Welch
Peter Willes

The British Film Institute
The British Theatre Association
The British Museum Newspaper Library
The Theatre Museum of the Victoria and Albert Museum
The Library and Museum of the Performing Arts, New
    York Public Library at Lincoln Centre
Boosey and Hawkes Ltd
Chappell and Co
Samuel French Ltd

The author wishes to make particular acknowledgement of
the help, advice and encouragement given by Mary Ellis and
Gordon Duttson

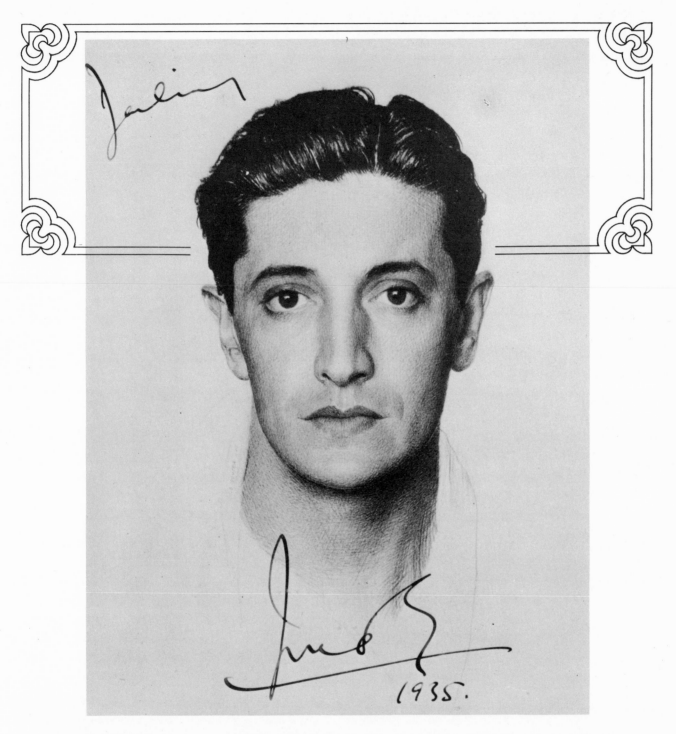

1935.

He was beautiful. And he was a darling. However opinions may differ about his other attributes, on these two there is total agreement: his good looks, and his good nature.

The good looks were almost, in the words of Beverly Nichols, 'too good to be true, with the impeccable nose, the raven locks, the huge eyes, the chiselled lips and all that neck'. They embodied, in one face, all the romantic ideals of his age: the Latin Lover, the Sheik of Araby and the Vagabond Gypsy. And they also possessed, in the modelling of the mouth and the flare of the nostrils, a dash of the Byronic aristocrat combined with the more aesthetic breed of Royalty—Ludwig of Bavaria, say, or Richard of Bordeaux.

To whom did he owe them? His mother quite naturally claimed them for her side of the family, asserting in her autobiography that her father's 'shining black curls, handsome flashing eyes and olive complexion bore out the suggestion that in Wales there is to be found a strong Spanish strain, whose ancestry on the distaff side', she coyly adds, 'apparently extended a most cordial welcome to the rescued members of the ill-fated Spanish Armada.' But all those who knew Ivor's father as a younger man say that his son's resemblance to him was unmistakable, and when, in his play *Proscenium*, Ivor made himself up as a grey-haired officer with a moustache, there was no gainsaying from whom he inherited the face that was to be, if not his entire fortune, at least a large part of it. And it was in his face that his physical appeal lay. The rest of him was unremarkable: narrow shoulders, an undeveloped chest, wide hips, presentable legs but rather large feet, and height some inches below the six foot ideal. But unlike the male heart-throbs of today, who rely on their physique to the extent of exposing as much of it as they may as often as possible, Ivor projected his magnetism from the neck up. A glance from those eyes, a glimpse of that profile was enough to excite the yearnings of a multitude of feminine hearts.

But if he was an object of passionate adoration to millions of fans, he was also, for those who knew him and worked with him, the most genuinely *loved* man of the Theatre of his, or perhaps any other, age. Seeking to assess his character, one is overwhelmed, almost to monotony, by repeated expressions of affection and admiration, all of them totally sincere, until one begins to question if such a paragon of kindness, humility, tact, tolerance and generosity could ever have existed—and in a profession which tries all these virtues to their limit. Where, one wonders, did these bottomless resources of goodness spring from? Adrian Brunel, who directed Ivor in three of his films, supplies a clue. While on location in Austria with *The Constant Nymph*, he and Novello took a stroll together: 'I remember Ivor telling me of the great influence ... that Ernan Forbes-Dennis and his wife, Phyllis Bottome, had on him. He told me of the conscious control ... that he had learned from them. His theory (and theirs?) was that one should always practise a kind and considerate behaviour to everyone, that the "meaningless symbols" of courtesy should be cultivated, that even at the risk of the charge of insincerity one should persevere, for these attitudes gradually influenced one's instinctive actions and one's outlook.' In other words, Ivor worked on his character just as he worked on his other assets, to develop and improve them as instruments of self-fulfilment; and if this sounds calculated, it is the calculation of a man who preferred to make his talents multiply rather than hide them under a bushel.

Were there no flaws in the perfection? Yes, he *could* be angry. He could even lose his temper. There were the times of what Mary Ellis describes as 'the little black beads', when the lustrous eyes became gimlets of fury and the language flowed thick, fast and purple. But it was soon over, and as often as not it was caused by one of the few things Ivor hated: inefficiency. Something else that aroused his anger, particularly if it interfered with work, was drunkenness. The only time that another of his leading ladies, Roma Beaumont, ever saw him behave discourteously was when, at a party, he came face to face with the actor, Robert Newton. 'Hello, Ivor!' said Newton, putting out his hand. 'Don't *ever* expect me to shake hands with you,' replied Ivor and turned away. Some years before, while playing the juvenile in *I Lived With You*, Robert Newton had been drunk onstage with him and it was never forgiven or forgotten.

Ivor himself only drank occasionally; his vices were cigarettes, sixty or more a day, and Nescafé, of which he consumed cup after cup when he was working. He was also an avid, and indiscriminate, film fan. According to some people, including his mother, he could be lazy; but his laziness was apparent rather than actual. He never worked set hours, only when the fancy took him; but since what he fancied most was his work, even away from his piano and his notebook the creative process continued in his mind. His lack of method led to accusations of indiscipline, and here it is appropriate to introduce the man with whom he is often compared and who is sometimes referred to, mistakenly, as his rival. 'If it wasn't Noël, it was usually Ivor,' says the forgetful actress dictating her memoirs, in a revue sketch by Herbert Farjeon. 'I hardly knew which was which.' In fact it would be hard to think of two people less similar than Coward and Novello and, so far from being rivals or even remotely jealous of each other, they had, as Coward described in his autobiography, 'a friendship which has lasted hilariously until now (1937) and shows every indication of enduring through any worlds which may be beyond us, providing that those worlds are as redolent of theatrical jokes and as humorous as this one is'. As is often the case, it is their humour that not only unites them but differentiates between them. Coward's wit sprang from his intellect and produced epigrams of such polish that they will be quoted for years to come; Ivor's relied on a chance concatenation of time, place and personality, to inspire a remark which reduced the whole company to tears of laughter but which seldom improved with repetition. 'He could make that poker funny,' said Zena Dare, 'but I really can't tell you how.' And in the dark moments of his life his humour rarely deserted him. Two of his closest friends, Robert Andrews and Olive Gilbert, went to fetch him at dead of night from Wormwood Scrubs, where he had been serving a four week sentence for an offence against the war-time transport regulations. They left the car a little way from the prison gates and the chauffeur drove on to collect Ivor. When the car returned, Bobbie and Olive, prepared for a tearful reunion, were greeted by Ivor saying, 'It's just like Marie Antoinette's flight to Varennes!'

Like Noël, Ivor moved with an entourage—'He went around in a *gang*' is how Sybil Thorndike describes it—and, while a few of the courtiers of these two reigning monarchs moved between their territories, those closest to the throne remained the same year after year. For Ivor, it seemed, the company of his friends was not only a comfort and a protection but an emotional necessity, and although he would withdraw from them at any moment of the day or night if his work called him, he would rely on them still to be there as companions and as audience when he re-emerged. Even on

On holiday in Jamaica in 1949. (l to r) Noël Coward, Graham Payne, Ivor, Ivor Dennis, Olive Gilbert.

The South African tour of *Perchance to Dream*: Ivor with (l to r) Zena Dare, Roma Beaumont, Robert Andrews and Olive Gilbert.

holiday he would arrange for at least three or four of them to accompany him, at his expense, and it is hard to imagine that he could ever have devoted himself exclusively to one person alone. Throughout his life there were, as was to be expected, constant speculations about whom he was in love with and whom he would marry, and as many theories advanced about why he never did. This is not the place to contribute another. Even today, nearly twenty-five years after his death, it is possible to sense a slight closing of the ranks among the inner circle whenever one approaches too near, as if one were threatening to tear away the mask and reveal some hideous truth. But the apprehension is misplaced. The man, as did Lord George Hell in *The Happy Hypocrite*—Ivor's best rôle, became in the end the mask. The truth about Novello is there for all to see, in his life and—which comes to the same thing—his work. That *was* Ivor. There was nothing else.

2

From the day he was born Ivor was influenced, though never dominated, by women, starting with his mother, Clara Novello Davies. Her great-grandfather was a Revivalist preacher, the Rev. William Evans, a star in his profession, from whom she must have inherited the mixture of evangelism and exhibitionism that was the driving force of her existence. Both her father, Jacob Davies, and her mother, Margaret Evans, were musical: she was named after a diva whom her father had admired when he saw her at the Cardiff Opera House, and she was encouraged from her earliest years to play the piano and sing. While still a child, she acted as accompanist to her father's choir and first met, among its members, the man who was to become her husband, David Davies. In order to pay her school fees when the family's fortunes were failing she gave piano lessons to her fellow pupils and later, at her father's suggestion, took up choral conducting and formed her own choir. She became unofficially engaged to David Davies at the age of fourteen but, owing to her mother's disapproval, he had to wait eight years to marry her. He was, in the words of Bobbie Andrews, 'a darling old peasant', handsome, easy-going and bone lazy. With Clara's assistance he obtained a job in the rent-collecting department of Cardiff City Council, where he would undoubtedly have stayed for the rest of his life had not his wife and son ordained otherwise. He was known to his friends and work-mates as Honest Dave Davies, and in later life he confessed to a journalist, 'I have never had any ambitions. I have been content to enjoy their success.'

Dave and Clara's first child was a daughter, Myvanwy, who died at six weeks. Clara was so distressed by her loss that she swore she would never have another baby and flung herself and her Welsh Ladies' Choir into concerts and choral competitions, winning a reputation as both conductor and singing teacher. One day her dress-maker, while fitting a gown for a visit to London,

Ivor's 'Mam': Mme Clara Novello Davies.

The infant Ivor.

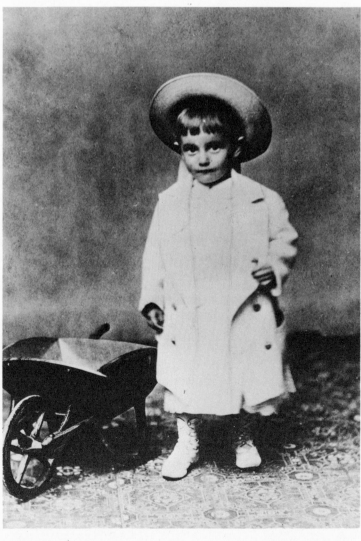

remarked on her increased girth. Clara at first refused to believe her and then, on discovering the woman was right, realised that somehow or other she had become pregnant again. This time, she decided, it would be a boy—but not just any boy: she was the Bride of Heavenly Music and he was to be her Messiah. In her autobiography, *The Life I Have Loved*, a work as flamboyantly romantic as any of her son's operettas, she wrote: 'I would have him made to order, a beautiful "Bubbles" sort of creation, with every gift, especially of music, in his soul.' When the baby arrived, on January the fifteenth 1893, at the Davies' house, Llwyn Yr Eos (Home of the Nightingales), Cowbridge Road, Cardiff, he was indeed a boy, but, to her distress, far from beautiful, with wispy black hair and an enormous nose. That was to be adjusted within a few years; her other requirement was fulfilled in abundance, although she could hardly have realised it at the time. David Ivor Davies, as he was christened, most certainly had the gift of music in his soul.

Within six months of his birth she was off again, this time to the Chicago World's Fair, where her choir won a gold medal, and this was to be the pattern of Ivor's childhood: tearful partings and joyful reunions with a mother who was now a celebrity, the self-styled Madame Clara Novello Davies. Glitteringly caparisoned and coroneted, in striking contrast to her Welsh Ladies' witch hats and aprons, and adorned with as many brooches, bracelets, medals and orders as she could dispose about her person, she wielded her baton tirelessly for any audience who would listen, from crowned heads (including Victoria's, at Osborne) to cow-punchers. Every now and then, even as a baby, Ivor would be snatched up at the last minute to accompany her and when she opened a studio in Maida Vale, in London, she could not resist taking him there for prolonged visits. This was a mistake. To the boy, Ivor, London meant only one thing: the Theatre. Somehow, through heaven knows what alien strain in his character, he had become infected with an addiction that was quite outside her calculations, and to the end of her days she would slightly resent the fact that Theatre, while bringing her son both fame and wealth, had interfered with his true vocation: to make music. When she discovered that his passion for the stage was verging on precocity, she packed him off to friends in Gloucester who were musically inclined and set about obtaining him a place at Magdalen College Choir School in Oxford, for he was developing into a promising boy soprano and nothing but the best would do. At this moment, for the only time in his life, Dave attempted to put his foot down. He wanted Ivor to go into a safe job, in business in Cardiff, and he arranged for the application forms from the Choir School to be 'mislaid'. But Clara found them in the nick of time, Ivor was awarded a scholarship and at the age of ten was whisked off to Oxford by his triumphant 'Mam'.

One of his school-fellows, though several years his senior, was the actor, Felix Aylmer: 'I remember the day that he arrived and we discovered that he already had a remarkable musical talent. We put him on a table and made him sing to us. I don't know whether he and I had similar vocal chords or what, but we always used to get our diseases at the same time of year. So we were constantly in the sick-room together, and when we were convalescing we used to make for the music-room and play duets. I remember him producing the first copy of *The Merry Widow*.' So, despite Mam's precautions, the Theatre still came first with Ivor, and Lily Elsie, Gertie Millar and the Dare Sisters, Zena and Phyllis, were, after his mother, the women he worshipped most in the world. His career as a singer was cut short when his voice broke a few years later, and he was never to sing professionally again, except briefly, for fun, in a 'cod' opera sequence in *Careless Rapture*. But he was already beginning to compose and Clara ensured that he would continue to grow up in a musical atmosphere by employing him as accompanist for her choral concerts and singing classes. One of her pupils was Gwen, the daughter of an old friend, the famous baritone, Ffrangcon-Davies, who attended classes at her new studio in George Street, Hanover Square: 'She was a formidable lady—dynamic, very kind, but adamant. Her great slogan was: No such word as "can't"! She had a curious system of voice

At Magdalen College Choir School, 1903.

In the Royal Naval Air Service, 1916.

production which was to make us beat ourselves on our diaphragms and say "Me-me-me-". One day Ivor came into the studio to play the piano, and we all swooned because he was so attractive.'

In 1910, when he was seventeen, Ivor had his first song published. It was called *Spring of the Year* and he wrote both the music and the words, which he would only do occasionally in future. This was still the period when after-dinner singers would regale the company with *Pale Hands I Loved* and other ballads of an Oriental, Middle Eastern or Medieval flavour, and for the next few years Ivor collaborated successfully with various aspiring imitators of Amy Woodford Findon.

But it took no less an event than the outbreak of war in 1914 to make him famous, literally overnight. The story of the composition of *Till The Boys Come Home* (later known as *Keep The Home Fires Burning*) varies according to who is telling it. But it seems fairly certain that Clara urged him to write a patriotic song and, when he declined, threatened to compose one herself. The result, we are told, was so appalling that Ivor immediately retaliated, as she hoped he would, by improvising the melody that was to become the most popular song of World War One. An acquaintance, the American writer, Lena Guilbert Ford, was summoned to complete the lyric which Ivor had half-written, and the number was first performed by a Miss Sybil Vane at a Sunday night concert at the Alhambra Theatre a few weeks later. Ivor accompanied her, and as he launched into the repeat chorus he heard, to his astonishment, the voices of the audience joining in. A legend had been born.

3

At about this time Ivor had composed his first operetta, entitled *The Fickle Jade*, and if women played a large part in his life, so too did luck, both good and bad. 'You've had a sort of satin-lined career, haven't you?' suggested a lady journalist on his arrival in New York in 1923. 'I have, haven't I?' he agreed, with 'a gracious smile', and up to that point it was certainly true. By the beginning of the Twenties, Ivor had established himself in the London theatre as the composer of highly agreeable melodies for musical comedies such as *Theodore and Co*, *Arlette* and *Who's Hooper?*, and for that new form of entertainment which had gained such popularity during the war, revue. In the latter field he had contributed to *See-Saw, Tabs* and one of André Charlot's greatest successes, *A to Z*. He had also found a permanent home in the heart of the West End, a flat (later to be known as The Flat) above the Strand Theatre at 11, Aldwych, which looked out onto the Gaiety where his first score, *Theodore and Co*, was performed. Here he began to form the nucleus of what later became his 'gang'. A founder member, Viola Tree, the eccentric actress daughter of Sir Herbert Beerbohm Tree, introduced him to one of the few male influences in his life, Edward (Eddie) Marsh, Winston Churchill's private secretary, a connoisseur of extreme sociability and impeccable taste, who, while attemping to be from time to time Ivor's most perceptive critic, was for the rest of his life his most devoted admirer. At a first night Eddie, in his turn, introduced Ivor to a young actor, Robert Andrews, who became his closest friend and—although the term fails to do justice to his mordant wit—Court Jester, who is privileged, when he thinks fit, to puncture His Majesty's self-importance.

Clara had, in the meanwhile, opened another studio in New York, and it was during Ivor's absence there in 1919 that luck intervened again in his career. The French director, Louis Mercanton, was in London looking for a leading man for his new film, *The Call of The Blood*. On a visit to the Daniel Mayer agency, who represented Ivor, he picked up a photograph of a devastatingly handsome youth. 'That's the actor I want!' he exclaimed. 'But he isn't an actor,' he was told. 'He's a composer.' 'Never mind,' insisted Mercanton, 'I want him.' A cable was despatched to the ship on which Ivor was returning from America and by the simple expedient of sending a reply in the affirmative he embarked on his new career as a film star.

It is fascinating to speculate what might have become of Ivor Novello if his screen career had been better handled than it was—fascinating and also alarming, because we might have been deprived of his most important achievement. Fortunately for posterity the state of the British film industry through most of the Twenties was only slightly less precarious than it is today, and, while Ivor's popularity reached gigantic proportions in this country, he was never established as an international star. The nearest he came to it was in 1922 when D. W. Griffith was visiting London and, thanks again to luck, happened to be dining at the Savoy on the same night as Ivor. His companion was the journalist and critic, Hannen Swaffer: ' "Who was that handsome young man?" Griffith said. "What a fine face!" "That's Ivor Novello," I said ... "I'd like to see him," said Griffith. I followed Novello and said, "Griffith would like to see you. Don't worry him for a day or two. Just now he is busy." A delighted smile split Novello's face nearly in two. "I shan't sleep tonight for excitement," he said. "It's a life's dream come true!" ' The dream come true was not, after all, quite what he had hoped for. Griffith brought Ivor to America, but gave him an unsuitable part—an erring ordinand who spends most of the movie in an agony of remorse over his affair with a waitress—in one of his least successful films, *The White Rose*. The Press had announced that Ivor would make seven pictures for Griffith, but the other six never materialised and his Hollywood career came, to all intents and purposes, to a full stop.

But his early success on the screen had also whetted his appetite for the Theatre and he made his début on the West End stage in a small part in *Deburau* at the Ambassadors Theatre in 1921. He followed it with modest achievements as a juvenile lead in *The Yellow Jacket* and *Spanish Lovers* and a spectacular flop, playing a rôle for which he was not equipped either by years or experience in *Enter Kiki*, opposite another of the important women in his life, Gladys Cooper. They had been teamed successfully in the film of *The Bohemian Girl* and so closely linked were they in the public's mind that when Miss Cooper visited New York while Ivor was there in 1923 the Press announced their engagement. Some of those who knew them both at the time consider there was more to the story than just a publicity stunt. 'I think he might have married Gladys,' said a fellow actress, 'but one day when they were sitting down to lunch at her house she said, "Ivor, go and wash your hands," and that was that.' Whatever the truth of the matter, they remained devoted to each other, but ironically the only play of his that they appeared in together, *Flies in the Sun*, was one of his few total failures.

Also in the cast of *The Bohemian Girl* was the classical actress, Constance Collier, whom Ivor had met briefly in New York in 1912, on his way back from Canada, where he had been involved in composing the music for an abortive Pageant of Empire. They met again in London, when he was introduced to her by Fay Compton at a costume ball, and became close friends. Besides being an accomplished Shakespearian, Miss Collier was conversant with every aspect of Theatre and sensed that Ivor might profit from her experience. After his success in Adrian Brunel's fim, *The Man Without Desire*, he had concocted a screenplay for himself to star in as a Parisian apache, with Gladys Cooper playing opposite him in a dual rôle, as a vicious demi-mondaine and an adoring waif. Brunel took an option on the property but was unable to raise backing for the film and the story reverted to Ivor. Constance Collier then suggested that he and she should collaborate on turning it into a stage play. Their nom-de-plume was to be his first Christian name and her married name, David L'Estrange, and the play was to be called *The Rat*.

In Jamaica, with Gladys Cooper and Zena Dare.

In fancy dress at the Albert Hall: Ivor and Fay Compton.

4

'None of our friends believed we were seriously writing ... and going to produce a play,' wrote Constance Collier in her book of memoirs, *Harlequinade*, 'They thought we were mad ... The only bit of sympathy we received during the whole undertaking was from Noël Coward.' For stage purposes it was impossible to double the two female leads; Zélie, the demi-mondaine, was to be played by Madeline Seymour, and the rôle of Odile, the waif, was offered to a young actress fresh from touring the provinces, Dorothy Batley: 'I went to The Flat and I was given some coffee and the scene to look at, and I really didn't think an awful lot of it—it wasn't Bernard Shaw, you know! But I said "Oh, yes!" What else could I have said—to Ivor Novello?' The play opened in January 1924 in Brighton, beset by every portent of disaster. 'Gladys Cooper was there in a box with Noël Coward, and after the first act Ivor rushed into my dressing-room and said, "There's a note from Gladys!" and he read it to me: "It's going well. Keep it up!" ' It was going more than well. Constance Collier, who was acting in *Our Betters* in London, arrived in Brighton by the last train to discover that their mad venture was a triumph. The story was repeated everywhere throughout the tour and in the summer they were offered the Prince of Wales Theatre in London. Madeline Seymour, who had not been happy in her rôle, was replaced by Isabel Jeans, whose feline elegance exactly suited it, and on June 9th *The Rat* opened in the West End to wild applause. With one play Ivor had established himself both as actor and dramatist.

Established himself, that is to say, with the public. With the critics it was a different matter, and this divergence persisted with greater or lesser emphasis until the day he died. There is nothing that arouses the disapproval of an English critic quite so much as early success, and Ivor, at the age of thirty, had succeeded in every field of his endeavour, both as composer, writer, screen actor and stage actor. In none of these capacities was he claiming to be great; he was only trying to be good, and sometimes managing to be excellent. His greatest asset as an actor was his sincerity, and it is apparent even today in a film such as *The Bohemian Girl*, where the rest of the cast, most of them far more experienced than he, flounder about with elaborate gestures and facial expressions, trying to bring conviction to a nonsensical script, while Ivor, by sheer force of feeling, makes one believe.

Another thing that told against him in the critics' eyes was his looks. 'His face was his misfortune,' wrote Phyllis Bottome. 'Ivor was tripped up by his beauty.' This is a little unfair. Ivor himself never relied upon his beauty, but others did, and he was too often cast in romantic rôles which required the kind of sensitivity he did not, as an actor, possess. When he wrote himself the part of Pierre Boucheron, The Rat, he knew what he was doing. The play was turned into a film in 1925 and probably benefited from being silent. Until the end, when he is called upon to display near-hysteria, Ivor's performance is electrifying: with no concessions to glamour, he portrays the apache to the life, tawdry, cocky, conceited and crafty—and full of fun. If producers had capitalised more on the fun in his personality and less on the sex-appeal, he might again have been lost to Hollywood. As it was, he was used in the cinema rather than exploited to his advantage and, with the exception of his two Hitchcock movies and perhaps *The Constant Nymph*, his silent screen career was artistically unprofitable. In any case his heart was, as it always had been, in the Theatre, and in 1928 he wrote his first play single-handed, *The Truth Game*, under the name of H. E. S. Davidson ('He's David's Son').

Now both Ivor's guiding influences, luck and a woman, threatened to turn against him. He had written a leading part for Constance Collier and on the eve of rehearsal she withdrew without explanation. The play was to be directed by Gerald du Maurier, but he also vanished inexplicably. Ellis Jeffreys took on the Collier rôle of Mrs Brandon, but after a few days rehearsal demanded a meeting with Ivor and du Maurier. Lily Elsie, the idol of Ivor's youth, was the star and, impatient to get on with

With Constance Collier at Redroofs, 1946.

Ivor approves a caricature by the Swedish artist, Nerman, 1929.

the job, she burst in on the meeting to discover, to her horror, that not only was Ellis Jeffrey also withdrawing but du Maurier, who had urged Miss Elsie to do the play, had never even read it. In a fury of loyalty to Ivor, she announced that they would find the best actress in London to play Mrs Brandon. She turned out to be perhaps not the best, but certainly an inspired choice: Lilian Braithwaite, whose air of acidulated graciousness was to adorn Ivor's plays for the next decade. *The Truth Game*, under the direction of Marie Tempest's husband, W. Graham Browne, finally opened at the Globe Theatre and was a hit. From then on Ivor would have no trouble finding a theatre for his plays, and the programme would read: 'by Ivor Novello'.

In 1932 three of them, *I Lived With You*, *Party* and *Symphony in Two Flats*, were published in one volume, and Eddie Marsh contributed a preface. 'If he (Ivor) will give himself his due,' he wrote in his final paragraph, 'and put his main reliance on those among his many gifts which distinguish the dramatist from the entertainer, he will surely win a high place in the theatre of his time, and perhaps write a play that will survive it.' But, despite this advice, Ivor failed to see the distinction and none of his plays have survived so far—although it would be interesting to see a revival of *I Lived With You*, if the right actor could be found to play the lead. It was filmed as a talkie in 1933, with several of the stage cast repeating their rôles, and is still extremely funny, while at the same time contriving to suggest the underlying bitterness of class feeling in England's suburbia. In a scene interpolated into

With his parents in the twenties.

Ivor takes Mam to the first night of *Fresh Fields*, 1933.

the movie version, Ivor, as the emigré Russian prince, Felix, is sent upstairs to have a hot bath. Reluctant to subject himself to what he considers an unnecessary ordeal (as was Ivor himself, on occasion, in real life) he supplies all the appropriate noises—splashes, gurgles and a snatch of song—lets out the bath water and emerges triumphantly from the bathroom. It is a delicious solo turn, performed with a mastery that makes one wish, for a moment, that Lubitsch or Capra could have got their hands on him.

Otherwise Ivor's plays were very much products of and for their time. Sumptuously set and costumed, and superbly cast from his stable of thoroughbred actresses—Fay Compton, Zena Dare, Edna Best, Lilian Braithwaite, Isabel Jeans, Heather Thatcher, they gave the public not just what they wanted but what he knew they would appreciate: full value for their money, gift-wrapped, and inscribed 'From Ivor, with Love'.

5

His father died in 1931 while Ivor was in Hollywood, under contract to MGM as a screen-writer. Honest Dave had retired at the earliest opportunity and lived out the rest of his life in the background, a bemused but uncomplaining spectator of the unlikely exploits of his wife and son. Clara continued to

18

With Beatrice Lillie and Robert Andrews at Redroofs, 1947.   L to r: Nat Woolf (Edna Best's husband), Ivor, Ronald Colman, his wife, Benita Hume and Edna Best.

occupy her full share of the foreground and sometimes rather more. 'He was wonderful to her' is the inevitable reply to any inquiry concerning Ivor's relationship to his mother, and wonderful he most certainly was, often, during her bouts of extravagance, intemperance and self-aggrandisement, well beyond the call of duty. But he never betrayed the least sign of anger or irritation with her, even to his friends, and while he sometimes made fun of her pretensions ('Mam ruined more voices than any other teacher in the business,' he once remarked), he never forgot the debt he owed to her single-mindedness, a debt which, in one respect, he had yet to pay. Plays and films were all very well, Mam reiterated, but she had brought her son into the world to compose beautiful music. She was soon to have her wishes fulfilled in abundance.

The Theatre Royal, Drury Lane, is one of London's most imposing theatres; it is also one of the most difficult to run profitably. During the Nineteen Twenties it had been kept solvent by a series of imported American operettas: *Rose Marie*, *The Desert Song* and *Showboat*. In 1930 Noël Coward gave it, in *Cavalcade*, one of the greatest successes of its history. But since then it had housed one flop after another and the board of directors were at their wits' end. One day at lunch the manager, Harry Tennent, was bemoaning Drury Lane's predicament to Ivor. 'Why don't you,' said Ivor on the spur of the moment, 'ask me to write a show for it?' and then proceeded to outline, off the cuff, the story of a musical extravaganza called *Glamorous Night* in which the gypsy mistress of a Ruritanian monarch, who is also a diva, becomes involved with a young Englishman who has invented a new kind of television, and which included, among other events, a performance of grand opera, a Romany wedding, a revolution and a shipwreck. Rather to his surprise, Tennent took him up on his suggestion and asked him to submit a scenario to the board of directors immediately. Ivor could barely remember what he had so impulsively fabricated, but he put it together on paper in record time and it was accepted. In the spring of 1935 *Glamorous Night* went into rehearsal.

The book and music were Ivor's, but as lyric-writer he chose a young man, Christopher Hassall, who was understudying him in his latest play, *Murder in Mayfair*, and who, he discovered, was a much better poet than he was an actor. The other two pillars in this, Ivor's most ambitious structure so far, were, true to his tradition, women. As his director he chose Leontine Sagan, a German who had made an international reputation with both the stage and film versions of *Children in Uniform* and whom he had first employed on *Murder in Mayfair*. As his leading lady he chose an American actress, Mary Ellis, who had starred in opera, drama and musical comedy in her own country and had conquered London in both Jerome Kern's *Music in the Air* and Eugene O'Neill's *Strange Interlude*.

Glamorous Night opened at the Theatre Royal on May 2nd and was, in the words of one critic, 'wildly, inspiringly, intoxicatingly triumphant'. Its story, it was generally agreed, was bosh, but bosh put over with such flare, bravura and, above all, sincerity that it became magnificent. Ivor had fused all three of his rôles—writer, composer and star—into one incandescent whole and made himself, at the age of forty-two, the single most potent personality in the entire British Theatre. At the party at The Flat after the first night, Mary Ellis noticed, across the room, Noël Coward wagging his finger in Ivor's face. 'He was telling him all the things that were wrong with *Glamorous Night*. And Ivor was roaring with laughter.' As well he might.

Now his kingdom was secure, both onstage and off. Besides The Flat he had his country home, Redroofs, where he spent every week-end, working when he felt like it and enjoying the company of his friends. His life and his career were organised and protected by a devoted staff: 'Lloydie' Williams, a childhood friend, who had become his secretary on leaving the Army in 1919, Fred Allen, who had managed first Mam's financial affairs and then Ivor's, Morgan, his chauffeur from the days of *The Rat*, and Bill Wright, his valet and dresser. And always at hand, to advise, encourage and, when necessary, to mock him, was Bobbie Andrews. 'It was a merry gathering from beginning to end,' said Dorothy Dickson, his leading lady in *Careless Rapture*, the show that succeeded *Glamorous Night* at the Lane. 'There was nothing to cross our paths at all.' Even World War Two caused only a temporary halt in Ivor's triumphant progress. His current, and perhaps greatest, success, *The Dancing Years*, had to close, but it reopened on tour within a matter of months and returned to London for a two-year run at the Adelphi.

In the February of 1943 Mam died. Her last grand project, never realised, was to fly her Welsh Ladies' Choir to Berlin and sing Hitler into surrender. After he had recovered from her loss, Ivor confided to Eddie Marsh that he still had 'bad moments, when he remembers that Mam was the only person who thought *everything* he did was perfect. I was struck by his saying it was a good thing to have one such person in one's life, provided it was *only* one.' She had shared fully in her son's many moments of glory; now she would at least be spared having to share in his moment of humiliation. The full story of his conviction and sentence for the illegal use of his car during war-time has been told elsewhere, and to debate the rights and wrongs of it at this remove in time seems fruitless: the authorities decided to make an example of someone prominent and Ivor Novello was the obvious choice. What is more to the point is the effect the whole experience had on Ivor himself. Some say that he put it behind him as soon as he left Wormwood Scrubs, others that it hastened his death. What is certain is that so far from disgracing him in the public's eye, the injustice of it enhanced, if that were possible, his already tremendous popularity. One of his favourite women, Phyllis Monkman, came to support him on the night he returned to the cast of *The Dancing Years*: 'It was the first time I had ever seen Ivor nervous. I said I'd just looked in to say hello. Then Tom Arnold arrived, and I left them and went to the back of the stalls. And of course Ivor walked on and the house came down. There was no need for *me* to be there!' The applause lasted for nearly three minutes.

Ivor has always been firmly associated by the critics with Ruritania; in fact only two of his musicals, the first and the last, took place there. After *Perchance to Dream* he began to write a show set in Wales for his new discovery, Vanessa Lee. Then he changed his mind. The year was 1949: 'We've had so much austerity,' he told her, 'we haven't seen any beautiful things. I think I'm going to do the last of Ruritania, and we can have the lot: Kings and Queens, Princes and Princesses, church music, everything. I shall naturally write a lovely part for myself—for my old age.' He was fifty-six and tired of having to dye his hair—an operation that was performed for him by 'Maison (Olive) Gilbert'. The result was *King's Rhapsody*, and it opened in Manchester on August 25th. After the first night he said to Winifred Newman, his company manager: 'Win, I think I've got my biggest success ever, but, oh dear, I do feel so ill.'

Shortly after the war he had followed Noël Coward's example and bought himself a house in Jamaica. At Christmas 1950, when *King's Rhapsody* had been running for well over a year to packed houses, he flew there for a holiday with a small group of friends, among them Phyllis Monkman: 'I was sitting behind Ivor on the plane, and I looked at the back of his neck. You know that when a man is ill—it doesn't happen to women—his neck gets thin. I looked at Bobbie's and I looked at Ivor's, and I could see the difference.' On his return he insisted, against doctor's orders, on attending the first night of the musical, *Gay's the Word*, which he had written for Cicely Courtneidge with a new collaborator, Alan Melville. Ten days later he returned to the cast of *King's Rhapsody*. The year before he had told a journalist, Elizabeth Frank, how he would prefer to close his career: 'I should like to make an enchanting curtain speech at the end of a wildly successful first night, and—to the sound of cheers and applause—drop gracefully dead. If possible, *before* the curtain falls.' He did not quite manage that, but within a few hours of the curtain falling at the Palace Theatre on March 5th 1951, and after having supper at The Flat with his producer, Tom Arnold, he died in his bed from a thrombosis.

The reign had come to an end, and there was to be no successor. The world that Ivor ruled, a realm of glamour, gaiety and romance, where everything was a little larger than life and at least twice as lovely, had gone for ever. All that was left was the music. Soaring, lilting, caressing, and as beguiling as the man who wrote them, his melodies are his memorial. Mam had, for once, been absolutely right.

A party at The Flat: Ivor, Tyrone Power, Gordon Duttson, Robert Andrews, Robert Bishop, Clifton Webb and Olive Gilbert.

At the window of The Flat.

Mam.

SONGS

(Photograph)   (Rita Martin)

MADAME CLARA NOVELLO DAVIES.

During Harrods' Fashion Display Week

TUESDAY, APRIL 27th to FRIDAY, APRIL 30th

RECITALS WILL BE GIVEN

Each Afternoon in the Restaurant

BY THE

ROYAL WELSH LADIES' CHOIR

Including many eminent Soloists

CONDUCTED BY

MADAME CLARA NOVELLO DAVIES

(Accompanist — IVOR NOVELLO)

The Programme and Songs are sold to Benefit
Queen Alexandra's Field Force Fund.

HARROD'S, LTD.   RICHARD BURBIDGE, Managing Director   LONDON, S.W.

Opposite: Programme for a war-time Charity Concert, which included, beside *Till The Boys Come Home*, Ivor's *The Little Damozel*, *Megan*, *Slumber Tree* and another patriotic number, *Soldiering*.

Above: The Royal Welsh Ladies' Choir. Ivor, as accompanist, sits at his mother's feet.

Little Clara was looked on as being a Child Prodigy. Not only could she play the piano with a certain amount of efficiency; she could also sing. Her father was in charge of the choir at Salem Chapel, and nothing pleased Clara better than to take his hand and go to the Choir Practice. And soon, of course, she had to have a choir, like father's. Every doll she possessed was a member, even down to twenty-four tiny ones, bought—I regret to say—with a two shilling piece stolen from the house-keeping purse by a too sympathetic maid! No matter what their size and shape, Clara would arrange them in rows and solemnly conduct them, pencil in hand, singing with them herself, of course. And woe betide the doll who sang a false note!

For one day, Clara told her father, the Dolls' Choir was going to sing before the Queen. Jacob was greatly intrigued by this: 'How many singers have you in your choir?' he asked. 'Oh, there are a HUNDRED,' Clara replied grandly, 'but you can't *see* the others, I have to THINK them.'

That was typical of Mam. She always thought on a big scale. And her ability to do so is perhaps one of the most valuable legacies I have from her.

Ivor Novello, in a BBC
Radio play, *Madame Clara*.

25

Ivor's first published song.

A gay and fanciful valse song, entitled *Spring of the Year* and composed by Mr Ivor Novello, the bearer of a name much esteemed by the musical profession, was entrusted to Miss Evangeline Florence, who dealt in such a persuasive fashion with its light-hearted phrases that she easily achieved success.

Daily Telegraph,
1 July 1911

According to Mam, however, the occasion was not quite the success Ivor had hoped it would be. He refused to accept her suggestions for altering the ending of what she referred to as 'a florid waltz song', and also insisted on accompanying Miss Florence against Clara's advice: 'His touch,' she considered, 'was too light for the Albert Hall.' She herself was to accompany the following singer, one of her pupils, and Ivor felt that if his mother could do it, so could he. In the event, Clara was proved right. The song received only a 'scattered clapping of hands', and not only was Ivor disappointed by its reception but he also had to suffer Miss Florence's complaints about his poor accompaniment. Mam's pupil, of course, had a triumph, and for encore gave one of Clara's own songs, *Friend*, which was immediately taken for publication by Boosey and Hawkes, who later published Ivor's songs.

'So it was through the public,' wrote Clara, 'that Ivor was given his first lesson of failure, and had his early ideas of easy success rudely shaken. And I was glad to have it so . . . I also felt that soon I should no longer be his adviser, as, after one or two such painful falls, like a young bird first essaying to fly, this son of mine would be spreading his wings for greater flights than a mother bird could follow.'

This incident, besides revealing an incipient rivalry between mother and son, also has a bearing on the Strange Case of Wilfred Douthitt, the young man whom Clara accompanied at the Albert Hall concert and for whom she appears to have felt rather more than the teacher's pride in a favourite pupil. Shortly after this he suddenly disappeared, under suspicious circumstances, which caused Madame Clara such distress that Ivor swore to find him and bring him to retribution. He was unsuccessful, and the next they heard of Douthitt was that he had joined the Canadian Army and been killed in Flanders. But some years later, while in New York, Clara was attending a recital at the Aeolian Hall with another pupil, Sybil Vane, and when 'the New Belgian Baritone', Louis Graveure, walked onstage, they both recognised him at once as Wilfred Douthitt, despite a heavy beard, a suspicion that was confirmed when he began to sing. But although challenged about his identity in the Press, Graveure refused to admit either that he was Douthitt or that he had been taught by Clara Novello Davies, and continued to keep up the deception for many years, making a reputation for himself as Louis Graveure in America and Europe. It was not until 1939, when Ivor's *The Dancing Years* was in rehearsal, that he wrote to Clara and confessed that he was indeed Wilfred Douthitt. He begged her forgiveness and was later invited to share her box at

Drury Lane. Whether he ever paid her the fees he owed her for his training is not recorded.

For some years past Madame Clara Novello Davies has been recognised as among the teachers of singing who have had great success with their pupils. Many who have studied with her took part in her concert last night at the Aeolian Hall and are well known to the musical public. Madame Novello Davies's son, Mr Ivor Novello, has already made a name as a song-writer in this country and in America, where he is at present for the production of his new opera. Mr Charles Mott sang the *Song of Exile* and *Hindu Lullaby*, from the song cycle, *Syria*. Throughout the long programme, Madame Davies played the accompaniments with untiring zeal and efficiency.

Evening Standard,
14 June 1913

Ivor's 'opera' was, in fact, an operetta, *The Fickle Jade*, which he had written for a competition organised by Chappell & Co, the music publishers, who would eventually publish his most famous compositions. He won second prize, but *The Fickle Jade* was never performed, although some of its melodies re-appeared in later shows (The Skating Waltz in the second act of *Glamorous Night* is one of them).

Some people considered it was the words which made this song. This may or may not be so, but the fact remains that all the words, including the title, were written by me, with the small exception of the last two lines. The authoress of these was poor Lena Guilbert Ford, an American woman living in London.

Ivor Novello, talking
about *Keep The Home Fires*
Burning in the News of the
World in 1933

Mrs Ford was 'poor' in more than one sense. Whatever her contribution to the lyrics of *Till The Boys Come Home*, as the song was originally called, owing to her lack of business sense she never received any royalties for it. And then, on March 18th 1918, she and her young son were killed by a bomb dropped on their home in Warrington Crescent, Maida Vale, during a Zeppelin raid. Curiously enough, the bomb nearly disposed of a neighbour, Adrian Brunel, who later directed Ivor in three of his films, *The Man Without Desire*, *The Vortex* and *The Constant Nymph*. But he insisted on taking his wife and mother to shelter in Warwick Avenue Underground Station. 'We had hardly installed ourselves below before we heard a bomb dropping and saw the tube lights swing: "That's us!" I said cheerfully. And it was ... Actually no bombs had fallen directly on our house; about four or five fastened together, so the experts said, had fallen on the Fords' house, and our damage was done by concussion. Young Ford and his mother were killed.'

Ironically the song was parodied two years before, when a German Zeppelin was shot down over the mouth of the Thames:

The great gas-bag reposes in the river's slime and the baby-killers who manned it repose in the arms of the people they came to slay ...

> Keep the Zeppelin turning,
> Good boys, you are learning
> Just the range that's needed
> For to bring them down.
> Plug the baby-killers,
> Slaughter the grave-fillers,
> Show them what we're made of
> Here in London Town.

Sunday Herald,
2 April 1916

It was to be parodied again during the Twenties, when it was adopted by the Unionist Party as their campaign slogan for the General Election of 1923:

At the Unionist Headquarters yesterday there were many head-aches. Everyone was trying to find a new verse to the old tune of *Keep The Home Fires Burning* ... Anyone with a brilliant thought rushed off to Mr Cambray, only to find too often that the suggestion would not scan. However one catchy verse has been evolved. It will soon be sung at all Unionist meetings throughout the country:

> Keep the home fires burning,
> Keep our British earning
> Wages that the Foreigner would steal away.
> Stand for home and neighbour,
> Spurn all foreign labour.
> Baldwin's way's the British Way
> And it's bound to pay.

Evening News,
23 November 1923

In 1931 Madame Clara inaugurated the Women's League of Peace whose General Council included such renowned ladies as the Countess of Oxford and Asquith, Dame Sybil Thorndike, Dame Madge Kendall, Mrs Charles Cochran, Lily Elsie and Marie Tempest. A mass rally was held at the Albert Hall and Clara's own song, *No More War*, was sung with great success. It was followed by yet another version of *Till The Boys Come Home*: 'Keep the PEACE Fires Burning'.

The Way to Sing *Till The Boys Come Home*
by Ivor Novello

Start with a fairly bold attack, with a marked crescendo on the words, 'The COUNTRY found them ready', and give a growing crescendo towards the end of the verse, then drop down to a soft tone to start the chorus and try to get a sustained, soothing sound on the first two phrases, especially on the word 'yearning'. The chorus is fairly quiet till after the phrase 'through the dark clouds shining'. Then comes a big break and a marked change of tone on the words 'Turn the dark clouds inside out Till the Boys Come Home' ... But, whatever happens, don't overdo it.

(from a magazine article)

From all accounts the favourite pantomime song this year is the familiar soldiers' favourite, *Keep The Home Fires Burning*.

The Pelican

To Keep the Home Fires Burning.
Proposals for Coal Economy to be Considered.
Evening News

Cigarette-smoking among women has increased during the War. It is the way they Keep the Home Fires Burning.

The Star

Keep the Home Fires Burning, but let the copper fire go out and stay out, for it never need be lighted again if you use Rinso, the cold water washer. When the Boys Come Home, they will find wives and sweethearts smiling and happy on wash-day.

Advertisement
in The Passing Show

It is more than possible that we may be greeted, from the gutter, by the strains of Ivor Novello's *Keep The Home Fires Burning*, played by a derelict ex-soldier on a cracked mouth organ. All over London there were these tragic bands of forgotten men, playing Ivor's tune to passers-by who were heartily sick of it. Ivor once told me that it nearly drove him mad. 'I made eighteen thousand pounds out of that tune,' he said, 'and if I hadn't spent the lot, I'd give it to these poor devils.'

Beverly Nichols,
The Sweet and Twenties

Opposite: Ivor in uniform as a Flight Sub-Lieutenant in the Royal Naval Air Service, with Mam, in 1916.

Ivor Novello has followed up his phenomenally successful song, *Till The Boys Come Home*, with another fine effort entitled *Laddie in Khaki*, the lyric, in this case, written by himself, being set to a forceful march theme with so arresting a refrain—'Laddie in Khaki, I'm waiting for you'—that it is certain to bring it into as great a public favour as the former.

Daily Mail

On joining the Royal Naval Air Service in 1916, Ivor was sent to the Crystal Palace for training and then posted to Chingford, where he was involved in two air crashes—fortunately not fatal. During his convalescence in Portsmouth he performed in some local amateur theatricals:

The Edith Cavell Hospital Bed Fund should materially benefit from two entertainments given in St Peter's Hall, Bournemouth, on Saturday, if the largeness of the audience is any criterion. The principal attraction was an Italian scena entitled 'La Serenata'. The part of the Fisherman, Beppo, was played by Mr Ivor Novello of the R.N.A.S. and composer of *Keep The Home Fires Burning*, whose presence and fine acting made his impersonation a conspicuous success. Mr Novello, who has a rich tenor voice, sang the Serenade and 'Sunset' with much expression and feeling. The songs in question were composed by Miss Dulcie Huntingdon and the words were written by the late Lt. Jocelyn Huntingdon who was killed in action in November 1914.

Bournemouth Echo

The composer of the famous Song of the Trenches, *Keep The Home Fires Burning*, has also had remarkable success with a number of new compositions, prominent among them *The Radiance of Your Eyes*. This charming piece is said to be a second *Sunshine of Your Smile*. Another, *The Garden of England*, which is being featured by the Alhambra revue, *The Bing Boys Are Here*, is whistled everywhere in England.

The Musical Courier

Ivor's contribution to *The Bing Boys*, one of the most popular entertainments of war-time London, was listed in the programme as *Keep The Home Flowers Blooming*, in order to cash in on his current hit. The show was an adaptation of a French revue, *Le Fils Touffe* by Rip and Bousquet, and its best-known song was, of course, Nat D. Ayer's *If You Were the Only Girl in the World*, sung by George Robey and Violet Loraine.

After his unfortunate aerial debut, the authorities decided to keep Ivor grounded and he was given a clerical post at the Air Ministry in London. This was much more convenient for his theatrical activities and he was asked by Grossmith and Laurillard to contribute some songs to Jerome Kern's musical comedy, *Theodore and Co*, at the Gaiety Theatre.

Opposite: Alfred Lester and George Robey on the cover of *The Bing Boys* programme.

Song: "Every little girl can teach me something new"—AUSTIN MELFORD.

Published by Ascherberg, Hopwood & Crew, Ltd., 16, Mortimer Street, W.

SEE-SAW

Music by
Ivor Novello & Philip Braham

André Charlot's
Successful
Musical Production.

The
Comedy Theatre,
London.

Selection
for
Pianoforte

Arranged by
Henri Jaxon

Price 2/- net cash.

Full Orchestra 5/- net.
Small „ 4/- net.
Revised Price
2/6
A. H. & C. Ltd.

Opposite: One of Ivor's songs in *Theodore and Co*, at the Gaiety, 1916.

Above: The first of André Charlot's revues to which Ivor contributed. The cast included Jack Hulbert, Phyllis Monkman, Billie Danvers and Winnie Melville.

The music of Messrs Ivor Novello and Jerome Kern is pleasant and catchy rather than remarkable. There is no number of the distinction of *They Wouldn't Believe Me*, but Miss Julia James . . . charms with a song, the title of which may be *Your Eyes* . . . Mr Leslie Henson has all to himself a long, curious song, *My Friend John Did the Same as Me*, with which he caused much laughter.

Morning Post

Only the war economy of words precludes a string of laudatory superlatives. Enough to say that *Theodore and Co* made a thumping success.

Daily Mail

Theodore and Co seems to be on for the duration. The soldiers, from Edward P. (the Prince of Wales) to the gallery private, who go at least once every time they are on leave, would miss it horribly if anything happened to it. It had a jovial birthday party on the stage the other night when Gaiety men in khaki and blue and Special Constable rig revisited the glimpses of the limelight and danced with the beauties once more.

Sunday Herald

The original music of this piece is said to have been composed by Miss Jane Vieu; but of Miss Jane Vieu's music only two numbers are left . . . The rest of the music has been written by Mr Ivor Novello and Mr Guy le Feuvre, who have each produced some light and pretty numbers, without much character, but with plenty of agreeable melody.

The Times review of
Arlette

Arlette was tried out at the Prince's Theatre, Manchester, in the summer of 1917. Also in Manchester, playing a small part in a play called *Wild Heather* at the Gaiety, was an aspiring young actor called Noël Coward:

Ivor's Trio from *Arlette*, another Grossmith and Laurillard show, which opened at the Shaftesbury Theatre on September 16th 1917.

I stepped off a tram outside the Midland Hotel on my way to play a matinée and met Bobbie Andrews and Ivor Novello . . . (Bobbie) introduced me to Ivor, and we stood there chatting while I tried to adjust my mind to the shock. My illusion of this romantic, handsome youth who had composed *Keep the Home Fires Burning* drooped and died and lay in the gutter between the tramlines and the curb. The reason for this was that I had caught him in a completely 'off' moment. He was not sitting at a grand piano. He was not in naval uniform. The eager Galahad expression which distinguished every photograph of him was lacking. His face was yellow, and he had omitted to shave owing to a morning rehearsal. He was wearing an old overcoat with an astrakhan collar and a degraded brown hat, and if he had suddenly produced a violin from somewhere and played the 'Barcarole' from *The Tales of Hoffmann* I should have given him threepence from sheer pity.

Noël Coward
Present Indicative

Waters (MR. JOHNNIE FIELDS).   Cherry (MISS ADRAH FAIR).   Duke (MR. LEONARD MACKAY).

Trio   -   -   -   "Let] Cousinly Love Continue."

CHERRY :—" We'll be nice to one another,   Oh, its quite all right to love me
Like a sister and a brother,   In a cousinly kind of way."

Arlette was an adaptation from the French and was Ivor's first excursion into Ruritania. It took place in Porania, whose ruler, Prince Paul, played by Joseph Coyne—the original Danilo in *The Merry Widow*—loses his heart to a commoner, Arlette (Winifred Barnes), and eventually gives up his throne for love of her. A sub-plot involved Cherry (Adrah Fair), the daughter of an American millionaire, who also falls for the Prince but ends up by marrying his cousin, the Duke of Ariosto, and becoming Princess of Poania, thus incidentally solving the country's financial problems.

Ivor's contribution to *Arlette* consisted of about a third of the score and gave evidence that he was finding his own style and breaking away from the atmosphere of the concert hall and the choir which pervaded his earlier songs. *Just a Memory* is a hauntingly plaintive ballad in the contemporary manner, *Cousinly Love* has the same jaunty tunefulness as *Primrose*, Roma Beaumont's song in *The Dancing Years*, while *The People's King* (listed in the score as *His Country First of All*) gives a foretaste of the weight and feeling he brought to another patriotic number, written twenty years later: *Rose of England* in *Crest of the Wave*.

Tabs, at the Vaudeville in 1918, was the second Charlot revue to which Ivor contributed, and starred Beatrice Lillie, Hal Bert and Guy le Feuvre, who composed several of the songs in *Arlette*. Miss Lillie's understudy was a promising young lady known as Gertrude Lawrence. Fourteen years later she recorded one of Ivor's best tunes in the show, *When I Said Goodbye to You*, which Miss Lillie had sung dressed in soldier's uniform:

It is just the song of a soldier boy, who said goodbye to the old folks without worrying much about it; but who nearly broke his heart when he had to say goodbye to his 'girl'. Of course this kind of sentiment is always a little artificial; but the girl likes to believe it is true, and in times like these they will swallow pretty well anything. Miss Lillie, however, renders the song in a simple, straightforward style without any trimmings, just as if its message were a self-evident truth: and it goes, as it deserves, to loud and prolonged applause.

The Bystander

The Bystander, June 19. 1918

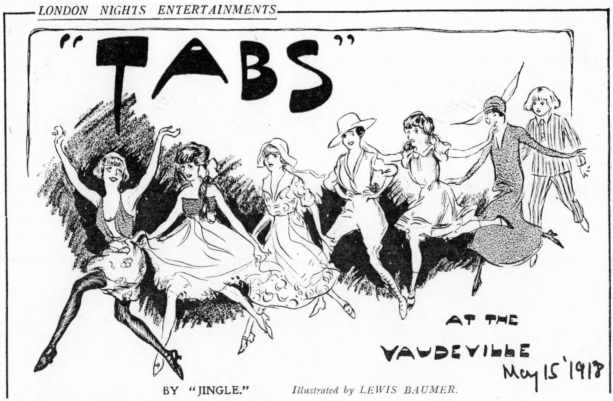

LONDON NIGHTS ENTERTAINMENTS

BY "JINGLE."   *Illustrated by LEWIS BAUMER.*

35

SUNG BY MISS MARJORIE GORDON

If you were King in Babylon

FROM THE MUSICAL COMEDY

"WHO'S HOOPER?"

ALFRED BUTT'S Production at the

Adelphi Theatre

Revised 2/6 Price

Words and Music by   IVOR NOVELLO

Price 2/- net

Ascherberg, Hopwood & Crew, Ltd.,
16, Mortimer Street,
London, W.1.

B. Feldman & Co.,
2, 3 & 4 Arthur Street, New Oxford Street,
London, W.C.2.

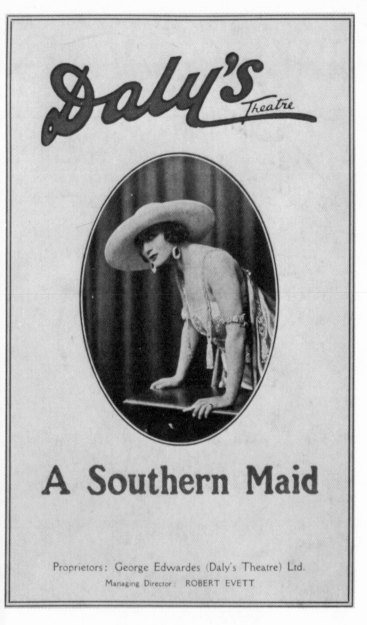

A Southern Maid

Proprietors: George Edwardes (Daly's Theatre) Ltd.

Managing Director: ROBERT EVETT

José Collins, on the programme cover, as Dolores in *A Southern Maid*, Daly's, 1920.

When once they (Robert Michaelis, recently demobilised, and Marjorie Gordon) had been welcomed back with rapturous enthusiasm, they certainly had a good deal of work to do, for the composers had been particularly kind to them ... Miss Cicely Debenham was wholly delightful and she has a Wedding Jazz which is going to be a perfect nuisance before the public weary of its haunting refrain.

The Times review of
Who's Hooper?

Opposite: The music cover for *Who's Hooper?*, Ivor's first post-war musical comedy, based on Pinero's *In Chancery* and starring W. H. Berry, Adelphi, 1919.

The first question everybody asks you after you have been to *A Southern Maid* is—is it as good as *The Maid of the Mountains*? And for the life of me it is extremely difficult to answer ... But this much can be said here and now—Miss José Collins is even finer in the new piece than she was in the old one.

The Tatler

The Maid of the Mountains had been a tremendous success at Daly's Theatre in 1917 and made an undisputed star of its leading lady, José Collins, whose waltz song, *Love Will Find a Way*, was one of the decade's most popular tunes. *A Southern Maid* was intended to duplicate that success, and the same composer, Harold Fraser-Simpson, was engaged to do the score. The director was Oscar Asche, whose oriental spectacle, *Chu Chin Chow*, had been the long-running hit of the Great War, and every care was taken to make the new show live up to the reputation of its predecessor; but, despite quite favourable reviews, it did not appeal to the public and closed after a few weeks.

The truth was that the operetta had had its day. With the increasing popularity of Jazz, audiences were drawn towards the snappier rhythms of musical comedy, where the songs, such as Ivor's *Wedding Jazz* in *Who's Hooper?*, reflected the beat to which the younger generation preferred to dance. Although operettas continued to be produced, the trend was more and more towards the American-style musical, as represented by George Gershwin's *Lady, Be Good* and *Funny Face* and Vincent Youmans' *No, No, Nanette*. Instead of the exotic backgrounds of Spain, Italy or Ruritania, their settings were New York or London, and the characters, no longer princes, duchesses or bandit chiefs, were recognisably contemporary.

For *The Golden Moth*, his next show, Ivor was for the first time asked to contribute the entire score. It was set in the night-club of the title and dealt with gangsters—among them a character called Dipper Tigg, played by the popular comedian, W. H. Berry, who had taken the lead in *Who's Hooper?* and whose song, *Dartmoor Days*, although a comedy number, had one of Ivor's most appealing melodies. Another was *Give Me a Thought Now and Then* which does not appear in the programme, but was published in the score, as what was then known as a Supplementary for the romantic leads, Nancy Lovat and Thorpe Bates. With *The Golden Moth* Ivor proved that he was as at home in the present day as he had been in the never-never land of operetta.

It was good to hear Mr Thorpe Bates, Mr Michaelis and Miss Nancy Lovat, as dainty a heroine as one could wish for, so well provided with tuneful music. Mr Ivor Novello, the composer of the score, has given generously of his best and practically every number which they sing had some haunting lilt of its own which will make for popularity. *Dear Eyes That Shine*, *Fairy Prince* and *My Girl*, to mention a few, will be heard on many a gramophone during the coming winter.

The Times review of
The Golden Moth

We lunch at Maxim's,
And her mother comes too!
How large a snack seems
When her mother comes too!
And when they're visiting me,
We finish afternoon tea,
She loves to sit on my knee—
And her mother does too!
To golf we started,
And her mother came too!
Three bags I carted
When her mother came too!
She fainted just off the tee,
My darling whispered to me—
'Jack dear, at last we are free!'
But her mother came to!

Dion Titheradge

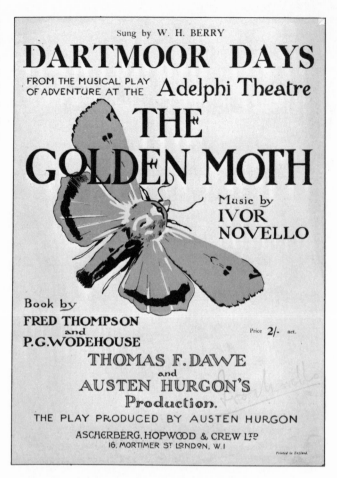

Above: W. H. Berry's hit song in *The Golden Moth*, Adelphi, 1921.

Below: Jack Buchanan, one of the stars of *A to Z*, Prince of Wales, 1921.

Of the many songs Ivor wrote for revue, this is the one that has had the longest life. It was sung, in his inimitably casual style, by Jack Buchanan. 'The title,' wrote Beverly Nichols in *The Sweet and Twenties*, 'does not sound musically inspiring, but Ivor invented a melodic line for it that was as clean and buoyant as an air by Schubert.'

A to Z was one of Charlot's most successful revues and when he took it to New York, under the title of *André Charlot's London Revue of 1924*, it made international stars of both Buchanan, Gertrude Lawrence and Beatrice Lillie.

Revue, nowadays a lost art, continued to be popular in London right through the Twenties, Thirties and Forties and only faded out finally in the Sixties when the so-called 'satirists' of Television pre-empted the field with more immediate and outspoken political comment than was possible in the Theatre. While the revues of C. B. Cochran, with their chorus of Young Ladies and interpolated ballets and production numbers, relied more on spectacle, those of André Charlot tended to be on an intimate scale, with a small company of versatile artists who could turn their hands to a song, a sketch or a dance number with equal ease. Charlot often discovered unknown talent which Cochran appropriated and expanded: as Douglas Byng—who worked for both—is quoted as saying, 'Charlot made stars—Cochran turned them into planets.'

A to Z may be said to have three component parts— Charlot, Charm and Chinatown (a reference to Philip Braham's *Limehouse Blues*) ... There is a delightful, and beautifully lit, setting for *The Oldest Game in the World*, in which one sees a parade of lovers from Cupid and Psyche to Darby and Joan.

The Times

The Oldest Game in the World

Prince of Wales Theatre

Sung by
Josephine Trix
and
Marcel de Haes

Words by
Ronald Jeans

Music by
Ivor Novello

Andre Charlot's *Revue*

Price 2/- net

ASCHERBERG, HOPWOOD & CREW, LTD.,
16, MORTIMER STREET, LONDON, W.1.

For Foreign Agencies see back page.

Printed in England.

DUSKY NIPPER

SUNG BY MISS BINNIE HALE
AND DANCED BY MR CYRIL MAUDE AND MISS BINNIE HALE IN
THOS. C. DAGNALL'S PRODUCTION OF

"THE DIPPERS"

BY BEN TRAVERS
AT THE CRITERION THEATRE, LONDON

Words
by
BEN
TRAVERS

Music
by

IVOR
NOVELLO

PRICE 2/- NET.

Photo: Hana

MISS BINNIE HALE.

ASCHERBERG
HOPWOOD &
CREW, LIMITED.
16 Mortimer Street, London, W. 1.

(FOR COLONIAL & FOREIGN AGENTS SEE BACK PAGE.)

PRINTED IN ENGLAND.

"PUPPETS!"
ACT I.

"PUPPETS!"

The Showman	ARTHUR CHESNEY
The Boy	FRANK LAWTON
Terpsichore	FAY COLE
The Policeman	REX CALDWELL
Euterpe	NETA UNDERWOOD
Harlequin	PAUL ENGLAND
Thalia	CONNIE EMERALD
The Londoner	STANLEY LUPINO
Columbine	BINNIE HALE

"THE PUPPET STRUT"
PAUL ENGLAND, FAY COLE AND CHORUS

"AUTO-SUGGESTION" (STANLEY LUPINO)

The Waiter	ALBERT WALLACE
Jim	STANLEY LUPINO
Mr. Graves	ARTHUR CHESNEY
Mr. Bury	REX CALDWELL
Lily	CONNIE EMERALD
Mr. Cherry	PAUL ENGLAND

"APRIL'S LADY"
BINNIE HALE AND CHORUS

"WHAT DO YOU MEAN?"
STANLEY LUPINO AND CONNIE EMERALD

"THE NEW PORTIA"

Kate	BINNIE HALE
Arthur	ARTHUR CHESNEY
Hopkins	JOSEPHINE DENT

"THE SAME OLD MOON"
NETA UNDERWOOD, PAUL ENGLAND AND CHORUS
(Staged by MADAME ASTAFIEVA)

"SLEEPING OUT"

Potty	STANLEY LUPINO
The Char	BINNIE HALE

"HOOPS AND SAWDUST" (Melody by LLOYD WILLIAMS)
ARTHUR CHESNEY

"A MUSICAL INTERLUDE" (Devised by STANLEY LUPINO)
STANLEY LUPINO AND BINNIE HALE

"RAGGEDY DOLL"
Sung by NETA UNDERWOOD
THE DANCERS: FAY COLE, PAUL ENGLAND, CONNIE EMERALD,
BINNIE HALE, STANLEY LUPINO
AND ENTIRE COMPANY
INTERVAL

P.T.O.

ACT II.

"TAPPING"
PEGGY HEATHER, PAT KENDALL, DORMA WARD, JOAN
ELKINS, MOLLY NEAME, INNIS SHAWEN, EVELYN
PUXON, VIOLET HANBURY

"A DOG'S LIFE"

A Shady Character...	ALBERT WALLACE
Wilfred	ARTHUR CHESNEY
Rosie	CONNIE EMERALD
Philip	REX CALDWELL

"ITALIAN LOVE" (STANLEY LUPINO AND LESLIE SARONY)
STANLEY LUPINO AND CHORUS

"SHE NEEDS ANOTHER NOW"
PAUL ENGLAND

"BROADCASTING"

The Manager	ARTHUR CHESNEY
The Typist	BINNIE HALE
The Office Boy	STANLEY LUPINO

"BARBARY"
NETA UNDERWOOD AND CHORUS
Dance by FAY COLE
(Staged by Madame ASTAFIEVA)

"PENELOPE" (Lyric by RONALD JEANS)
BINNIE HALE

"PROPS!"

The Call Boy	FRANK LAWTON
The Electrician	ALBERT WALLACE
The Producer	ARTHUR CHESNEY
Props	STANLEY LUPINO
Miss Gladwin	CONNIE EMERALD
Mr. Inchpin	REX CALDWELL
Mr. Dalroy	PAUL ENGLAND

"AND THAT'S NOT ALL"
PAUL ENGLAND AND BINNIE HALE

"PLEASE LAUGH!"
STANLEY LUPINO

"AULD ACQUAINTANCE BLUES"
THE ENTIRE COMPANY

Opposite: Binnie Hale had appeared at the Criterion in 1922, in the play *The Dippers*, for which Ivor wrote one song.

Above: Programme for André Charlot's *Puppets*, at the Vaudeville, 1924.

Miss Binnie Hale is good in everything she does. She sings, acts and dances with equal charm. But her pleasantest moments are when, with Mr Lupino, she begins to imitate well-known artists. She gives, in rapid succession, impressions of Miss Evelyn Laye, Miss José Collins and Miss Beatrice Lillie, and all are admirable.

The Times

I have a burning desire to know if Mr Novello knows *Tristan*. The general structure of his music would not be called 'like Wagner's', but there is a phrase of one song of his, a leading phrase, with very curious and unusual intervals, that is repeated with exactitude, that recurs over and over again in *Tristan*.

Observer

Ivor Novello, listening from a box at the Vaudeville to the music he has composed for *Puppets*—mostly very pretty stuff—is not to be idle for long. Having admitted to me in an interval that the likeness to a famous phrase in Act Two of *Tristan and Isolde* in his duet *The Same Old Moon* was intentional—'Moon, love—love, Tristan,' he said, 'I hope people will see the point'—, he spoke of his next production, *The Rat*.

Evening Standard

41

Our England, one of three songs written by Ivor for José Collins to sing in *Our Nell*, Gaiety, 1924.

The first song to raise the enthusiasm of the audience to Gaiety first night pitch was *Our England*, which seemed a judicious mixture of Shakespeare, *God Save the King* and *Keep The Home Fires Burning*. It was sung by Miss José Collins as Nell Gwynn, who also for the occasion had become a symbol of patriotism, a sort of Cockney Joan of Arc.

Evening News

Our England, patriotically suited for Empire Year, will be the rage of the Season.

The People

The best of the sentimental songs, *Land of Might-Have-Been*, was by Ivor Novello, who has also been responsible for its stirring march song, *Our England*. It will be played by every military band.

Daily News

1924 was the year of the Empire Exhibition at Wembley, and patriotic ardour was running high—at any rate in the newspapers. The melody of *Our England* had in fact been composed some years before as a war-time song but was rejected by Ivor in favour of the tune that became *Keep The Home Fires Burning*. Fear of Bolshevism was still rife in some sections of the community, and the following announcement appeared in the Press shortly after the first night of *Our Nell*:

'Leaders of the British Fascisti have become so enamoured of *Our England*, the stirring song by Reginald Arkell and Ivor Novello which forms the finale of the First Act of *Our Nell* at the Gaiety Theatre . . . that they have asked permission of the management to adopt it as their official anthem. *Our England*, they say, with its inspiring theme and its loyal sentiments would make an ideal Fascist anthem and would serve as an excellent antidote to *The Red Flag*.'

What Ivor felt about this appropriation of his song is not recorded, but it must be remembered that Mussolini and his Blackshirts were regarded at that time as heroes and saviours of Italy. The British Fascist movement gained momentum in the Thirties, under Oswald Mosley, but by then *Our England* had given way to *Horst Wessel*.

Land of Might-Have-Been was also an earlier composition. Ivor was improvising one afternoon at The Flat, while some of his entourage, including Eddie Marsh, were having tea, when the tune emerged and attracted everyone's attention. Ivor suggested that Marsh should try his hand at writing the words and also suggested the title. 'So then I sat up all night,' recounted Marsh, 'with a wet towel round my head. Next day I took him the result. The song was a great success in our circle, and either Olga Lynn or Fay Compton or somebody would sing it at every party.' When it was put into *Our Nell*, the lyric was credited to 'Edward Moore'.

Opposite: José Collins as Nell Gwynn, Arthur Wontner as Charles II.

CHARLES: "Do you know I could have your head off for that?"

NELL: "Maybe you could. But you won't!"

Photo, Stage Photo Company.

Cicely Courtneidge as 'The Dowager Fairy Queen', set to Ivor's music, in *The House that Jack Built*, Adelphi, 1929.

This delicious performer ... gives an imitation, almost too real to be burlesque, of a Fairy Queen in a provincial pantomime. In numbers such as these Miss Courtneidge has no peer.

Sunday Times

And above all, perhaps, see her in a brilliant (and not too cruel) burlesque of a fairy queen who has seen better days ... (Ivor Novello's) frankly unassuming tunes, like those of Mr Vivian Ellis, show a neat touch and are quite up to revue standard.

Daily Telegraph

'I met Ivor during the first World War, through Phyl Monkman, when she was doing revues with Charlot and Jack (her husband and partner, Jack Hulbert) was in a couple of them with her. Ivor was always in and out of the dressing-rooms, and I used to be in Phyl's dressing-room quite a lot. In those days I was very shy, and didn't like to go anywhere unless I was asked! Ivor was the most delightful person—almost the most delightful person, I think, that I've ever met—always so sincere and easy to talk to. He used to give parties, and that was the first time I ever went to parties—at The Flat. I used to go there continually and he used to be sitting at the piano, composing numbers. I couldn't get a job at all, but later on I got on the Music Halls, and Ivor wrote a number with Jack for me and it was called *And the Little Dog's Tail Went up.* I used to do a show with three cameos: I was myself in the first, then I was a nurse, and then I did a male impersonation, an Air Force officer. When I got to Birmingham, in those days there was a Watch Committee and they would see the first house, and if they didn't approve of something, they would say, "That must come out." But that didn't happen to me. I did the two houses, and the following morning I was told that my number had to come out, that it was vulgar. "What do you mean?" I said, and they said, "It's got a double meaning." I told them they must be a lot of dirty old men if they could find a double meaning in it, but they just said, "It's got to go." So I said, "It can't. I'm billed to do three cameos, and I can't just do two. Besides, this is my act, I've got nothing else to do. If my song goes, I go too." I was terrified! But I got on to my agent, and I left. It was the only time I ever walked out on a show, and the only time I was barred—and because of a song by Ivor Novello!'

Cicely Courtneidge

The last show that Ivor wrote was a musical for Cicely Courtneidge: *Gay's the Word*, at the Saville Theatre, in 1951.

In the late Twenties and early Thirties Ivor became too busy with films and with writing and acting for the straight theatre to give as much time as before to his music, and it was not until 1935, when he started work on *Glamorous Night*, that he began composing seriously again, although he continued to produce melodies spontaneously whenever he felt in the mood.

There was so much good light music being written in the Nineteen Twenties, on both sides of the Atlantic, that Ivor's contribution tends to have been overlooked in latter years, while that of Coward, Gershwin, Porter and Rodgers is still performed, and admired even more than it was at the time. Partly this must be due to the small regard given to the scores of revue and musical comedy in this country by the theatre critics who tend to dismiss anything less weighty than an oratorio as 'thin' or 'tinkling', and partly to the lack of adequate exploitation by the music publishers and record companies. Also, revue is by nature an ephemeral form, and many of Ivor's melodies were teamed with lyrics whose humour and point have probably vanished. All the same a revival of his songs of this period would undoubtedly produce some pleasant surprises and bear out the contentions of such ardent admirers of Novello's music as Beverly Nichols, who wrote, in 1959:

Music poured out of Ivor: there was more music in his little finger than in the whole fraternity of contemporary English composers. To prove this you need only refer to the score of any of his works in the Twenties—revues such as *A to Z*, or musical comedies like *The Golden Moth*—and compare them with the 'scores', if they can be dignified by such a term, of some of the successes of the Fifties. If Ivor had conceived anything so pedestrian as the monotonous jog-trots on the tonic and the dominant to which we have recently been treated, he would have thrown the manuscript into the waste-paper basket. But then, of course, Ivor couldn't have conceived such things, for he happened to be a fine musician. Nor, in the Twenties, would audiences have listened to them.

Ivor, as seen by Nerman, one of the most gifted and successful cartoonists of the Twenties and Thirties.

FILMS

Below: A charming love scene with Gladys Cooper in "The Bohemian Girl," the first of the two films they made together.

"Carnival," one of the most famous of earlier films, had Hilda Bayley and Ivor Novello as the lovers.

□   □

A game of chess with June, themselves pawns in the game played by Dan Cupid, in "The Lodger."

The Call of the Blood (*1920*)

This was a tale of adultery and revenge, set in Sicily, where the film was made, and adapted from the novel by Robert Hichens, an author celebrated for such highly coloured romances as *The Garden of Allah* and *Bella Donna*. It concerned Hermione (Phyllis Neilson-Terry), a young English bride, and her husband, Maurice, played by Ivor, who are spending their honeymoon in Sicily. She leaves to nurse a rich friend, Emile Artois, and in her absence Maurice consoles himself with a Sicilian girl, Maddelena (Desdemona Mazza). The inevitable happens and the girl's father, in order to avenge his daughter's honour, kills her seducer. Hermione returns and comes upon her dead husband's body lying across a rock on the mountainside. Maddelena also dies, and, accompanied by Emile, whom she is about to marry, Hermione places flowers on both graves in a gesture of forgiveness.

One day my lucky star caused him (Louis Mercanton, the film's director) to take up my photograph. 'That's the man I want,' he said. 'But that is Ivor Novello, the composer,' replied Mr Lambert who was with him. 'I don't care what he is, if he will take the part,' returned Mercanton. When he wrote offering me the part, I was just waiting for an excuse to go to Paris. I took the first aeroplane over and arrived in Paris the day Peace was signed.

Ivor, interviewed in the
Bioscope.

The Remorseful Adulterer. Ivor as Maurice with Phyllis Neilson-Terry as Hermione.

Ivor on location in Taormina, with Desdemona Mazza.

Sarah Bernhardt was present at a private showing in Paris of Louis Mercanton's film, *The Call of the Blood*. (She) was enraptured with the thrilling situations and the romantic acting ... Phyllis Neilson-Terry and Ivor Novello came in for a generous measure of her appreciation ... Many of the scenes were taken in and around Mr Robert Hichens' private residence in Taormina in Sicily where M. Louis Mercanton engineered a wonderful festa among the townsfolk that was essential to the story.

The Football Post

Ivor Novello's first screen appearance ... is a signal success and it is thought by Parisian experts that the handsome young composer-screen star will cause quite a flutter among fair film-goers in England.

The Illustrated Chronicle

A number of well-known people were present yesterday evening, by invitation of Ivor Novello, to see the release of the new and thrilling film *The Call of the Blood* ... The Duke and Duchess of Sutherland, the latter in her girl-guide uniform, Lady Diana Cooper, Lady Dudley, Lady Churston, Mrs Winston Churchill, Lady Howard de Walden, in a chinchilla-trimmed suiting, were a few of those present.

The Daily Sketch

The success of the film is really due to Mr Ivor Novello ... His task of inspiring his audience with sympathy for the gay, impressionable young husband of Mr Hichens' novel is not an easy one. But Mr Novello's fine interpretation not only shows why the young husband is more to be pitied than despised but also it carries conviction with it—no mean success when psychology can only be conveyed by gesture and facial expression.

The Sunday Times

Miarka (1920)

Subtitled *Daughter of the Bear*, this was an adaptation of a novel by Jean Richepin, and was also directed by Louis Mercanton. The leading lady was again Desdemona Mazza, who took the part of Miarka, a gypsy whose foster-mother was a performing bear. Ivor played a character called Ivor, the adopted son of a village squire, with whom Miarka falls in love, although she is betrothed to an unknown Romany Prince. Kate, Miarka's grandmother, played by the great French tragedienne, Réjane, removes her to Stes. Marie de la Mer, to the church of the gypsies' patron saint. But the lovers are reunited when Ivor turns out to be a gypsy prince himself, and Kate dies while giving thanks to the Madonna. Réjane herself died shortly after shooting was completed.

M. Louis Mercanton, the producer of *The Call of the Blood*, is now in the South of France selecting locations for his screen version of *Miarka, the Bear Girl* by Jean Richepin of the Académie Française. *Miarka* was written by Richepin nearly fifteen years ago and is one of his most fascinating works ... M. Mercanton, who has already secured a wonderful cast for his 'super' film, including Réjane, Novello and Desdemona Mazza, has just telephoned from Paris to say that he has persuaded the famous author of *Miarka*, Jean Richepin, to enact the part of Ivor Novello's father in the film. Richepin's consent to appear on the screen marks an epoch in kinema history. It is the first time a pre-eminent literary genius and poet has agreed to become a film actor. Richepin was last seen in *La Dubarry*, produced by Mrs Brown Potter at the Savoy Theatre in 1905. He is at the moment with Louis Mercanton, making researches into gypsy customs.

The Arts Gazette

The film of *Miarka—Child of the Bear* in which the great French actress, Mme Réjane, made her last historic appearance attracted a most distinguished audience when it was privately screened on its arrival in London. Lady Tree issued invitations on behalf of Mme Sarah Bernhardt, who found the journey to London too arduous ... Since then it has been shown by Royal Command at Marlborough House. Réjane gives a wonderful performance, but in the scene where the old Romany, Kate, dies, her acting is almost uncannily real—an effect which is the more poignant in that she died so soon afterwards. Ivor Novello, the young English composer, plays in this picture ... but next to Réjane the most astonishing actor is the bear, who must be seen to be believed.

Our Home

Desdemona Mazza and Ivor Novello make the most of their straightforward rôles ... For the splendid bear—whose fight with the villain is a masterpiece of animal stage-management—no praise can be too high. The great creature will be a universal favourite.

The Bioscope

Before 1920 ?

"To LADY TREE:
Ma charmante amie, voulez vous etre mon interprete ou ma voix pour me representer a la premiere apparition de " Miarka —la Fille à l'Ourse," dans lequel on verra pour la derniere fois notre merveilleuse Réjane. Aujourdhui, que je suis bien portante je serais allee moi meme a Londres si les difficultes du voyage n'etaient pas si agacantes. Je compte sur votre bonne grace pour tous votre amitie pour moi et votre admiration pour Réjane et je vous envoie l'expression de mon affecteux souvenir
SARAH BERNHARDT"

EMPIRE THEATRE

(Kindly lent by SIR ALFRED BUTT and his Co-Directors, and Mr. J. L. SACKS)

A Private Presentation of the Film

"Miarka—la Fille à l'Ourse"

Adapted by JEAN RICHEPIN
from his famous novel

Produced by LOUIS MERCANTON

The principal role acted by

MADAME RÉJANE

CAST

Romany Kate	- - -	Madame RÉJANE
Miarka	- -	Mdlle. DESDEMONA MAZZA
Octavia	- - -	Madame MONTBAZON
The Squire	- - -	Mons. JEAN RICHEPIN (of the Comedie Francaise)
Ivor *(his Nephew)*	- -	Mr. IVOR NOVELLO
Luke *(the Squire's Gamekeeper)*	-	Mr. CHARLES VANEL

Madame SARAH BERNHARDT desires to thank for their help and kindness, Mr. OSCAR BARRETT, of the Empire Theatre, for his arrangements, Mr. SYDNEY FFOULKES for his Music, and Mr. H. S. LAMBERT, of His Majesty's Theatre

The programme of the private performance of *Miarka*, sponsored by Sarah Bernhardt as a tribute to Réjane.

Carnival (1921)

Ivor's first English film was a screen version of a stage success which the actor, Matheson Lang, had written in collaboration with H. C. M. Hardinge for himself and his wife, Hilda Bayley. It was the first version of a theme which was to reappear in other movies—notably Ronald Colman's *A Double Life*—that of the actor playing Othello whose jealousy drives him to enact the story in reality. Ivor played the lover, Count Andrea, while Lang played the tragedian, Silvio Steno, and Miss Bayley the flirtatious wife, Simonetta. Much of the film was shot on location in Venice, where a surprising incident took place:

> 'Twinkles', otherwise Florence Hunter, a very clever child actress, recently went to Venice for a British company, to take part in *Carnival*. She had the unusual experience of being christened at St Mark's Cathedral in that romantic old town. During a 'wait' for one of the scenes it was discovered that she had not been christened. Hilda Bayley and Ivor Novello . . . suggested that the ceremony should take place at once. They both stood godparents. During the most solemn part of the proceedings it was discovered that Twinkles was wearing a wig as part of her film make-up. This having been removed, the service went on.
>
> The News of the World

Ivor's acting in *Carnival* received mixed notices, but The Cinema called his performance 'a great achievement' and considered that he played 'the cumbersome rôle of the lover in the only way it could be played'. On its first showing *Carnival* caused complaints about its excessive length and the lack of restraint in the love scenes between Ivor and Hilda Bayley, who appeared in a Carnival scene scantily dressed as a Bacchante.

> On Monday afternoon a revised edition . . . was shown at the Alhambra to an immense audience which received it with unbounded enthusiasm. It has been cut down to about two thirds of its original length and now goes with a swing from start to finish . . . In deference presumably to certain criticisms passed by very sensitive persons, the lover is not permitted to embrace the heroine with quite so much ardour.
>
> The Cinema

Ivor as Count Andrea in *Carnival*.

The Bohemian Girl (1922)

This suffered from one insurmountable drawback: it was an opera (by Balfe) without the music, but with all the absurdities and artificialities of an opera libretto. Ivor was again involved with gypsies, but this time was in reality the Polish Count Thaddeus, in hiding from the Austrian invaders. Gladys Cooper played the aristocratic Arline who had been lost in childhood by her nurse, and rescued from yet another bear by Thaddeus, to be brought up among the gypsies. But in the words of the opera's most famous song, she 'dreamt that she dwelt in marble halls' and the true identities of the two lovers are eventually revealed in an almost farcical climax during which Ivor is obliged to conceal himself in a cupboard in Arline's boudoir. But the film was beautifully photographed and the settings, particularly Arline's 'marble halls', were lavish and picturesque. Ellen Terry, as Arline's nurse, Buda, the cause of all the trouble, wanders in and out looking as if she felt she ought to be in another film—which, in fact, she was, simultaneously. *The Bohemian Girl* was nevertheless a great success commercially, and was re-released within a year or so of its initial screening.

Opposite top: 'I Dreamt that I Dwelt in Marble Halls'. Gladys Cooper as Arline relives her past—unaccountably in the eighteenth century—with Ivor in a powdered wig.

Opposite bottom: Ivor is married to Gladys in a gypsy wedding ceremony performed by Constance Collier and witnessed by C. Aubrey Smith. Ivor was later to go through the same ordeal, on a grander scale, in *Glamorous Night*.

Thaddeus was played by Ivor Novello, one of the most intense lovers on the screen America included. He has every quality under the sun to make a screen star: a perfect figure and features, dark hair and eyes, and all the poetry and music of his nature, helping to build up a personality that is making him a world-wide favourite.

Picture Show

The film was shown in New York to coincide with Ivor's arrival there to star in D. W. Griffith's *The White Rose*:

Our report to the public is that Mr Novello is as attractive as they make 'em and that Mr Griffith is some picker. A couple of years under good direction may see Novello as great an idol of the movie fans as—well, as certain other picture stars. Ivor Novello looks a little like Conway Tearle, a little like Ramon Novarro and a little like Dickie Barthelmess. He is natural and has no annoying mannerisms. We do not know whether he can act because he has had no chance to do so in the picture we saw him in.

The New York News

Ivor Novello seems bored with the whole thing, though there never has been such a gorgeous profile on the screen since Francis X. Bushman's.

The New York Tribune

Below: Constance Collier, Henri Vibart, Harley Knoles (director), Gladys Cooper, C. Aubrey Smith and Ivor, with Ellen Terry seated, on the set.

Gladys Cooper as Arline looks pretty and walks placidly through her part. Ivor Novello as Thaddeus looks handsome and fills his rôle in a similar manner. But both of them ... lack fire and consequently fail to achieve any real dramatic effects. Ellen Terry as the nurse fills her part efficiently, but her distance from the camera nullifies her ability.

Kine Weekly

Miss Cooper is lovely to look upon as the Bohemian Girl, but her lack of experience in the films is obvious: she has yet to learn how to register emotions. Ivor Novello however gives every indication of becoming another Valentino. He is not only one of the best-looking men on the screen today, but he is also a finished actor.

New York Evening Mail

Gladys Cooper and Ellen Terry.

The Man Without Desire (1923)

Ivor played Vittorio, a gallant in eighteenth-century Venice, who falls in love with Leonora (Nina Vanna), the wife of Almoro, an aristocratic voluptuary (Sergio Mari). A journalist—played by Adrian Brunel, the film's director—publishes a denunciation of Almoro and is punished by having his hands crushed. Luigia, Leonora's maid (Jane Dryden, in private life Mrs Brunel), who is in love with the journalist, poisons Almoro's wine in revenge, but Leonora drinks it and dies. Vittorio kills Almoro in a duel, but then, finding Leonora also dead, decides to undergo treatment at the hands of an apothecary, whereby he will be rendered lifeless for two hundred years, his body preserved in a tomb. In the present day, following the discovery of the apothecary's papers, Vittorio's body is exhumed and he is brought back to life. Returning to Leonora's palazzo, he meets her descendant, Ginevra, who is involved with a descendant of Almoro. She falls in love with Vittorio, but he finds that he cannot feel any physical passion for her, due to his long period of 'lifelessness'. Despairing of being able to return her love, he takes poison and dies in her arms. In an alternative ending, which was shot and offered to exhibitors who preferred it, Ginevra's embrace restores Vittorio to life and, presumably, potency.

This film, with its imaginative treatment of an unusual theme and its visual virtuosity, is often quoted as a landmark in the history of the British cinema by modern critics. Unfortunately it is almost impossible to judge its true merits from the copy in existence in this country, from which every title has been hacked, along with a considerable amount of footage. However, the sets are striking and the period costumes—some of them lent by the Baroness d'Erlanger—truly evocative of the Guardi and Longhi paintings on which the first half of the film is based. Ivor makes the most of his big moments, particularly of the waking in the tomb —at the première a woman in the audience screamed —and Nina Vanna, a White Russian refugee with no acting experience, quite justifies Brunel's choice of her for the lead. But the crux of the plot—that the hero, brought back to life after two hundred years, is incapable of feeling physical passion—is rather muffed, perhaps because of censorship problems. In some areas of the country the title had to be changed to The Man Without a Soul.

The film started life by being called It Happened in Venice, but ended up by being called The Man Without Desire. The original was mine, and the final one was from Miles (Mander, Brunel's partner). I still like mine better than his, but must admit that most people liked his (except the Censor). The story was evolved—a composite affair, with a host of literary parents, just like a modern film. Hugo Rumbold had said that we must have a story of Venice in the early eighteenth century—the Pietro Longhi period. Miles and I were afraid of a costume film: in spite of the fact that nearly all the biggest film successes had been period productions, the trade insisted that the public wouldn't go to see them. So I suggested a compromise—a story in two parts, the first part being two hundred years ago, the second part in modern times . . .

Adrian Brunel, *Nice Work*

Owing to the bad weather, the shooting schedule was continually being altered. Ivor's solution was to lie in bed, stark naked, but made up, with his various costumes laid out, ready to put on whenever he was called. 'Ivor's room was next to ours,' writes Adrian Brunel. 'The communicating door was left open during the day, and from my seat at my desk . . . I could see and talk to Ivor; and from his bed he could see the Campanile, which was the inspiration of a slightly rude song he composed, that began:

There's an angel at the top of the Campanile,
And she's got a lot of feathers round her rum-ti-tum-ti-tum.

I remember one day being particularly worried. I was already made up and dressed, working at my desk and

Right: Pietro Longhi: Bergamo—Maschere Venete.

Below: Ivor engaged in a duel, one of the scenes which shows how closely the film reproduced the Longhi originals.

puzzling out changes. Babs (his wife) and Ivor were both anxious to help me, so she and Nina sat on the bed and talked in whispers, while Ivor kept one eye on the Campanile, to see if the clouds cleared and the sun came out. Suddenly Ivor saw the sun. He bounded out of bed, wearing only a vest, seized his wig and dashed into my room, crying exultantly, "Adrian, Adrian, the sun's coming out!" Nina screamed, Ivor hastily held his wig in front of him, and, flourishing his free hand, bowed low, apologised to the "gracious ladies" for the intrusion, and retired backwards into his room.'

The unit then moved to Berlin, where the interiors were shot. As Ivor was already under contract to D. W. Griffith, shooting went on until midnight every night to enable him to leave on time. The film was first shown in a British Film Week at the Tivoli Cinema, between *Scaramouche* and Chaplin's *A Woman of Paris*.

Above: Ivor pays his respects to one of several dwarfs who appeared in the film.

Opposite top: On location in Venice. Beside Ivor stand Adrian Brunel and his wife, Babs (Jane Dryden), who also took part in the picture.

Opposite bottom: Ivor prostrate, on the same spot.

Ivor and Nina Vanna in the modern episode.

Lloyd Williams (right), Ivor's secretary, had a small part in the film.

In our primitive endeavour to groom Nina for stardom, we decided that her Russian surname, Yarsikova, should be changed, the main objection to it being that everyone would pronounce it differently, and that in some cases it might sound like 'you're sick of her'. Ivor said 'V' was a lucky letter, which influenced our superstitious Russian girl: he also said that there had been a lot in the papers about 'Monna Vanna' and thought that Nina Vanna would sound and look well, and seem familiar.

Adrian Brunel, *Nice Work*

Miss Vanna's career never blossomed, although she appeared opposite Ivor again in *The Triumph of the Rat*. But Ivor's was flourishing, as the following announcement in the Kinematograph Weekly indicates:

Get In On The Novello Boom!

An Apology: Owing to the recent absence of Ivor Novello with D. W. Griffith in America, the completion of this artist's most magnificent achievement, *The Man Without Desire*, has been delayed.

BUT—

We are now happy to announce that the Trade Show will take place at the new Tivoli Theatre Strand WC on Friday December 14th at 11.15 am.

As a composite whole, the production can take rank with anything that has been seen in London this year ... The plot is well conceived and cleverly worked out so that all the characters of two hundred years ago are able to appear as their own descendants. This calls for the most delicate acting on behalf of the three principals and each is so nearly alike and yet so utterly different in the two characters that there can be nothing but praise for their work. Mr Ivor Novello himself has done nothing better for the films and Miss Nina Vanna and Sr Sergio Mari are equally good ... Mr Adrian Brunel, the producer, is to be congratulated for his work as well. The film may not be popular but it is possible that it may attract a new audience to the picture theatres at which it is shown, and then it should convince unbelievers that the despised cinematograph can occasionally be artistic after all.

The Times

Ivor Novello is excellent. There are, in the earlier parts of the picture, touches of immaturity about his acting, but his sense of screen techniques is sound and his interpretation of a part full of contrasts is really good.

The Daily Sketch

The cameraman lines up the shot of Ivor's return to life

The film is directly modelled on methods of German production: the hands are as the hands of Brunel, but the voice is as the voice of (Fritz) Lang. *The Man Without Desire*, as a testimonial for native production, is worth all the British Film Weeks put together. It is physical, concrete proof that there is life within the industry yet. It holds a promise for tomorrow, it tells a grand story for today.

C. A. Lejeune, writing in the
Manchester Guardian

The acting of Ivor Novello is a revelation. No other director has been able to get into the work of this actor fifty per cent of the power and charm he displays under the guidance of Adrian Brunel ... Here there is both promise and fulfilment in his work.

Kine Weekly

It is interesting to note that both sad and happy endings for the film have been produced for use at the choice of the individual exhibitor ... Musically the film presents attractive possibilities. Directors should take advantage of the striking themes composed by Mr. Novello.

The Bioscope

Ivor himself was opposed to the use of the happy ending to the film, as he made clear in this interview:

After all, there is no such thing as a tragic ending, if the ending be a true one. In the case of *The Man Without Desire* there could only be a tragic ending, because the theme is sinning against God. We are told in the Bible that the days of our years are threescore years and ten, and if by reason of strength they may be fourscore years, yet is their strength labour and sorrow. What then could there be of happiness for a man who prolongs his life by two hundred years? ... Therefore the tragic ending please. I should be extraordinarily sorry to see a different ending, as Vittorio's death scene was generally said to be my best bit of acting.

Ivor's popularity was growing fast, and scenes such as this one in Scotland were soon to become commonplace:

A seething mass collected at the picture house and police assistance was necessary to regulate the crowds of ladies eager to see the handsome Ivor, as he is off. As one man remarked, 'It might have been the start of the White Sales.'

The Glasgow News

Above: Ivor's departure for America, to make *The White Rose* for D. W. Griffith in December 1922.

Will Love Find a Way?

That is the question movie folk are asking. This is the reason: Gladys Cooper, considered the most beautiful woman on the English stage, sailed from England Wednesday, bound for New York. Her sole purpose in making the trip is to marry Ivor Norvello (sic), the English dramatic actor who D. W. Griffith imported to star in his new production, *The White Rose*. But, unknown to her as yet, she will return to England in two weeks unmarried. It seems that Norvello casually mentioned to Griffith the purpose of her trip, and then and there Griffith gave some advice. He is reported to have said, 'Ivor, although there is no clause in our contract that can keep you from marrying, I wouldn't do it if I were you. In the first place I think you can't do justice to your work as a dramatic actor and be on your honeymoon at the same time. And another point I want to 'make: Wouldn't it impair your value as a star if it were known that you were married? I don't object to your marrying, but I do object if you marry before you finish *The White Rose*.' So it seems that Gladys Cooper will not wed Norvello for at least three months.

New York American

Below: Gladys Cooper's arrival in New York; left to right: Miss Cooper, Clifton Webb, Mme Clara, Ivor and Lady Tichborne, who accompanied Gladys Cooper from England.

Above: Ivor visits Coney Island with his co-stars in *The White Rose*, Mae Marsh (at the wheel) and Carol Dempster. 'Lloydie' Williams (right) keeps an eye on him.

Right: With Ethel Barrymore at a fancy dress ball, Ivor is dressed à la Valentino.

An unusual British type is Novello, an exceptional, totally exceptional young man. It won't take him long to find his way into the hearts of American fans, for he is sincere, talented and good-looking. What more can a girl ask of a screen star? And what love songs he could write, if he could only find the inspiration!

Movie Weekly

Miss Gladys Cooper, who is sailing today for England, was the guest of honour at a dance and entertainment given Monday night by Ivor Novello ... The guests included Lady Tichborne, Mrs Lydig Hoyt, Miss Elsie de Wolfe, Billie Burke, Laurette Taylor, Irene Bordoni, Jeanne Eagels, Ethel Barrymore, Lenore Ulric, Dorothy Gish, Haidee Wright, Blanche Bates, Marie Keen, Clifton Web, Leslie Howard, Edmund Goulding.

The New York Times

The White Rose (1923)

Ivor's arrival in America provoked a storm of speculation in the Press. Would he be the new Valentino, since Rudi himself was in trouble with his studio? 'Rudi Out, but Flappers Rejoice,' crowed one fan magazine, 'Three New Sheiks in the Beauty War: Charles de Rochefort, Joseph Schildkraut and Ivor Novello.' Ivor's surname caused some confusion. In one newspaper it was spelt Norvelli, in Boston he was labelled 'the handsome Swedish actor', in Philadelphia 'the Russian actor and composer'. Chicago got it right and announced that 'D. W. Griffith has secured the signature of Ivor Novello, said to be the handsomest man in England.'

'Please, please don't write me up as the Handsomest Man in England . . . I was never more embarrassed in my life. Promise me you'll cut out all that rot.'

Ivor, interviewed in
the New York Evening Telegram

Ivor in the throes of self-reproach.

The White Rose opened in America in the Spring of 1923 and, while the film itself was received rather coolly, Ivor's notices were encouraging. 'His work is fervent, earnest and sincere,' was the opinion of the New York Herald, 'his presence is pleasing, and he is endowed with a countenance which will show up well on the cover of any fan magazine.' 'Novello, a sincere actor with a pleasing personality and good looks, will appeal to American audiences,' wrote the critic of the New York Telegraph. 'If he has not done so, Mr Griffith should give him a contract to keep him in this country.' Griffith had in fact done just that: for seven films, with a three month break between each, to allow Ivor to return to England. All in all, Ivor's American début appeared to be highly promising.

He arrived wearing his black hair long, for Griffith had cabled him, 'Don't trim your hair. Important.' He began work on *The White Rose* with Mae Marsh today. Ivor has everything earlier sheiks had, and more. He is Grecian in form and features and fortunate enough to be taller and slimmer than Valentino . . . He wears those passionate clothes. His scarf is a deep wine red. 'I've come to America, my spiritual home,' he said.

The Washington Times

With Mae Marsh as 'Teasie', the waitress whom he seduces.

The White Rose was given a gala première at the Scala Theatre in London in November 1923—'It was a dark, shiveringly cold night,' one paper reported. 'A thousand roses of waxed paper were given away to the womenfolk in the audience. Sixty ounces of perfume were used, I am told, to scent them.' Despite this extravagance, the film failed to please most of the critics, who found Griffith's tale of a young trainee priest's ill-starred affair with a roguish waitress nicknamed 'Teasie' too hard to take. 'And the youth plucked a white rose,' ran the synopsis, 'and pinned it on her bosom. And their lips met . . . And on such a night . . . As the stars faded before the dawn Bessie hurried home—to her sorrow. And Joseph arose—a MAN OF SIN!' 'Ivor Novello is properly irritating as the priggish young clergyman,' wrote The Times. 'Mr Novello, as the minister, looked . . . far too good to be true,' was the verdict of the Daily Express. 'He fell from grace with an awkwardness which the power of his subsequent confession redeemed. *The White Rose* need never fail while there is a tear left to water it. It is an Armageddon of emotions.' But it was 1923 and the public had few tears left to shed over Griffith's dramas of transgression and redemption. Griffith's own star was in the descendant and he was having difficulty in finding backing. Ivor's other films under his contract never materialised.

Griffith Co. Inc. Sued for $11,200. Ivor Novello, English Actor, Claims Sixteen Weeks of Salary at $700 on an Alleged Agreement. Had Option for Two Pictures. Albert H. T. Banzhof, attorney for the Griffith Co., said last night he believed the reason Novello was not used was that (he) refused to work in other than Griffith pictures, objecting to being 'farmed out'.

The New York Telegraph

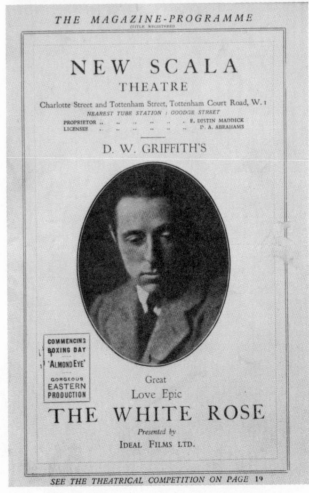

Opposite: Ivor in a fancy dress episode.

Top right: With Carol Dempster and congregation.

Bottom right: The programme for the London première.

Bonnie Prince Charlie (1923)

Despite the comparative failure of *The White Rose*, Ivor's popularity with the public, in this country at any rate, was unimpaired, as is borne out by this headline in Picturegoer of January 1924:

The Names of the Four Most Popular Movie Heroes of the Moment All End in O!

The article went on to list them: Antonio Moreno, Ramon Novarro, Rudolph Valentino and Ivor Novello.

And in the winning entry in a Popularity Contest in the same magazine, Ivor was the only British star nominated, coming sixth, after Valentino, Norma Talmadge, Ramon Novarro, Jackie Coogan and Harold Lloyd.

His next vehicle, *Bonnie Prince Charlie*, was a determined effort on the part of the producers to establish him and Gladys Cooper as a romantic team, although their real life attachment had apparently fizzled out. She had been a favourite of the theatre-going public for some years, mainly because of her extraordinary good looks: in fact, while Ivor was being fêted in New York as England's Handsomest Man, Miss Cooper was heralded on her arrival there as 'England's Most Beautiful Woman'. But success on the screen eluded her until much later in life, when she went to Hollywood in the late Thirties and became a character actress of considerable accomplishment.

The Young Pretender has also proved elusive as a screen hero, a later version of his story, starring David Niven and Margaret Leighton, being one of the costliest failures in British film history. The one in which Ivor appeared was more successful, mainly because of his tremendous following, although the casting was, on the face of it, hardly less unlikely. The story was largely fictitious and the publicity made no bones about admitting it, since the true facts would have barely satisfied Ivor's fans. Flora MacDonald first meets Prince Charles at a ball given in his honour in Holyrood Palace, when he occupies Edinburgh at the head of the rebel army. After defeating the English at Prestonpans, Charlie loses valuable time while dallying with Flora, who is also loved by an imaginary character, Robert Fraser, played by Hugh Miller. Fraser betrays the rebels' plans to the English, which results in their defeat at Culloden and Prince Charles' flight to Skye, aided and abetted by Flora, and at one point in disguise as her lady's maid.

Some of the film was shot on location in the Highlands. Ivor fancied himself in tartan and took to wearing his kilt outside working hours until his leading lady informed him firmly that it was upsetting the natives.

Opposite: The long trail to Skye. Ivor and Gladys on horseback.

Below: Ivor with Gladys Cooper as Flora MacDonald.

Gladys Cooper and Ivor Novello in "Bonnie Prince Charlie"

As the bonny young Prince whose handsome features won the hearts of all his hapless adherents, Mr Novello is the very man to fill the part. The irresolution he displays at important junctures in his fortunes is equally characteristic. Miss Gladys Cooper ... gives a most charming and sympathetic rendering of the heroine ... One can quite believe that, with greater experience, Miss Cooper will acquire a reputation on the screen equal to the popularity she has for long enjoyed on the boards.

The Daily Telegraph

Miss Cooper's delineation of the character was obviously painstaking. Indeed she seemed to me to depict every emotion by numbers, so to speak. I am not a Scot, but even if I were, I think I should still look upon the preliminary attempt to establish atmosphere by the introduction of a solitary piper as rather futile.

Encore

'Wha wouldna fecht for Charlie?' asks the old Scottish ballad-monger. Who indeed, if Charlie was anything like as gallant and handsome a prince as Ivor Novello makes him, or had so spirited and loyal an advocate as the fair Flora of Miss Cooper's creation? It is, alas, a sad historical fact that Flora MacDonald did not arrive on the scene of action until the final chapter in Charlie's enterprise had been reached, when she helped him in his flight to Skye.

The Sketch

Ivor Novello can be safely boomed. He is a great favourite with the ladies, who will be anxious to see him as the dashing Scottish hero. Mention the fact that he has composed for the film the themes, *Prince Charles* and *Flora MacDonald*. Decorate your lobby and the front of your house with tartan and obtain a collection of old Scottish weapons, which can be hung on your walls to advantage.

Advice to Cinema Managers
in the Kine Weekly

Opposite top left: Ivor and Gladys Cooper listen to the instructions of the director, C. C. Calvert.

Opposite top right: The scene as it appeared on the screen.

Opposite bottom: Prince Charles in drag. Flora MacDonald disguises him as her maid on the flight to Skye.

The Rat (1925)

This was a straight adaptation of the play which Ivor had written for himself in collaboration with Constance Collier. The original story had been conceived as a film for Adrian Brunel to make as a successor to *The Man Without Desire*, but Brunel's company had run out of money, and the property reverted to Ivor. As it had been for his career in the Theatre, *The Rat* was a turning-point in Ivor's progress as a screen star.

Quite frankly I think *The Rat* established him as a box-office name. When Griffith took him for *The White Rose*, it was just for his lovely profile. But to me a box-office name means only one thing: does it draw money at the box-office? And until *The Rat* I don't think he did.

Michael Balcon

Top left: Ivor as Pierre Boucheron, the Rat, and Isabel Jeans as Zélie de Chaumont.

Bottom left: The Rat with the devoted Odile (Mae Marsh).

Below: A moment of suspense for Pierre and Odile.

The Rat performs an Apache Dance in the White Coffin night-club.

Taken for what it is—a blatantly commercial melo-drama—*The Rat* is a thoroughly enjoyable film. It is well made and elaborately mounted: there is a good deal of location work in Paris, and a spectacular sequence shot at the Folies Bergère which Zélie attends with her protector and where the Rat steals her cigarette case. All the cast play to the hilt, including the bunch of thugs and floosies who inhabit the White Coffin and fight over the all-conquer-ing Rat. As a show-case for Ivor's personality it is infallible, his only lapse being the climactic scenes of dementia and redemption. Visually he makes no concessions: his 'Rat' costume is grubby, tight-fitting and unflattering, while his 'dress' outfit for visiting Zélie is ludicrous. Miss Jeans, on the other hand, is superbly gowned and slinks through the piece with a fine air of corrupt sophistication. Only Mae Marsh is permitted to overplay, in her customary 'little sister' manner, and milks her solo scenes of unrequited love for the Rat to the point of embarrassment. But the final episode, where she returns from prison to find that the Rat now realises he loves her—which was the weakest in the play—has been mercifully curtailed, to the advantage of the film.

If any ingredient is lacking to make this a first-class popular picture, we cannot think what it can be. Ivor Novello gets every chance out of the title rôle, and his improved histrionic abilities are marked: his bearing and looks are free from any effeminacy, and he is now surely one of the world's supreme young men of the screen. Incidentally, he gets over a semi-brutal swagger without appearing bounderish—a difficult thing in a character so theatrically romantic.

The Kine Weekly

Ivor Novello has not, up to the present, been exactly lucky in his screen rôles. Here at last he has found some-thing that really suits him: as the swaggering, ultra-romantic hero of the Gallic underworld he is thoroughly happy and makes the most of a rôle that offers much to the right man.

Picturegoer

71

THE
KINEMATOGRAPH
W E E K L Y
Registered at the G.P.O. as a Newspaper

JULY - 22 - 1926
Nº 1005 Price 1/-
VOL. 113
30/- PER ANNUM
POST FREE
U.K. & CANADA
U.S.A. - 12 $

IVOR NOVELLO
in
"The TRIUMPH of
THE RAT"
with
ISABEL JEANS
and
Nina Vanna
Directed by
GRAHAM CUTTS

W&F FILM SERVICE LTD. 74-76 Old Compton Street, London, W.1.

The Triumph of The Rat (1926)

The impact of *The Rat* was so tremendous that Sam Eckman, the representative of MGM in this country, sent for me one day and said that his chief, Arthur Loewe, had instructed him to offer me a deal for three pictures a year with Novello, because they felt he had great international possibilities. We were a bit sceptical at the time about American finances, but they made an offer of a premium—I think it was £20,000 on every picture they failed to distribute. I was very tempted to do this, but we had had a great deal of support up to that time from C. M. Woolf, so I felt it only proper to discuss it with him, and he persuaded me to stay with a company that was exclusively British. And he became the first chairman of Gainsborough Pictures . . .

. . . It would be silly to pretend that Novello's films had a success all over the world, but they were remarkably successful in this country. We always knew that he had limitations of course, but he was such an enchanting character: no side at all, none of the star nonsense, eager to learn and charming to the people he worked with. So I suppose one got carried away, and something of it came through on the screen.

Michael Balcon

Since Ivor Novello first set women's hearts a-fluttering to the tune of his stage love-making he has persistently told all interviewers that he hated being a 'Matinée Idol' and wanted to 'Act'. Without casting stones at any of his previous performances (stage or screen) in *The Triumph of The Rat* he definitely proves his right to shed the matinée idol pose, for—he *does* act, and act well!

Picturegoer

The Rat in High Society, now comfortably installed in Zélie's apartment.

T.173

The Rat attempts to seduce Madeleine de l'Orme (Nina Vanna) at a costume ball.

The film shows every sign of being hastily run up to cash in on the success of the original—which it did. The story—of how the Rat, now ensconced as Zélie de Chaumet's lover, the faithful Odile having apparently died, takes on a bet that he can seduce a virginal noblewoman—exhausts itself halfway through and becomes bogged down in banality and melodrama, specifically in the interminable sequence of the Rat's descent to the gutter, hounded by the vengeful Zélie, and his rejection by his old associates, where Ivor's inadequacy as a dramatic actor is mercilessly exposed. There is one episode in particular, when he staggers along the pavement and, discovering a scrap thrown from a restaurant table, falls upon it ravenously, which is almost a parody of itself.

The best part of the film, visually at any rate, is the opening few reels, during which we see the Rat at large in society, immaculately dressed and surrounded by admiring women, against the glittering background—shot presumably on location—of a vast Parisian restaurant. Isabel Jeans is even more elaborately gowned than in the first film, and her apartment is a paradise of period 'camp', featuring a stuffed leopard with which she makes great play. Nina Vanna is also exquisitely presented in a contrasting setting of aristocratic elegance, and the costume ball at which the Rat makes his first attempt to seduce her, is full of bizarre moments. But it is obvious that what is lacking is the sound dramatic structure which Ivor and Constance Collier hammered out for their first venture as playwrights, and it is not surprising that the third in the Rat series, promised for immediate production, had to wait for some years—until in fact it came too late—before it materialised.

The Lodger (1926)

It was the first time I exercised my style . . . In truth you
might say *The Lodger* was my first picture.

Alfred Hitchcock,
talking to François Truffaut

The Lodger, a novel by Marie Belloc-Lowndes, was a treatment of the Jack the Ripper murders, in which a mysterious
stranger takes a room in the house of a London family and,
by his suspicious behaviour, convinces them that he is the
Ripper. It was turned into a play called *Who Is He?* by H. A.
Vachell, which Hitchcock saw and felt would make a good
film; but he was still relatively unknown as a director. 'I
knew he was destined to be a great film man,' says Michael
Balcon. 'Although I was his boss, he knew a damn sight
more than I did. His mind was a camera.' After making
two films in Germany, Hitchcock suggested *The Lodger* to
Balcon, and was offered Ivor, then under contract to
Gainsborough, as a leading man. Owing to Ivor's tremendous following, Hitchcock was obliged to make him turn out
to be innocent at the end of the film, although he would
have preferred to leave the audience in doubt. But by a
series of visual suggestions, starting with the apparition of
the Stranger on the Buntings' doorstep, fog swirling behind
him and only his eyes visible over an enveloping muffler, he
transforms his star into an icon of such sinister potency that
one is almost disappointed to find that he is not the murderer. In the circumstances, Ivor becomes something of a
puppet in Hitchcock's hands, and it is not surprising to find
as harsh a critic as Lindsay Anderson saying of him, in a
note for the British Film Institute: 'Novello's performance
throughout is extremely crude (and often, now, very funny).'
But he goes on to add, 'This is partly due to his limitations
as an actor, but partly also to script and direction which,
with a quite unscrupulous dishonesty, require him to
behave in a blatantly "guilty" manner in order deliberately
to mislead the audience.'

When the film was completed, it was considered a disaster
and its distribution was cancelled. Then Ivor Montagu was
called in to re-edit it, Hitchcock was asked to reshoot a few
sequences, and McKnight Kauffer, the celebrated commercial artist, was commissioned to design the titles. The film
was shown to the critics and at once hailed as, in the words
of the Bioscope, 'the finest British picture ever made' and
went on to become one of the most successful films of the
year. Perhaps because of the compromises Hitchcock was
forced to make, *The Lodger* now seems a curiously uneven
film, combining passages of characteristic menace, in which
Hitchcock builds up suspense in a masterly manner, with
pedestrian sequences which could have been made by anyone. The opening fifteen minutes, where the latest victim is
dredged from the Thames and the news spreads round

Ivor's first appearance, out of the fog.

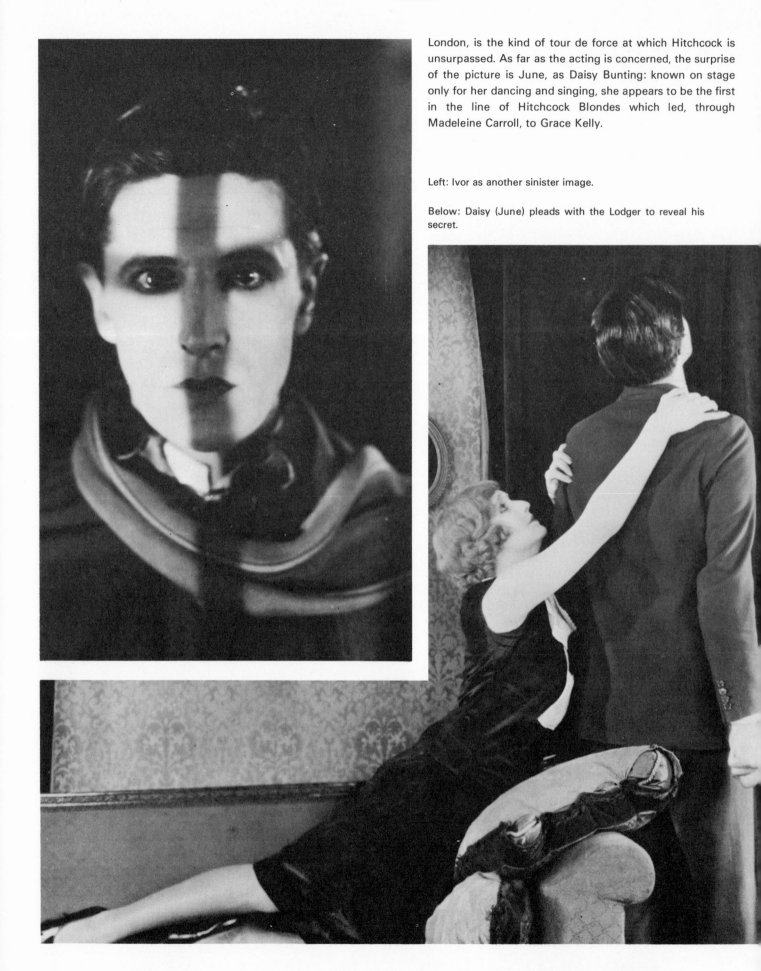

London, is the kind of tour de force at which Hitchcock is unsurpassed. As far as the acting is concerned, the surprise of the picture is June, as Daisy Bunting: known on stage only for her dancing and singing, she appears to be the first in the line of Hitchcock Blondes which led, through Madeleine Carroll, to Grace Kelly.

Left: Ivor as another sinister image.

Below: Daisy (June) pleads with the Lodger to reveal his secret.

Ivor, as Roddy, takes the blame. This scene contained the deathless title: 'Does this mean, Sir, that I can't play for the Old Boys?'

Downhill (1927)

Ivor Novello fans will love it, because they would love anything that featured their idol. And the people who do not go to see a film because of the personal attractions of the star will appreciate the clever direction. Mr Hitchcock believes in satisfying all portions of the public. He realises that the average 'highbrow' picture is seldom a good box-office proposition . . . He prefers to take a 'lowbrow' story and give it a 'highbrow' treatment.

Picturegoer

This is an apt summing-up of Ivor's second film with Hitchcock. It was based on another play which he had written in collaboration with Constance Collier, and concerned the ordeal of Roddy, a public school boy, who takes the blame for his best friend Tim's misdemeanour with a

shop-girl, is expelled and goes to the dogs. The film is an extraordinary example of Hitchcock's gift for making good cinema out of unpromising material. Titles throughout are kept to a minimum and, although the story still seems pretty ludicrous, one is constantly carried along by a series of marvellously visual episodes, linked by the 'Downhill' images—first an escalator descending to the Underground, and later an elevator descending from the flat where Roddy keeps his mistress, Julia (Isabel Jeans). There is a masterstroke of direction when we are led to believe that Roddy has taken a job as a waiter, only to discover, as the camera pans to the right, that he is playing a small part in a musical comedy.

From Isabel Jeans, Hitchcock induces a performance quite different from her usual soignée vamp: a cheap, predatory

The last step Downhill: Roddy on board ship at Marseilles.

blonde, whose every gesture betrays her greed and self-absorption. The scene where Roddy, having married her, discovers that she is continuing a former intrigue, is turned by Hitchcock from melodrama into near-farce: while Roddy and the lover (Ian Hunter) indulge in fisticuffs, Julia is intent on preserving a huge and hideous vase which she removes from its pedestal and into her bedroom. The following sequence—Roddy, again penniless, reduced to working as a gigolo in a Montmartre night-club—is the highlight of the film. Pale and expressionless, he steers a succession of ageing ladies round the floor on the instructions of a grotesque madame. A weird woman, with glaring eyes, asks him to her table and, touched by her apparent concern, Roddy pours out his heart to her. At another table an elderly roué has a seizure and when a waiter pulls back a curtain to give him air, the room is flooded with daylight and Roddy looks round with growing horror as the customers are revealed in all their ugliness. His gaze returns to his companion and he sees her for what she is: a hideous, raddled nymphomaniac. Roddy is next found on the docks of Marseilles, where he is helped on board a ship by some derelicts who discover his identity. As the ship's engines start up, he relapses into delirium and sees all the characters from his downfall merging into one mocking group. The photography of Ivor's livid face is at once beautiful and horrifying, and equal to anything in the most acclaimed 'art' films of the period. In fact, visually at any rate, *Downhill* is much more rewarding than the highly praised *Lodger*, simply because the variety of scenes and situations gave so much wider scope to the genius of Hitchcock.

The Vortex (*1928*)

Adrian Brunel was reluctant to take on the direction of *The Vortex*, because of both its unsuitability for the screen and the censorship problem presented by the two leading characters: a mother who has lovers and her son who takes drugs, and he gives the impression that Noël Coward's play had to be hopelessly bowdlerised. But this is an exaggeration. The story is in essence exactly the same as the play, the only alterations being that Florence at no time states that Tom is actually her lover (though her feelings for him are patently far from platonic) and Nicky only threatens to take drugs unless she mends her ways. The presentation of the characters at the film's opening is marred by facetious titles (by Roland Pertwee)—e.g., 'Florence Lancaster also had lofty ambitions—she had had her face lifted', and instead of returning from Paris, Nicky is now living in a flat in London, where his neighbour is a painter whose model (Julie Suedo) is attracted to Nicky and uses his music in a revue. (Stills exist showing her onstage while Ivor conducts in the pit, but the scene does not appear in the existing copy. Nor does one in which Nicky and Florence attend a mannequin parade.) Nicky discovers that she is a drug addict and confiscates her box of dope, which Florence comes across in their final confrontation. The film tacks on a happy ending where Nicky's fiancée, Bunty (Frances Doble), having been ordered out of the house by Florence when she is discovered in Tom's arms, looks up the time of the next train to London; Florence and Nicky, now reconciled, come downstairs and ask her to stay on, and the three embrace each other in a final tableau of mutual forgiveness. All the acting is of a high standard. Willette Kershaw, who was offered the part after Delysia and Edna Purviance had turned it down, is ideally cast as Florence—particularly when one remembers that, in the play, Bunty, on seeing her photograph, remarks that she has the look of 'a heroic little

The Author visits the set: l to r, Noël Coward, Ivor, Alan Hollis, Willette Kershaw, Adrian Brunel, Frances Doble.

boy'—and carries off all the dramatic highlights with distinction. An important—and helpful—addition to Coward's script is a sequence of a tennis party at the Lancasters' country house, during which Florence flirts outrageously on a secluded lawn with the reluctant Tom, while the other guests make mocking comments on her infatuation, some of which are overheard by Nicky, thus helping to precipitate the climax. Ivor is excellent in the earlier stages of the film, where his boyish charm is given full play, although he is deprived of much of the character's depth by the fact that in this version, instead of living it up on the Rive Gauche, Nicky is leading a comparatively harmless existence in London, his neuroses confined to an occasional bout of cocktail-shaking, while Bunty is no longer a hectic good-time girl but a working journalist-photographer who comes to interview Nicky. The violent emotions of the last act, where Nicky invades his mother's bedroom and forces her to come to terms with her age and position, are beyond Ivor—as they always were to be. Despite his romantically dramatic appearance, his strong points, as a film actor, were his charm, his humour and, above all, his sincerity.

But the film's main fault is nothing to do with alterations to the story or Ivor's deficiencies as an actor; it is simply that, being silent, it deprives the audience of the play's dialogue. Whereas this was undoubtedly a benefit to *The Rat* and *Downhill*, in the case of *The Vortex* it was an insurmountable drawback.

When I realised the difficulties I had before me in putting over my emasculated *Vortex*, I decided to borrow some of Hitchcock's tactics. It was too late in the day to reconstruct the whole script, but there was much that could still be done to embellish what I had, with a display of technical devices which might divert the critics who were expecting to see Coward's *Vortex* on screen ... It was just an extra coating of sugar for the doughnut—to make up for the lack of jam at its centre. These desperate measures were welcomed by my unit and Ivor Novello composed a joyous slogan, with musical accompaniment:

A cute shot a day
Keeps the critics at bay.

Adrian Brunel, *Nice Work*

Excellent as this production is in many details, it is another proof that the most successful of stage plays is not necessarily a fit subject for the screen.

The Bioscope

Top: Nicky lives the vie de bohème: The leg belongs to Julie Suedo.

Centre: With Willette Kershaw as Florence.

Bottom: Ivor with Frances Doble as Bunty.

Noël Coward's play has been filtered, and a mother's vanity and clinging to her faded looks quite well presented. Willette Kershaw is very good as Florence . . . Ivor Novello is quite good as Nicky. Considering the difficulties of the story, which is hardly suitable for screen purposes, Adrian Brunel has done very well.

Kine Weekly

You may take it that I am not interested in writing scenarios at all. I want to write words, not stage directions . . . As a dramatist, dialogue and its psychology are practically my whole career.

Noël Coward, interviewed
by Picturegoer, during the making
of *The Vortex*

At about the same time, Hitchcock was coping with the film of another Coward play, *Easy Virtue*, which Gainsborough had bought. Realising that his plays were intractable film material, Michael Balcon asked Coward to write an original screen story. The result, called *Concerto*, was never filmed, but became one of his greatest stage successes, *Bitter Sweet*. The problem of filming Coward was solved by Noël himself, in the mid-Forties, with *Brief Encounter*.

A scene missing from the final film: Nicky and his mother visit a dress shop.

The Constant Nymph (1928)

Margaret Kennedy's sentimental novel was one of the biggest best-sellers of the Twenties, and at that period, if a book was successful, it was almost inevitably dramatised. Basil Dean persuaded Miss Kennedy to let him make the adaptation with her collaboration, and the play was presented in London at the New Theatre in 1926. Edna Best played Tessa, the youngest daughter of the Bohemian Sanger family, who develops a child-like passion for the boorish but gifted composer, Lewis Dodd. Ivor had hoped to be offered this part, but it went instead to Noël Coward, who, after the success of *The Vortex* and several other plays, was currently the most talked-about man in the Theatre. Coward was reluctant to play the rôle, for various reasons, but Dean persuaded him, mainly by telling him that he need only appear for the first month of the run. The play was a hit and continued to be so, even though Coward left it a week early, suffering from a nervous break-down. He had been overworking for some time, and the gruelling rehearsals under Basil Dean for a part which he later confessed he hated, were too much for him. His understudy, John Gielgud, took over.

After the stage success, a film version was bound to follow. The rights were bought by Gainsborough, and the producer was again Michael Balcon: 'We must have acquired the rights in 1927 or 1928. I know it was to be the star film in our programme for 1928 and we spent a lot of money on it. We got the package of the play—and Basil. He had directed it so successfully on the stage and had become so identified with it that we gave him the chance of directing the film—well, he probably insisted on it, knowing Basil! But on the other hand we insisted on the countermeasure of having someone who would keep him right on the film side, and that was Adrian Brunel.'

When the film was announced, there was much speculation as to who would be cast in the leads. It was predicted that Noël Coward would again play Lewis Dodd, but it is unlikely that he would have considered doing so after his experience in the stage version, and he was not in any case a film name. When Ivor was first offered the rôle, he turned it down, because he was hurt at not having been asked to play it on stage. But it so happened that he had just seen a country house at Littlewick Green near Maidenhead which he had set his heart on buying:

'I bought Redroofs (as the house was later called) with the money I made from *The Constant Nymph* ... But there is a story in that and it happened like this. At that time I was terribly keen on playing Lewis Dodd, but when the play was cast, to my bitter disappointment I was not offered the part. Later, when Basil Dean started work on the film version, he had great difficulty in finding a Lewis Dodd for the screen. He tested fifteen actors without success and finally approached me. My reply was to ask for a big salary and I named the exact price of the freehold of Redroofs, yes, even to the odd shilling. So

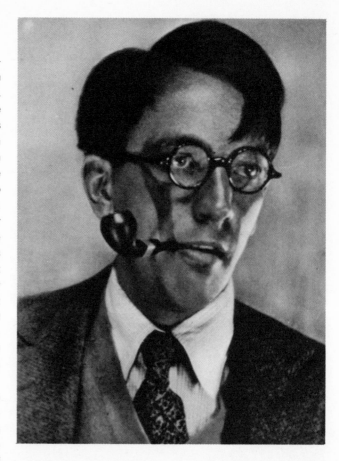

with one film I was able to achieve two of my ambitions: to play Lewis Dodd and to own Redroofs.'
Ivor, in an interview
in the New London Magazine

To celebrate this transaction, Ivor announced that he would actually call the house 'The Constant Nymph', but was fortunately dissuaded by friends from doing so.

For the part of Tessa it was reported that Dorothy Gish was being considered, simply because she had been seen at the play. Several girls were tested, among them Daphne du Maurier, but Adrian Brunel had already made his choice: a young English actress who had been under contract to Abel Gance in Paris, Mabel Poulton:

'I read the novel and fell in love with it, and was madly keen to play it, but Dorothy Gish was booked. Then she fell ill, and so I went rushing round to Michael Balcon. I didn't know him, but I'd read about him and I knew where his office was. Then Basil Dean said, 'Can you cry?', and I said, 'Oh, yes!' because I was rather emotional, and I think that helped me to get the part.'

'She possessed a quality of emotion,' wrote Basil Dean, 'that I have not seen surpassed on the British screen either before or since the coming of sound ... I can see her now wandering about the mountain paths in the Tyrol, a copy of the novel under her arm and an intense far-away look on her childlike face, living introspectively her neglected love. In short, *she was Tessa*.'

The location shooting in Austria, in the actual settings of the novel, took place in an atmosphere of considerable tension, largely because Brunel, though officially director, was 'supervised' by Basil Dean, who at that time had had no experience of the cinema. Ivor appears to have provided the calm centre in several storms, both on and off the set:

Everyone wanted Ivor to take his or her part against everyone else. Ivor did not take anyone's part and yet he appeared to take everyone's ... He played and sang enchanting will o' the wisp songs when awful pauses fell on the studio. Later on (he) managed with infinite adroitness to unloose the rigidity of the Producer. Nor did Ivor call it a day till he had treated the whole company to a remarkably hair-raising switchback and the joys of a rink where blunt-nosed imitation motors could batter each other murderously and with impunity.

Phyllis Bottome, *From the Life*

The three Lewis Dodds: Noël Coward (left), Ivor (below) and John Gielgud (right).

PICTURE SHOW ART SUPPLEMENT, *October 6th, 1928.*

At Florence's musical party Lewis disgraces himself by singing a song that begins, "There was a lady loved a swine," to the horror of the assembly.

Above: Lewis Dodd disrupts a musical soirée at the home of his fiancée, Florence (Frances Doble, *left*). Elsa Lanchester is a disapproving guest.

Right: Ivor and Mable Poulton.

The interiors were made in England, at the Gainsborough Studios at Islington, and the climactic sequence of Lewis Dodd conducting his symphony were shot in twenty-four hours at the Queen's Hall, where the numerous re-takes threatened to cause more upheavals. 'The orchestra groaned aloud at these interminable repetitions,' wrote Basil Dean, 'but Ivor's sweetness and charm prevented a major revolt.' There was one more battle to come, this time with the Censor, who objected to a child of thirteen, as Tessa was in the book, becoming a man's mistress. Brunel had to point out that there was no sexual relationship between her and Dodd and that Miss Poulton was in fact nearly twice that age. The film had an enthusiastic reception when it was first shown, and should have gone on to make a lot of money. 'In my view it was a very good silent film indeed,' says Michael Balcon, 'but talkies had just come in, and from the time it was started its commercial future was very much in doubt.' A few years later Basil Dean himself directed a talkie version with Victoria Hopper and Brian Aherne. In the Forties the rights were bought by Warners for a re-make, starring Joan Fontaine and Charles Boyer, and all copies of the first film were apparently destroyed.

At one stroke Miss Poulton takes a front rank among the international stars. Ivor Novello's Lewis Dodd is also a clever piece of work and if Dodd's surly manners have been insisted on at the expense of his underlying sincerity and hatred of shams, that is due to the limitations of the scenario rather than any fault of the actor.

The Bioscope

Beside being an excellent entertainment, with fun, romance and tragedy beautifully balanced, it is terribly interesting on other counts ... It stamps Mabel Poulton as a tremendous proposition. And it reveals what many

people may be excused for not knowing—that Ivor Novello can act.

Picturegoer

One wonders how even Ivor's patience stood up to these repeated discoveries of the fact that, although he was handsome, he was also an actor.

I didn't know who was Lewis Dodd. We all met at Liverpool Street Station to go to Austria, and Ivor was very charming and said I looked right and so on. He was most kind and helpful, and he was marvellous to act with because he was so really right for the part—playing the piano and being a composer himself. I didn't have an awful lot of technique in those days; I just had this very emotional part and loved playing it. Sometimes I had my face turned away from the camera and he used to gently turn it round and say, 'Come on, darling,' and afterwards, 'You didn't have your nose in the camera.'

Mabel Poulton

Mabel Poulton, Ivor and Tony de Lungo.

Above: Redroofs, the country house which Ivor bought with his fee for *The Constant Nymph*.

This photograph, taken in Germany, is one of the rare portraits of Ivor with a moustache. The appearance of this embellishment was as hotly debated by the fans as was the disappearance of Ronald Colman's a few years later. On the whole, they were against it, and he only wore it in two films, *The Gallant Hussar* and *South Sea Bubble*. He intended to have a moustache again for his play, *Murder in Mayfair*, and appears with it in photographs taken on the tour; but by the time the play reached London it had vanished again. It undoubtedly gives his face a new character, one which his admirers may not have welcomed. As he appears here, he could easily take his place alongside George Raft, Nils Asther or Ricardo Cortez as a Hollywood 'menace'.

The Gallant Hussar (1928)

Had this film been made a few years earlier, it would probably have been a great success. But by the beginning of 1929, when it was released, the public were completely converted to the talking picture, and even films that were made as 'silents' were being withdrawn and frantically refurbished with a musical soundtrack and snatches of dialogue, in the hope of saving them from oblivion. What is more, the story of a reckless lieutenant who falls in love at first sight with an American heiress thinking she is a penniless tourist, while she imagines he is a farm-hand, was hardly the sort of thing to interest an audience who had seen *The Gold-Diggers on Broadway* in sound and colour the night before. However, the part and the costume—he was always happy in uniform—obviously suited Ivor, and the reviews were, under the circumstances, quite favourable.

This charming picture is convincing proof that fragility of plot is no bar to enjoyment. Fortunately the star is endowed with a personality suggesting innocent irresponsibility rather than ingrained wickedness: consequently he never forfeits sympathy.

The Bioscope

The film has the scantiest of stories and lacks continuity; but it has a spontaneity and a charming irresponsibility which tide it over these weaknesses ... Ivor Novello manages to go the pace as thoroughly as may be without alienating our sympathy. Personal charm as much as acting ability enables him to achieve considerable success. His performance is reminiscent of Ramon Novarro in his lighter work, and the quality is much the same ... Beautiful scenery forms a conventional sentimental setting for the love affair, and the more sophisticated scenes are carried out luxuriously.

Film Weekly

Ivor with Evelyn Holt.

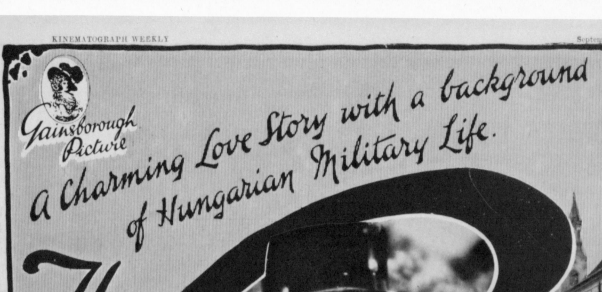

M.WOOLF & MICHAEL BALCON present
OR NOVELLO
EVELYN HOLT in
nt Hussar
rection
OLVARY
Art Direction
NO TIM. O.F.WERNDORFF.
ESENTATION
IPPODROME
MBER 18th at 3 p.m.

Return of The Rat (1928)

A further sequel to *The Rat*, with Ivor Novello again, but it is by no means up to the standard of the original film. The story is novelettish and unoriginal, while most of the situations can be anticipated. Ivor, as usual, relies more on his effective profile rather than acting ability.

Film Weekly

The film was made as a 'silent', but held back to have a sound-track dubbed in to make it a 'part-talkie'.

Right: The Rat returns to his old haunt.

Opposite: Ivor, in disguise, with Isabel Jeans.

Below: With Marie Ault, who played Mère Colline in all three of the 'Rat' films.

In this episode the Rat is now married to Zélie de Chaumet, but she is dallying with an old lover, Henri de Verrai (Bernard Nedell), to whom she agrees to grant her favours in repayment of a racing debt. Disgusted with her, the Rat returns to his old stamping ground, the White Coffin, where he meets Lisette (Mabel Poulton), the counterpart of his old love, Odile. Finding Zélie and de Verrai in flagrante, he challenges his rival to a duel and is left for dead, while the heartless Zélie gives a costume ball to announce her be-

trothal to de Verrai. The Rat attends in disguise, along with his confederates, and becomes involved in a scuffle, in the course of which the lights go out and Zélie, finally getting her just deserts, is stabbed to death. The Rat is suspected, but the murderer is actually the villainous crook, Morel (Gordon Harker), who also lusts after Lisette. With the help of his gang, the Rat evades arrest and rescues Lisette from the clutches of Morel, whom he hands over to the police. Understandably disillusioned with both high society and the

Above: Anton Walbrook in the sound re-make of *The Rat*.

Left: Ivor with Mabel Poulton and Gordon Harker.

underworld, the Rat retires from both and settles down to married life with the devoted Lisette.

The final appearance of the Rat, to date, was in a talkie version, produced by Herbert Wilcox for RKO Radio in this country, in 1937. The story was more or less the same as the original, and Ivor was approached to play the lead again; but he sensibly turned it down and the part was given to Anton Walbrook, who was just beginning to make his name in the English-speaking cinema, having recently played Prince Albert to Anna Neagle's Queen Victoria. Zélie was played by Ruth Chatterton, Odile by René Ray, and Mary Clare, Beatrix Lehmann and Felix Aylmer were also in the cast. But by now the whole conception had become an anachronism; the film made little impact and was shown, in most cases, as the lower half of a double bill.

A South Sea Bubble (1928)

This, Ivor's last silent film, came and went without causing much of a stir in the summer of 1928. It was originally a project of Adrian Brunel's, who was taken off it to direct *The Vortex*, and was an adaptation of a story by Roland Pertwee, a well-known novelist and short-story writer of the time. It concerned Vernon Winslowe, the descendant of a privateer, Roger Winslowe, who has left a buried treasure on a South Sea Island. Being bankrupt, Vernon induces a group of people to put up money for an expedition to rediscover it, but plants a fake treasure himself on the spot marked on his ancestor's map. To his surprise, the real treasure is discovered and leads to a series of disputes and brawls among the treasure-hunters. During a violent climax the booty is lost at sea, but the survivors have of course realised by this time that the True Treasure of Life is Happiness.

The film scarcely fulfils the promise of originality held out by the story ... If Hayes Hunter, the director, had kept to light amusement, *A South Sea Bubble* would have been a great success. Unfortunately he has introduced drama, which almost ruins it ... Ivor Novello's acting is sometimes quite poor and mechanical.

Film Weekly

Ivor Novello plays the part of Winslowe with a moustache and his usual attractive manner of well-bred immobility.

The Bioscope

It was really a load of nonsense, indifferently directed by Hayes Hunter. In fact it was a failure.

Michael Balcon

Below: Ivor with Annette Benson.

Opposite top: With Annette Benson.

Opposite bottom: With Benita Hume.

Above: Ivor with the leading lady in the American version, Jacqueline Logan.

Below: Ivor, in the same scene, with Benita Hume.

Symphony in Two Flats (1930)

Well, girls, here's Ivor Novello's first talkie! For my own sake I am glad to be able to say that *Symphony in Two Flats* ... is a good show, with Ivor Novello putting up a sincere performance and even giving it really clever acting in the emotional scenes ... Even if I didn't say so, you would be quite sure that his voice is very, very pleasant.

Film Weekly

This was the first of Ivor's plays to be filmed in a sound version and followed the original closely, except that the comedy episodes on 'The Floor Below', which featured Lilian Braithwaite and Viola Tree and counterpointed the dramatic events on 'The Floor Above', were eliminated, thus rather nullifying the point of the title. By way of opening the story out and also cashing in on current taste, the frustrated composer, David Kennard, played by Ivor, is persuaded to write a syncopated version of his symphony which is played at a concert by Jack Payne and his orchestra and is a resounding success. This music was specially composed for the film by Eric Coates. Benita Hume appeared as David's wife, Lesley, on stage, but an American actress, Jacqueline Logan, who had played, among other things, Mary Magdalen in Cecil de Mille's *King of Kings*, was cast for the film. This caused an outcry in the Daily Express, which accused Gainsborough Films of a lack of patriotism at a time of national crisis, and Miss Hume was engaged to make a duplicate version for distribution in this country.

Ivor Novello plays David with easy and natural charm, showing the self-centred nature of the musical genius without unduly stressing the selfishness of the character. He reveals also a delightful sense of humour, being more successful in his lighter moments than under strong emotion. Mr Novello's countless admirers will also deplore the fact that many of these scenes are played with his face concealed by a surgical bandage.

The Bioscope

The part of Leo Chavasse, acted on stage by George Relph, was played in the film version, at Ivor's request, by Cyril Ritchard, who had just appeared in Hitchcock's *Blackmail*, the first successful British talkie:

'I went down to the studios one morning, and Ivor's entourage were there, tip-toeing through the tulips. I asked what was wrong, and they said, "Ivor's seen himself in the rushes, and he isn't happy." Later, after the trade show at the Tivoli, I rang him and said, "It's very good, isn't it?" Ivor just said, very quietly, "No."'

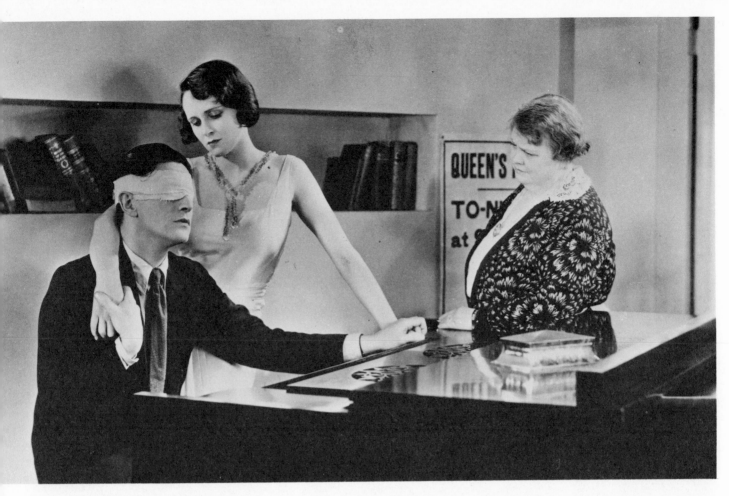

Above: Ivor with Benita Hume and Minnie Rayner.

Below: With Cyril Ritchard and Benita Hume.

Overleaf: Jack Payne congratulates David Kennard (Ivor) on the success of his Syncopated Symphony.

Once a Lady (1931)

The strong cast, which includes Ivor Novello, would lead one to expect much more entertainment than there actually is in this picture . . . Ivor Novello makes a debonair Bennett . . . Technically the picture is very good, with elaborate settings; but no amount of these hide the deficiencies of a plot which weakens as it progresses.

Picturegoer

As a result of the success of his play, *The Truth Game*, on Broadway in December 1930, Ivor was put under contract by MGM as a scriptwriter and went to Hollywood, where he was not particularly happy. Ruth Chatterton, an old friend, thinking that it might cheer him up to do some acting, suggested him as the second male lead in a film she was about to make for Paramount. Her thoughtful gesture had unfortunate consequences, since the film was an almost unqualified disaster and Ivor was never again invited to perform by a Hollywood studio.

The story was an adaptation of a German play, *The Second Life*, and Miss Chatterton played a White Russian emigrée, Anna, who marries an upper-class Englishman (Geoffrey Kerr) by whom she has a daughter (Jill Esmond). Tiring of country life, she runs off to Paris and has an affair with Bennett Cloud, the character played by Ivor, who is subsequently killed off in a train crash. Anna, hearing that her daughter is also about to make an unsuitable marriage, returns to her husband and is eventually forgiven.

The publicity read: The Kind of Movie that Does Wonderful Things to Your Heart.

With Ruth Chatterton.

The Lodger (1932)

An inferior re-make of Ivor's earlier success, this version had the Lodger, now called Angeloff, turning out to be the murderer. The hero, Joe Martin, was played by Jack Hawkins, then at the outset of a long and distinguished career. Yet another version, made in Hollywood in 1944, starred Laird Cregar and was mainly notable for the fact that in it Merle Oberon, then Lady Korda, danced a discreet Can-Can.

Right: Filming at Twickenham Studios.

Below: With Elizabeth Allan as Daisy.

Sleeping Car (1933)

An unhappy attempt at farce. I was completely lost among a lot of comics like Laddie Cliff. The only laugh I got was over a face-slapping scene. Ivor Novello hated having his face slapped, I got the giggles, and we had seventeen takes.

Madeleine Carroll, in a
review of her career in Film Weekly, 1939

Madeleine Carroll, one of the most beautiful, if perhaps not the most talented, actresses of her generation, was cast as Anne, an English girl of the madcap heiress variety so dear to the hearts of scriptwriters in the 1930s, who is threatened with deportation from France after being convicted for what the synopsis refers to as 'furious driving'. In order to stay in France she advertises for a Frenchman to marry her and one of the applicants is Gaston (Ivor), a flirtatious sleeping-car attendant with whom she has already had a stormy encounter. The marriage takes place, as a purely business proposition, but Anne inevitably finds herself falling in love with Gaston and, after the usual complications, a happy ending is arrived at.

Ivor, presumably locked out of Madelèine Carroll's bedroom, makes do with a bearskin rug.

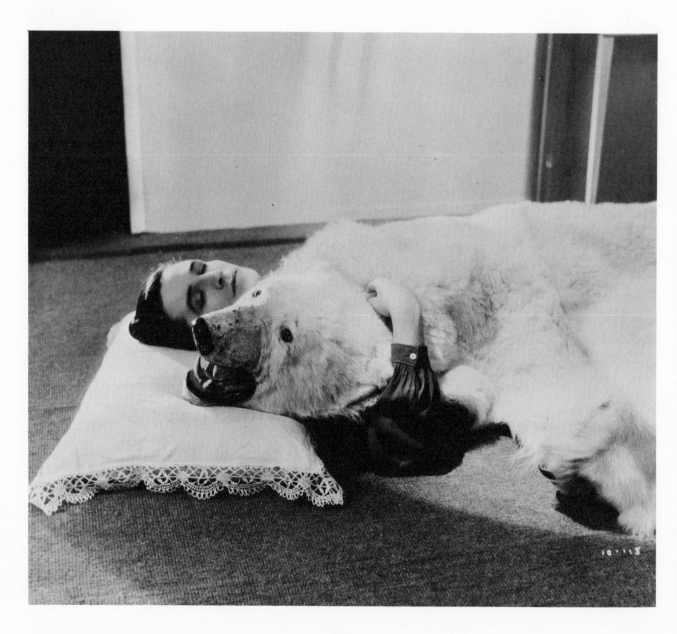

The comics referred to by Miss Carroll included Stanley Holloway and Claude Allister, and a young comedienne who was later to make quite a name for herself, Kay Hammond, also had a featured rôle. In the right hands the film could well have had the same kind of appeal as the slightly risqué comedies which Ernst Lubitsch and others were making in Hollywood, but it suffered somewhat in production from the fact that the director, Anatole Litvak, was rather more interested in his leading lady personally than in the outcome of the film as a whole. In spite of that, the reviews were moderately good, but the film did not appeal to the public. Unlike Ivor, Madeleine Carroll went on to have a successful career in Hollywood, where she appeared as several more madcap heiresses, usually opposite Fred MacMurray.

Sleeping Car is a gay comedy, with a wealth of laughter arising from its many original and piquant situations.

Sunday Pictorial

Ivor Novello has a rôle which suits him admirably and he carries it off with easy charm. Madeleine Carroll is good too, as Anne. These two share the acting honours and practically hold the stage all the time.

Kine Weekly

For various reasons this might almost be called a comedy *Rome Express* ... It is a curious tale, because it starts off as a flirtatious comedy and reaches its climax somewhere in the more dubious by-ways of bedroom farce. But there are some bright moments between the light comedy beginning and the farcical finish-up ... The film has comedy, if not wit, and piquant characters, if not real people. Pictorially, it is lavish and ingenious ... Ivor Novello does his best with the flirtatious Gaston.

Film Weekly

With Madeleine Carroll.

The tea-party scene where Felix outrages the neighbours. Ida Lupino is next to Ursula Jeans at the left, while Minnie Rayner presides at the tea-table with Eliot Makeham beside her.

I Lived With You (1933)

This was Ivor's first play on the London stage after his return from Hollywood and his biggest success up to that point. The film version follows the play closely—too closely at times—and several of the stage cast repeat their rôles. Like Pierre Boucheron in *The Rat*, the part of Felix Lenieff, the White Russian prince who moves in with the suburban Wallis family and transforms their lives, was tailor-made for Ivor's special brand of mischievous charm and it is probably his best performance in a 'talkie'. But all the acting is good, and Minnie Rayner, in particular, in her stage rôle of Mrs Wallis, comes across very strongly on the screen as a kind of miniature Marie Dressler, Cockney-style. Although some attempt is made to open out the play in the early sequences, the latter half of the film is hopelessly stage-bound and, after a hilarious first half, tends to drag. But it still holds up a good deal better than most other domestic comedies of the period.

The star, who acts exceedingly well, is supported by first-class players, and the atmosphere and direction, which reveals shrewd observation, leave nothing to be desired. Ivor Novello has no difficulty in acquiring an intriguing accent, and his good looks help him to bring conviction to a difficult part.

Kine Weekly

Ivor Novello has created that rare thing—a really original story, and those who have not seen the play should find definitely unusual entertainment in this talkie version of his stage production . . . If Novello's own mannerisms . . . are a little obvious at times, his characterisation of the Russian prince who innocently plays havoc with an English middle-class home is still a clever study, and it is impossible to imagine anyone handling the part better than the author himself.

Film Weekly

Ivor with Fay Compton.

Autumn Crocus (1934)

The play by Dodie Smith, produced on the stage by Basil Dean, was the first version of a story—spinster tourist awakened to life and love by a romantic foreigner—which was to do service on other occasions, notably for Katharine Hepburn in *Summer Madness*. Fay Compton created the part of Jenny in the theatre, and her leading man, Francis Lederer, became a star overnight as Steiner, the inn-keeper for whom Jenny falls, only to discover that he is married, with children. Lederer was whisked off to Hollywood at the end of the run, and Basil Dean, who was directing the film version, offered the part to Ivor. He was appearing with Fay Compton in his own play, *Murder in Mayfair*, during the shooting, and, according to Dean, both their performances suffered as a result. 'With the applause of the previous night still ringing in their ears,' he wrote, 'it was difficult to hold the full attention of Fay and Ivor to their parts; by four

o'clock in the afternoon their thoughts were turning to their approaching night's work.' Because the two stars were working in London, it was impossible to take them on location and the film is marred by some obvious back projection of the Tyrol and inefficient sound-mixing. Nevertheless it is a moving, if unimaginative, presentation of a sentimental subject, and Ivor makes a creditable job of a difficult part. Once again he is at his best when the script requires charm and humour and only fails to convince in the emotional scenes. It must be admitted that at times he does look a little old to get away with the 'boyishness' of the part (he was now forty) and rather too exquisite to be running a village inn. But there is no doubt that he was still a potential asset to the Cinema, and it is sad that from now on he decided to work exclusively in the Theatre.

PLAYS

Miss Edna May.

'Lily May': Ivor as a picture postcard beauty.

One of Ivor's earliest and most convincing acting performances took place at the age of twelve, when he and his mother were staying with friends in Bristol. On the back of the picture postcard above (*right*) is written:

Ivor Novello in the donor's garments and flaxen wig, in which attire I walked with him down Whiteladies Road, Clifton. 'Lily May' was his name for me. The story of how, with my connivance, the parlourmaid introduced him into our drawing-room after dinner, hoodwinking my mother and his own, makes a tale worth telling.
Miss M. Kerle Harvey

On the following day, Miss Harvey and Mam took Ivor to a photographer's studio to have his picture taken, in the style of the postcard beauties of the day whom he worshipped: Edna May, Gertie Millar, Lily Elsie, and Zena and Phyllis Dare. The photograph was printed on postcards and Ivor tinted them himself and distributed them to his friends.

Opposite: Ivor in costume for a school play.

108

A SILENCE THAT CAN ALMOST BE FELT

A tense moment at a rehearsal of " Not So Bad As We Seem," Lord Lytton's comedy, which is to be revived at Devonshire House to-day (November 30). Mrs. Asquith is cast for the part of the Silent Lady of Deadman's Lane. Mr. Ivor Novello plays Lord Wilmot, and Colonel C. P. Hawkes Mr. Shadowy Softhead, who is described in the play as "a young gentleman from the city, friend and double to Lord Wilmot"

Ivor in rehearsal with Margot Asquith.

Not As Bad As We Seem (1921)

Ivor's first London appearance was in an amateur production of a play by Bulwer Lytton, written in 1850 (also for amateurs), which was directed by Nigel Playfair and put on for one performance at Devonshire House, to raise funds for the David Copperfield Library in Johnson Street. Also in the cast were Compton Mackenzie, who played a Watchman, Alfred Noyes, who spoke the Epilogue, and Tennyson Jesse, Rebecca West and Adeline Genée.

Mam never encouraged Ivor to act, and at one moment actively prevented him. He had auditioned for the chorus in a tour of *The Count of Luxembourg* and got the job; but she intercepted a letter calling him to rehearsal, and when he failed to turn up, someone else was cast.

Opposite: The Profile makes its first appearance.

Ivor as the Young Man, Armand Duval.

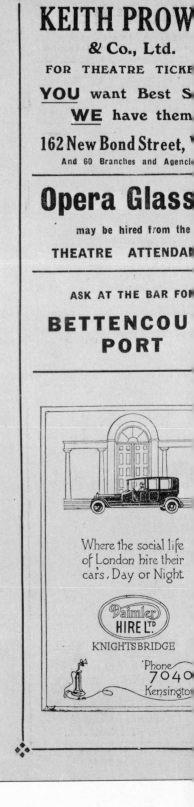

Deburau (1921)

Although he appeared briefly in a revue at the Little Theatre called *As It Used To Be* in 1914, Ivor's first professional engagement in a 'straight' play was in *Deburau* at the Ambassadors Theatre in 1921. This was an adaptation from the French of Sacha Guitry by Harvey Granville Barker and was produced by H. M. Harwood. The leads were Madge Titheradge, Robert Loraine, Leslie Banks and Jeanne de Casalis, and Bobbie Andrews (as he was then known professionally) was also in the cast. Ivor received a mention from no less a critic than Desmond McCarthy:

Mr Ivor Novello as the Young Man, her (Madge Titheradge's) new lover whom, having caught the act of adoring from her Pierrot, she really worships, put into his wooing the respectful ecstasies of 1840. He did very well.

AMBASSADORS THEATRE.

Proprietors - - THE AMBASSADORS THEATRE LTD.
Licensee—HERBERT JAY   Sole Lessee—H. M. HARWOOD
General Manager   ..   ..   B. A. MEYER

EVERY EVENING AT 8.30.

First Mat.: Sat. Nov. 5th, at 2.30.

H. M. HARWOOD

PRESENTS

By arrangement with Charles B. Cochran

DEBURAU

A Comedy by
SACHA GUITRY.
in an English Version by
HARLEY GRANVILLE BARKER.

Jean Gaspard Deburau		ROBERT LORAINE
Marie Duplessis		MADGE TITHERADGE
Monsieur Bertrand		MICHAEL SHERBROOKE
Robillard		JOHN HOWELL
Laurent		LESLIE BANKS
Laplace		J. HENRY TWYFORD
Justine		GLADYS GAYNOR
Madame Rébard	Of the Follies	COLETTE O'NIEL
Clare	Theatre	JEANNE CASALIS
C'ément		EDWARD MERVYN
The Barker		BRUCE WINSTON
The Money-taker		CHERRY CARVER
The Prompter		HARLEY MERICA
Madame Rabouin		BEVERLY SITGREAVES
Charles Deburau		BOBBIE ANDREWS
A Young Man		IVOR NOVELLO
A Doctor		THOMAS WEGUELIN
A Lady		CATHRYN D'ELAINE
A Journalist		STAFFORD HILLIARD
Marie Duplessis' Maid		CHERRY CARVER

Prologue. Outside the Follies Theatre.	**ACT III. An Attic.**
ACT I. Inside the Follies Theatre.	**ACT IV. Inside the Follies Theatre.**
Scene 1. The end of the performance.	Scene 1.} As in Act I.
Scene 2. After the performance.	Scene 2.}
A few months elapse.	*Evening of the same day as*
ACT II. Marie Duplessis' Boudoir.	*Act III.*
Seven years elapse.	

The scene is laid in Paris about the year 1840.

The pantomime arranged by MAESTRO ENRICHO CECCHETTI.

The Scenes for Acts I. and III. designed by J. CROSBIE-FRAZER.
The Scene for Act II. designed by PAUL GILL. Costumes by L. & H. NATHAN.
Miss Titheradge's dresses by MADAME HAYWARD.
Scenery painted by J. CROSBIE-FRAZER at the Ambassadors Scenic Studio.
Shoes by A. FRANKS.   Wigs by CLARKSON.
Furniture by J. and S. LYON.

OVERTURE							
ENTR'ACTE I.	..	..	..	..	..	..	*John H. Foulds*
BALLET MUSIC	..	..	..	..	..	..	
ENTR'ACTE II.							
ENTR'ACTE III.	..	..	..	..	..	..	*Chopin*

Orchestra under the direction of JOHN H. FOULDS.

Stage Director	STAFFORD HILLIARD
Stage Manager	ALFRED BLACKMORE
Asst. Stage Manager	HARLEY MERICA
Acting Manager	PAUL GILL

Ambassadors.   November 4th, 1921

OPERA GLASSES MAY BE HIRED FROM THE THEATRE ATTENDANTS.

The programme for *Deburau*.

Ivor as Wu Hoo Git, with Ann Trevor as Plum Blossom.

The Yellow Jacket (1922)

In the following year Ivor took the juvenile lead in two plays for the Benrimo management at the Kingsway. The first was a revival of a pseudo-Chinese folk play, not unlike the long-running *Lady Precious Stream* of the Thirties, in which everything, including the scenery, was symbolical, and the most significant character was the comic Property Man. Benrimo, who collaborated on the play as well as directing it, was a Belasco-like figure of the period of whom one actress remarked, 'He makes artists out of mud.'

Ivor Novello scarcely justifies the villain's accusations of 'vulgar manliness', but did well enough.

The Daily Sketch

I expect it was the engaging personality of Mr Ivor Novello, who has taken up acting in deadly earnest, that helped to fill the Kingsway with such a 'precious' audience on Tuesday night. He played the young lover . . . exceedingly well, and it looks as though he might have the reversion of the beautiful Bellew, handsome Harry Conway, Alexander, Waller and other matinée idols.

The Sunday Chronicle

Mr Novello, a frank and good-looking romantic youth, showed too obviously a sensibility to the absurdities of the part, forced the pace emotionally, and occasionally lost the heroic in the effeminate.

The Sunday Times

Spanish Lovers (1922)

Ivor's second rôle for Benrimo was in a translation by Christopher St John from the French, in its turn a translation from the Spanish of J. Feliu y Cordona. He played the tragic hero, Javier, whom the heroine marries against her will and who finally, relinquishing her to the man she loves, expires from a wasting disease. After the end of the run at the Kingsway, Ivor took the play out on tour with some of the London company, presenting *The Constant Lover* by St John Hankin as a curtain-raiser.

Mr Ivor Novello played the part of Javier with pathos and languishing grace. His starts of helpless fury were admirable.

Desmond McCarthy
in the New Statesman

Mr Ivor Novello furnished a most interesting and carefully finished study of the feverishly feeble Javier, at one moment torn by passion, at another yielding to an uncontrollable access of despair.

The Daily Telegraph

He gave a representation of a doomed weakling as poetic, as courageous, as graceful and vigorous as could be expected from him. I think he made a big step upward as an actor by his handling of this part. We have none too many men capable of playing juvenile leads and if Mr Novello can step into the breach, his good looks, pleasing voice and engaging manner should carry him a long way in his work.

Sydney Carroll
in the Sunday Times

Ivor, as Javier, attacks Malcolm Morley, his rival for the love of Doris Lloyd.

Enter Kiki (1923)

Ivor and Gladys Cooper, as has been already noted, were publicised as a romantic team both on and off the screen, but their stage ventures together were not so happy, and of all of them *Enter Kiki*, which was presented at the Playhouse under Miss Cooper's own management, was probably the most unfortunate. As *Kiki* simply, in an adaptation by Sidney Blow and Douglas Hoare from the French of André Picard, it had been a great success on Broadway two years previously, when the dynamic brunette, Lenore Ulric, had played the title rôle. But Gladys Cooper was an entirely different type of performer, and Ivor, still a relatively inexperienced juvenile, was hardly suited to the part of Victor

Leroux, the debonair and worldly theatrical manager to whom an aspiring chorus girl lays relentless siege. The part of Kiki, who forces herself on Leroux, makes him take her home for supper, spends the night on his sofa and the next morning, when Mme Leroux appears, threatens to murder her and then fakes a cataleptic coma to retain Victor's attention, was a show-case for the right actress—which Miss Cooper was not, any more than Ivor was the right actor to play opposite her. Nevertheless, although one critic reported that he acted 'in a sort of dreary trance', others found much to admire in his performance.

Victor's kiss awakens Kiki from her 'trance'.

It may be that if the play were done with the touch of Sacha Guitry and Yvonne Printemps, a greater liveliness would creep into it. Miss Gladys Cooper plays it with great gusto, but perhaps because Mr Ivor Novello, as the solemn Victor, is as solemn as a cathedral, the pathos seems to weigh a little heavy on her.

The Times

Ivor Novello walked through the piece with more surety than he has yet shown, and now and then he acted with considerable force.

The Daily News

To many of us the most successful performance of the evening was that of Ivor Novello as Victor Leroux. He was one of the few players that seemed to realise he was not acting in *Charlie's Aunt*. There is an intellectual quality about Mr Novello's acting which gives promise of brilliant development, if he resists the temptation to become a matinée idol.

The Weekly Dispatch

Kiki (Gladys Cooper) auditions for Victor Leroux (Ivor).

The Rat (1924)

The Story of an Apache, by David L'Estrange

You know the Apache: he wears peg-top trousers and a grey muffler, and his favourite haunt is the cabaret of the White Coffin where Rose and Mou-Mou sigh for him because he knocks them about in the intervals of crime. To the cabaret comes the ineffectual Detective-Inspector who has never succeeded in running the Rat to earth. Comes also a shimmering empress of the demi-monde, bored by her banker-lover, no wonder, and in quest of new sensations. Comes also Odile, the little mistress of the Rat, representing from the first all that is good in his nature. Why the banker-lover of the demi-mondaine should fix amorous eyes upon the heroine is hard to understand, but he always does, it is part of the plot . . . Why he should persevere in his attentions after being half-strangled by the Rat is still more mysterious: the plot

Right: Ivor as Pierre Boucheron, the Rat.

Below: *The Rat* Company on Tour: Morgan, Ivor's chauffeur, is second from the right at the back, beside his wife, Vi. 'Lloydie' stands behind Ivor's right shoulder.

MR. IVOR NOVELLO.
As "THE RAT".

has him fairly in its clutches. It is easier to be convinced by the passion of the demi-mondaine for her Apache, new sensations being always alluring. While the Rat visits her in the Avenue Victor Hugo, the banker pesters the little mistress in her humble lodging. The Rat returns and kills him. The little mistress confesses to the crime to shield her lover. A tense scene in the ante-room of the examining magistrate, and the Rat appears in the guise of a reformed character, spurning the demi-monde and its follies and declaring for humble blessedness with his Odile.

The Sporting & Dramatic

As a work of art the value of *The Rat* is about ninepence, at a liberal estimate, but as a box-office attraction I should think it ranks at about £1,500 a week.

London Opinion

Left: The Rat in derisive mood.

Below: A caricature by Hicks.

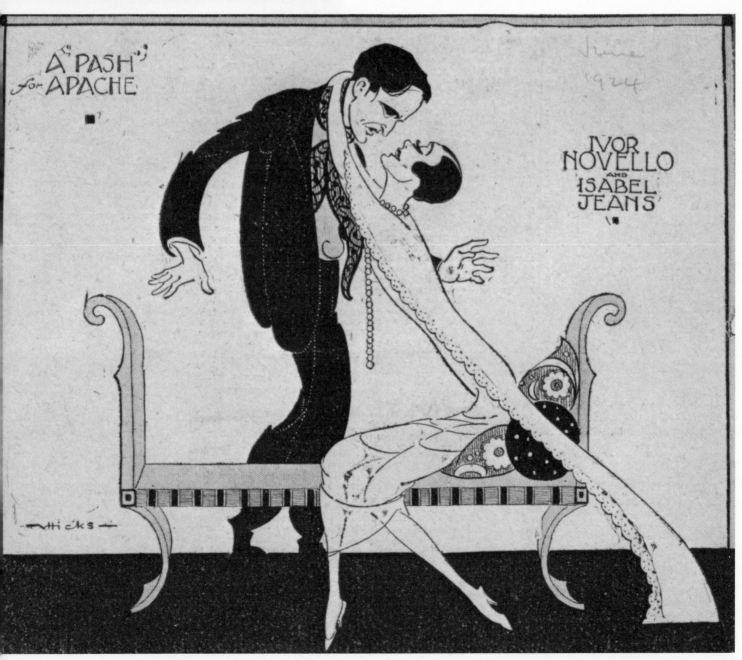

A "PASH" for APACHE

IVOR NOVELLO AND ISABEL JEANS

This is a good melodrama, written in red ink and served piping hot, a trifling foolish mixed metaphor perhaps, but no matter. It were a foolish thing to despise the medium of which this is an excellent specimen... Mr Ivor Novello plays the Rat very much in the tradition of Sir John Martin-Harvey, that is to say, worthily and well. His cinema following, present, one gathered, in force, might have been excused for fearing lest the stage words of Mercury should prove harsh after the screen poems of Apollo, but they trembled needlessly. Miss Dorothy Batley, a new-comer, played injured innocence very well indeed. A few more parts like Odile and she can be trusted to hold her own in something that makes sense ... This play should have a long run. It is a collector's piece, complete in every detail. No cliché in the way of phrase has been omitted and no tag of sentiment neglected. David L'Estrange may possess his soul in peace: the home fires will be kept burning throughout the summer.

James Agate
in the Sunday Times

Mr Ivor (David) Novello and Miss Constance (L'Estrange) Collier are responsible for *The Rat* ... and no single unassisted mind could conceivably have put together so much stock situation stated in so many hoary platitudes as the combined efforts of these two clever people have produced. They must have written *The Rat* with tongue in cheek all the time and they must chuckle a great deal together on the tremendous success of their appeal to the multitude. Mr Novello is the Rat all the time, and six or sixteen or sixty lovely ladies in the cast kiss him with intention at and between the various curtains, and he dances, and laughs, and slays, and makes love, and even goes mad and babbles of green fields, and the audience is swayed by his joys and sorrows, and it is all incredibly humiliating to the intelligence and exciting to the emotions of the crowd. It must be seen to be believed.

The Queen

You will not find all this on a week-end trip organised by Doctor Lunn, but why cross the Channel when Paris is so much more colourful at the Prince of Wales ... ? Mr Ivor Novello is half the authorship and Miss Constance Collier is the other half, but where, as a member of the Younger Generation, did Mr Novello get all those funny old-fashioned ideas?

The Daily Herald

The plot is childish, not to say sugary, but what of that? It is theatrical, it provides a vehicle in which ... a set of clever and handsome people can show their best airs and graces, and it is pleasantly flattering to our human natures ... There is no guillotine in this play. The Parisian police are a friendly lot, and when little Odile, the foster sister, looking like Joan of Arc when she heard the voices, says 'I did it', and the guiltily splendid one, in spite

of the scandal, comes and swears that the Rat was in her arms at the time of the murder, it is decided that the murder was justifiable. You couldn't guillotine Odile.

The Evening Standard

The last act is very poor wish-wash, but as there are bad good plays, so there are good bad ones, and *The Rat* is not at all a bad good bad one. Perhaps a pinch of salt should be given away with every programme just to show that it is only a bit of fun.

The Sphere

120

The Rat dances with America (Dorothy St John), observed by Det-Insp Caillard (James Lindsay), Zélie de Chaumet (Isabel Jeans), Herman Stetz (W. Cronin Wilson) and Madeline Sornay (Nancy Pawley).

Left: The Villain gets his just deserts: Ivor with W. Cronin Wilson and Dorothy Batley.

Below: Isabel Jeans and Ivor.

Opposite: The Rat Redeemed: Ivor and Dorothy Batley.

Feminine admiration was divided between the perfection of Ivor Novello's profile and of Isabel Jeans' Reville-made garments in general and in particular perhaps of the superb chinchilla cloak which she wore in the first act over a gown all of shining silver tissue and lace, embroidered with diamonds, long diamond earrings in the form of tassels, and one choker necklace of huge pearls and another long rope of small pearls being completing details of a toilette that dazzled all eyes.

The Sporting & Dramatic

At every tragic moment at which her lines were colourless rather than absurd Miss Batley produced a feeling of reality and emotion quite foreign to the piece. Mr Ivor Novello, like so many English stars, is an actor whose stage personality is attractive to you or unattractive. It is not immediately clear to me why that personality should have tended to make the Rat seem rather harmless—not quite a guinea-pig, you understand, but something more like the virtuous mongoose.

The Spectator

"RAT": "Can't you come a little closer?"

"THE RAT" STEP

(FOX-TROT)

As danced by Ivor Novello and Dorothy St. John in "THE RAT"

PHOTO · FOULSHAM & BANFIELD

Music by

IVOR
NOVELLO

Price 2/- Net.

ASCHERBERG · HOPWOOD & CREW · LTD
16 · Mortimer Street · London · W·1.
(FOR COLONIAL AND FOREIGN AGENTS SEE BACK PAGE.)

PRINTED IN ENGLAND.

The Fifty-Fifty Club is now being formed in the West End and it is hoped to open it, in its premises in the neighbourhood of Wardour Street, about October the first. It will be a club primarily for theatrical people, where they will be able to go before and after the shows, and where they will be able to dance, sip cocktails, dine or sup at a reasonable rate. 'The Club is to be so called,' said Ivor Novello, one of the prime movers in the venture, 'because one will get out of it as much as one gives.' The Club and its members will go fifty-fifty in fact ... Though the outside public will not be excluded, the first three hundred members will be exclusively stage folk. The decorations, which will be most striking, will be done by Nerman, whose work in clubs in Stockholm greatly impressed Novello.

The Evening News

On the opening night it needed a battering ram to get you in and a vacuum cleaner to get you out. The inside of the Fifty-Fifty is orange and blue, and there are theatrical caricatures around the walls that have any amount of punch; indeed they almost hurt you after the first half hour.

The Graphic

All too soon the news got around and various social liaison officers began to appear with representative groups, and the small part actors, who were the basic reason for the club's existence, were seen to be shrinking away into the shadowy corners of the room until finally they no longer came at all. Personally I mourn to this day the loss of the Fifty-Fifty Club.

Noël Coward
Present Indicative

Opposite: The cover of the music Ivor wrote for his Apache dance.

Below: Ivor in the Fifty-Fifty Club, in front of his caricature by Nerman.

Old Heidelberg (1925)

The Rat transferred from the Prince of Wales to the Garrick, where it completed its run at the end of 1924. Ivor then went into rehearsal for a revival of *Old Heidelberg* at the same theatre, with Dorothy Batley again playing opposite him. The play was an adaptation from the German of Wilhelm Meier-Forster, and had been presented by George Alexander at the St James's Theatre in 1903 with himself and Eva Moore in the leads.

While *Old Heidelberg* was in rehearsal, an American comedy called *Six-Cylinder Love* with Bobby Howes and Edna Best was presented at the Garrick, but was such a flop that it had to close after a few performances and the management begged Ivor to re-open *The Rat* as a stop-gap—which must be the soonest any play has ever been 'revived' in the West End.

Old Heidelberg was subsequently turned into a musical play under the title of *The Student Prince*, for which Sigmund Romberg wrote the score.

Mr Ivor Novello has youth and good looks as the Prince, but somehow lacks the distinction with which Alexander invested the character when he was no longer young.

The Times

The play was moderately well done at the Garrick. It was much too long and should have been cut a full hour. As it was, the evening was half spent before Mr Novello was called upon to begin acting, which in the end he did gracefully and at times movingly, even to the point of surviving a uniform reminiscent of a municipal bandsman from Southend.

James Agate
in the Sunday Times

Opposite top: The Prince as Student: William Kendall stands at the other end of the table, with Morgan, Ivor's chauffeur, on his left.

Below: Ivor and Dorothy Batley demonstrate love-making techniques for the London Magazine.

Opposite bottom: Ivor, as Prince Karl Heinrich, foreshadowing his last appearance, as Nikki in *King's Rhapsody*.

Iris (1925)

Old Heidelberg closed after a few weeks, and Ivor went into this revival of a Pinero play which Gladys Cooper had put on at the Adelphi. Her leading man was Henry Ainley. Ivor replaced Anew McMaster in the rôle of Laurence Trenwith.

Ivor as Laurence Trenwith, with Gladys Cooper.

Iris (1925)

The Firebrand (1925)

Ivor's one stage appearance with his close friend, Constance Collier, was much less successful than their writing collaborations. The play, by Edwin Justus Mayer, was a fanciful treatment of the life of Benvenuto Cellini and had been a hit on Broadway in 1924, when another 'matinèe idol', Joseph Schildkraut, played Cellini, and Nana Bryant, Frank Morgan and Edward G. Robinson were also in the cast. The London version was presented by the

Ivor as Cellini, with Constance Collier.

American impresario, Gilbert Miller, and was lavishly produced, with costumes by the brilliant French designer and illustrator, Georges Barbier; but the public did not respond and the run was only ten weeks.

The play was filmed in the 1930s under the title of *The Affairs of Cellini* with Fredric March, Constance Bennett and Fay Wray, and with Frank Morgan repeating his stage rôle, and later still it became a Broadway musical, *The Firebrand of Florence*, with a score by Kurt Weill and Weill's wife, Lotte Lenya, appearing as the Duchess of Florence, the part played in London by Constance Collier.

'The author has utilized rather than chronicled Benvenuto Cellini,' that is to say, turned him into a handsome gallant (with the easy co-operation of Mr Ivor Novello), brave to fantastic extravagance in his apparel, with two legs never of the same colour, an incomparable braggart and universal lover. But then Mr Novello is always, as the Americans say, 'easy to look at', and the author's way of utilising him is to keep us looking at him all the time, to the general satisfaction.

The Times

I remember so well going round after the first night to Constance's dressing-room. She had this long wig on, and she just took it off and said, 'It's a flop!'

Dorothy Batley

Downhill (1926)

For their second collaboration as 'David L'Estrange' Ivor and Constance Collier devised a story every bit as sentimental and melodramatic as *The Rat*, and, if anything, rather more improbable: Roddy Berwick, Captain of the School, is accused by a local waitress of being the father of her child. The culprit is really Roddy's best friend, Tim, but Roddy takes the blame and is expelled. Ostracised by his father, he takes a job as a chorus boy, has a love affair with the leading lady, and when she ditches him, goes from bad to worse, ending up on the docks of Marseilles. Returning to England, he is about to drown himself in the Thames when Tim, who has confessed his guilt, rescues him and Roddy's name is cleared.

But although it had a respectable run, it failed to repeat *The Rat*'s success and did much better business on tour, when Ivor's film fans flocked to see him, than in the West End. In it Phyllis Monkman, a close friend of Ivor's, who had previously appeared mainly in revue and musical comedy, made her dramatic début as Julia Blue, the gold-digging actress who seduces Roddy at one stage in his progress Downhill, and then leaves him when she has spent all his money. Preposterous as the plot was, it was put across in deadly earnest—although it appears that Ivor himself occasionally failed to take it seriously:

We were playing a scene together on a settee, when suddenly something caught his attention and he dried up—in his own play! I gave him the cue again, and nothing happened. I gave it him three times and he took not the slightest bit of notice. Then suddenly he got up and went off, leaving me onstage all by myself. So I got up and said, 'I wonder where Minnie is——?'—she was my dresser in the play—'Minnie! Minnie! Where are you?' And then I started doing my hair. After several minutes Ivor put his head round the door, with a Harry Tate moustache on. I was gone—and so was he! Talk about discipline—that's what he did in his own play!

Phyllis Monkman

Downhill or (if we may suggest an alternative title) From Public School to the Embankment—a drama in nine short but lurid reels featuring (there is no other word) Mr Ivor Novello in a rough but graceful descent from the splendours of 'Soccer' to the miseries of 'Marseilles' . . . Miss Phyllis Monkman is in great spirits in Julia's dressing-room, and Mr Ivor Novello has all the glitter and emphasis that the piece requires. We do not doubt that his spectacular descent will be frequently repeated.

The Times

When Mr Novello washed his legs in the first scene of this play, one heard the sound of indrawn breath coming from the maidens in the pit. Here was a thrilling spectacle to be described with the utmost particularity on the morrow to the unfortunate maidens who had missed it. His knees, his shins, even his thighs, and his dear little wiggly toes! If there were palpitations in the pit, there were sighs of satisfaction in the gallery. Hitherto life had seemed to be full. Could there be anything more delightful than Ivor's famous profile which he so engagingly and so frequently exhibited? . . . How could any maiden hope for more? And then—oh, delicious!—someone discovered that Ivor had knees, and immediately Mr David L'Estrange sat down and wrote a play so that they might be publicly washed at the same time that his profile was exhibited. Not in vain had the maidens stood in queues for hours! At the end of the weary night they saw his toes.

St John Ervine
in the Observer

Opposite: A page of scenes from *Downhill* in the Sketch.

Plays of the Moment: "Down Hill," at the Queen's.

ONE OF THE GOOD INFLUENCES IN THE RAKE'S LIFE: RODDY (IVOR NOVELLO) WITH VIVIEN (FRANCES DOBLE).

THE BOY AND THE REVUE STAR: RODDY (IVOR NOVELLO) AND JULIA (PHYLLIS MONKMAN) IN THE THEATRE DRESSING-ROOM SCENE.

EXPELLED FROM SCHOOL, AND ABUSED BY HIS FATHER: RODDY (IVOR NOVELLO) AND TOM BERWICK (EVELYN ROBERTS).

MOTHER AND SON: MRS. BERWICK (JESSIE BATEMAN) AND RODDY (IVOR NOVELLO).

"Down Hill" is by David L'Estrange (otherwise Mr. Ivor Novello) and Miss Constance Collier; and it is a modern "Rake's Progress." Mr. Ivor Novello is the boy who is expelled from school for the misdeeds of his friend Tom. He runs away from home, becomes a chorus man in a revue, and falls in love with the star, Julia—a rôle taken by Miss Phyllis Monkman. (This is this popular actress's first appearance in "straight" comedy, and she has a strongly emotional part to play.) Miss Frances Doble, the beautiful young American actress, is the Vivien, one of the good influences of the boy's life, and Miss Jessie Bateman is his sympathetic and loving mother.

Photographs by Stage Photo. Co.

Liliom (1926)

Under the title *The Daisy* this play had already failed once in London in 1920, and this version, directed by Komisarjevsky, fared little better, but did at least serve to establish Charles Laughton in the West End. As the eponymous hero, a bullying fair-ground barker who is loved by a good girl, dies in a brawl, and eventually goes to heaven, Ivor was patently miscast. The play later had much more success as Rodgers and Hammerstein's musical, *Carousel*.

Mr Ivor Novello continues his uneven but, I think, on the whole, upward course. He is surprisingly good at moments; surprisingly conventional or careless or obvious at others. Liliom was alive, however, and that is much to achieve.

Punch

An Interview with Mrs Compton MacKenzie:
'I cried so much over some of the scenes, but I enjoy crying at the theatre.' What interested me most was to hear that Fay Compton is wearing wonderful Balkan peasant dresses, voluminous skirts and brilliant colourings and embroideries ... I asked Mrs Compton Mackenzie how shingled hair fits the picture of a Balkan peasant girl and she told me that Fay Compton is wearing her hair parted in the centre, thus disguising her smart new shingle.

The Daily Chronicle

Surely it must be obvious to everyone that this hulking brute must be a brute who hulks and that to present him with the aquiline grace and Latin effrontery of Mr Novello at his most accomplished is to court disaster. As a blustering, throat-slitting bully this charming actor failed charmingly; as Mr Bernard Shaw's Louis Dubedat he was delightful ... The fellow should be totally unable to explain himself, whereas Mr Novello, one felt, could have explained anything and everything from Lord Beaverbrook's politics to the esoteric mystery of the Black Bottom.

James Agate
in the Sunday Times

With Charles Laughton.

With Fay Compton.

The festa scene: Ivor on the bar and Frances Doble seated down-stage.

Sirocco (1927)

The events on the first night were so startling that for many years thereafter the name became a synonym in theatrical circles for disaster: one actor to another, 'How was it last night?' 'Sirocco, old boy.'

Basil Dean,
Seven Ages

Sirocco was an early unproduced play of Noël Coward's which Basil Dean decided to present, in a revised version, with, at Coward's request, Ivor in the lead. It is not a particularly good play, but nor is it a bad one: a romantic melodrama about an English wife on the loose in Italy, who has a passionate affair with the local Romeo, which ends in violence. But from the moment the curtain rose on the first night at Daly's, there were signs of animosity in the gallery—directed mainly against Coward, whose early success was bringing the inevitable reaction—and at the climax of the second act, when Ivor and Frances Doble made fervent love on the floor, the scene was greeted with laughter and cat-calls. From then on the disturbances increased until the final curtain which fell to a storm of booing. Basil Dean, who made it a rule to go out and have dinner during a first performance, returned to the theatre at this point, and, mistaking the uproar for cheers, ordered the stage manager to keep raising the curtain. Coward, in desperation, went onstage to face the audience, whereupon the din increased to riot proportions. He then led Frances Doble forward, and the unfortunate creature, apparently unaware of the situation, uttered the—under the circumstances—memorable phrase: 'Ladies and Gentlemen, this is the happiest night of my life.'

'This was received with shrieks of incredulous laughter,' writes Basil Dean, 'at which I lost my head completely and went onto the stage in a fury. There was a momentary silence as people waited to hear what I had to say. I began, "Ladies and Gentlemen—if there *are* any gentlemen in the house ...?" And then the kettle boiled over.'

"God bless our home": Sirio (Mrs. Robinson up), being an artist, goes round the furniture in quest of beauty: Frances Doble and Ivor Novello.

Ivor's behaviour throughout was remarkable . . . With full realisation that all his trouble and hard work had gone for less than nothing, his sense of humour was still clear and strong enough to enable him to make a joke of the whole thing. Nor was he apparently in the least ruffled by the inevitable Press blast the next day. He made no complaints, attached no blame or responsibility to anyone, and accepted failure with the same grace that he has always accepted success.

Noël Coward,
Present Indicative

Top: The End of a Love Affair: Ivor and Frances Doble.

Bottom: The same scene, as observed by Hynes in the Sporting & Dramatic.

How dreadfully silly and solemn it became—the solemner the sillier! There was a time when it seemed that a derisive gallery would put an end to our discomfort, but the curtain to the second act was happily quicker than their impatience . . . A more uncomfortable conclusion to an evening may we never experience. The worst of it was that Mr Coward had brought it on himself.

The Times

Mr Novello's and Miss Doble's performances were both good ones—each a rather surprising revelation of the capabilities of the actor and actress. But the predominant performance of the evening was that of the gallery, and it was not to the gallery's credit.

The Evening Standard

The behaviour of the Gallery, the uppermost section of the theatre, where seats were unreserved and had to be queued for—often, for a big attraction, throughout the previous night—was a subject of controversy right through the Twenties and Thirties and up until the last decade, when the increasing price of theatre tickets led the managements to make all seats bookable. The camaraderie of the 'Gallery First Nighters' and along with it the displays of partisanship which could make or break a play vanished, and it is many years since the dreaded—and occasionally merited—sound of booing has been heard in the West End.

Ivor and Noël (*r*) assist at a Theatrical Garden Party.

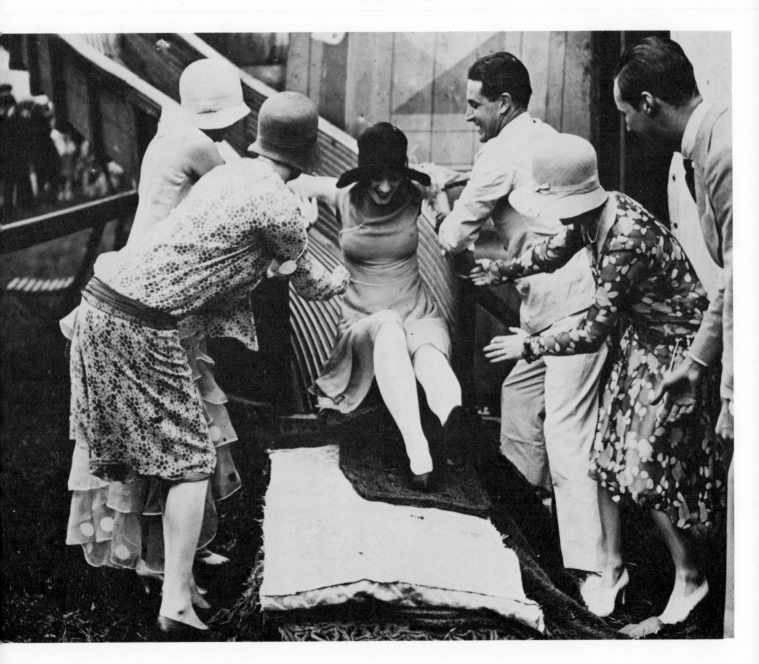

135

The Truth Game (1928)

After several near-failures and the disaster of *Sirocco*, Ivor's status in the Theatre was rather in question, and it was against the advice of most of his friends—including particularly Noël Coward—that he decided to launch his first solo venture as playwright, under the nom-de-plume of H. E. S. Davidson. It was written as a vehicle for one of the idols of his youth, Lily Elsie, who had recently come back to the Theatre after several years' retirement. He wrote the male lead, Max Clement, for himself, and the part of Mrs Brandon for Constance Collier. Thinking that it would deter him from going ahead with the production, Miss Collier retired from the cast after a few rehearsals. But she was replaced by Ellis Jeffreys, who also departed, and the part was finally played by Lilian Braithwaite and was the first of many that she was to take in Ivor's plays. After some delay, *The Truth Game* opened at the Globe Theatre and was an immediate success. Unlike his previous plays, it was the lightest of comedies and revolved round two cast-iron themes—sex and money.

A Punch cartoon of Ivor and Lily Elsie.

Lily Elsie and Lilian Braithwaite.

Ivor and Lily Elsie.

136

Sir Joshua Grimshaw	Vera Crombie	Evelyn Brandon	Max Clement	The Lady Joan Culver	Lord Straffield
(Frederick Volpe)	(Mabel Sealby)	(Lilian Braithwaite)	(Ivor Novello)	(Viola Tree)	(Glen Byam Shaw)

The House Party conspires to play the truth game.

A scene from the second act.

Lily Elsie played Rosine Browne, a wealthy widow who finds herself being pursued by a penniless adventurer, Max Clement. With the assistance of Mrs Brandon, a 'ten per cent' lady who lives off the commissions she makes from the shops to whom she sends rich customers, Max presses his suit, and Rosine falls in love with him, only to find that he is a distant relative who, if she remarries, will inherit her fortune. Disillusioned with Max, she announces her engagement to the wealthy Sir George Kelvin. But Mrs Brandon again intervenes and all ends happily. A sub-plot involved the gauche Lady Joan Turner, played by Ivor's friend, Viola Tree, for whom Mrs Brandon is seeking a rich husband. The 'Truth Game' of the title takes place at a house party in the second act and enables Max to reveal his feelings for Rosine.

Lily Elsie and Ivor Novello are the most picturesque pair that feminine playgoers could wish to see, and as women form the greater part of any given audience, their complete satisfaction with the entertainment is practically guaranteed in advance.

Theatre World

This light comedy (with heavy patches) shows sound promise, for the author, Mr. 'H. E. S. Davidson', has a sense of fantastic character and a fair hand for lively dialogue—promise, I think, rather than quite satisfactory achievement. He ought, I consider, to jettison his over-sentimental cargo.

Punch

The Third Act was all more inane than it need have been, and it is pleasanter to remember the earlier acts which are full of good-humoured nonsense and the ingenious decorations of impudent dialogue. Mr Novello is in high spirits; Miss Lily Elsie has a firm and charming grip on the not very subtle intricacies of Rosine's character; Miss Viola Tree gives a remarkably entertaining caricature of a Duke's daughter . . . and Miss Lilian Braithwaite . . . gives a performance more polished than them all. In brief, though the play is shallow and scattered in its conclusion, the trimmings are often very good fun.

The Times

After six months' run, *The Truth Game* went on tour and then returned to the West End for a further season, at Daly's.

Right: Ivor and Lily Elsie 'listening in'.

Below: The first night party onstage: Ivor stands between Lilian Braithwaite, Madame Clara and Lily Elsie, behind whom is Viola Tree.

'The Flat' sat, and still sits, on the very top of the Strand Theatre, and in order to reach it a perilous ascent was made in a small, self-worked lift. Ivor's guests crushed themselves timorously together in this frightening little box, someone pulled a rope, there was a sharp grinding noise, a scream from some less hardy member of the party; then, swaying and rattling, the box ascended. Upon reaching the top, it would hit the roof with a crash and, more often than not, creak all the way down again ... The big room of the flat had a raised dais running across one end. Upon this were sometimes two, at other times no grand pianos, sometimes a gramophone, and nearly always Viola Tree ... The high spots of the parties were reached in this room. Charades were performed, people did stunts, Olga Lynn sang, and Fay Compton immediately did an imitation of Olga Lynn singing.

Noël Coward,
Present Indicative

Left: Ivor and the false bookshelves that concealed his gramophone records.

Below: In the sitting-room.

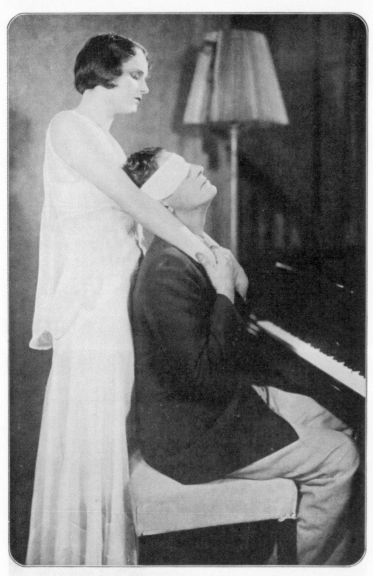

DAVID : " Oh Lesley ! What if I never saw you again ?"
LESLEY : " Of course you'll see, better than ever. I'll be here to look after you."

DAVID (*pretending he can see*) : " I can get along now. Good-bye, my dear."
LESLEY : " Don't you want me, David?"

Symphony in Two Flats (1929)

This was Ivor's first play to be produced under his own name, and for the main theme he returned to sentimental melodrama. He played David Kennard, a struggling young composer, who meets Lesley (Benita Hume) at the Chelsea Arts Ball and marries her. They set up home in a flat in Tadema Studios, and Lesley takes a job as a model while David works on a symphony which he is entering for a competition sponsored by the Gramophone Company. He is also helped out by Leo Chavasse (George Relph) a rich friend who is in love with Lesley. To add to his problems, David finds he is going blind and by the time the results of the competition come out he has almost lost his sight. But Leo conceals a letter from the Gramophone Company turning down David's symphony, and with the connivance of Lesley makes him believe he has won. But David buys a radio and, listening to the concert, hears someone else's symphony being played. Tearing the bandages from his eyes, he sees Leo and Lesley in what he assumes to be an adulterous embrace. He turns Lesley out and takes to writ-

ing popular songs to make a living, and when she returns, pretends that his sight is restored and he no longer needs her. But Lesley finds out the truth, and they are reunited in the hope that David will eventually regain his sight. In contrast, the goings-on in the 'Flat Below', told in alternate scenes, are wholly comic and concern a widow, Mrs Plaintiff (Lilian Braithwaite) and her two daughters by different marriages, Salmon (Viola Tree), an eccentric artist and keep-fit enthusiast, and Beryl (Ann Trevor). Various farcical situations result in Beryl marrying the house agent who found them the flat and Mrs Plaintiff marrying an Australian millionaire.

The part of Mabel, the 'all-in-all' (as Ivor describes her) who 'does for' David and Lesley and sympathises with them in their troubles, was played by Minnie Rayner, a Cockney comedienne who became Ivor's mascot and appeared subsequently in nearly every play and musical that he wrote until her death.

Lilian Braithwaite and Viola Tree.

To me, for one, the scene where the blind musician learns that it is not his symphony which has won the prize—though of the theatre theatrical—never lost its shattering poignancy ... With all its own considerable merits (*Symphony in Two Flats*) is chiefly interesting as a measure of the progress the author has made in the two or three years since it was written.

Edward Marsh

Unless we are to believe that Mr Novello was prompted by the lack of matter in either of them to tell two stories instead of one, we are driven to decide that the moral of the play is that you do not get to know people unless you happen to meet them. Nine scenes are a long journey for such a prize.

The Times

Each of his two separate plays has an odd effect of distracting from the other. The people in the top flat are so unrelievedly intense, and the people below are so painstakingly comic, that one wishes they could be allowed to mix and so mitigate each other's crudeness. For all that, the play is a thoroughly competent piece of work. Its serious scenes give Mr Novello himself good scope to

show once again that he is an enormously improved actor, whose range of expression has improved out of all knowledge in the last few years ... These two (Lilian Braithwaite and Viola Tree) made Mr Novello's last play for him and, in this one, though the material they are given is rather coarse in texture, they keep us laughing almost continuously.

The Daily Telegraph

To read nowadays, *Symphony in Two Flats* seems painfully contrived and mawkish, but one has to admire the confidence with which Ivor interlarded the dramatic tale with farcical comedy to produce a concoction which, while it may not have impressed the critics, certainly entertained the public. The play lasted for five months—a considerable run in those days. The film rights were bought by Gainsborough, and, more important, the Shuberts offered to present it on Broadway, with Ivor and most of the London cast, apart from Viola Tree who had other commitments. Joyce Carey, Lilian Braithwaite's daughter, had been living in America and came to see the play on her return to London: 'When Lilian told me they were going to New York, I was very surprised—*and* worried.'

Symphony in Two Flats opened at the Sam S. Shubert Theatre on September 16th 1930, in the middle of a heat-wave, but to luke-warm notices. Richard Watts in the Herald Tribune called it 'an ambitious and often interesting attempt that doesn't quite work out', while John Mason Brown of the Evening Post wrote, 'The two plays which combine to form it only tend to make it seem twice as unsatisfactory as it might ordinarily have seemed.' The Times attacked Ivor as both author and actor: 'Composing under the influence of two contrasting moods, Mr Novello has indulged himself in an exercise more mannered than substantial . . . His is a performance—and a play—coloured with preciosity.' The play was withdrawn after forty-seven performances, but, rather surprisingly, the Shuberts gave Ivor a second chance on Broadway. Billie Burke, the wife of Florenz Ziegfeld, and a much loved comedienne, was coming out of retirement to assist her husband's deteriorating finances and was looking for a suitable play. The Shuberts offered her the part of Mrs Brandon which Lilian Braithwaite had played in London, Miss Burke accepted, and *The Truth Game* opened at the Ethel Barrymore Theatre two days after Christmas 1930.

This time the critics were kinder, although the Herald Tribune called the play 'Just another semi-lollipop, more interesting in appearance than substance.'

Mr Novello (is) one of those prodigious Jack-of-all-arts who have provided Londoners with song and quip from the war days onward . . . I am glad we are having a second look at him and his ten talents.

New York American

A superb example of what can be done with a thin story by brilliant acting and direction. The author of this charming bit of fluff is the clever young Englishman, Mr Ivor Novello, whose acting in the principal male rôle is going to give many a husband something to think about for several months to come . . . Miss Burke gives a show that is a constant ripple of joy.

The Theatre Magazine

Ivor joins a backstage party for Joan Crawford and Douglas Fairbanks Jr who were visiting New York on their honeymoon: it includes Fred and Adele Astaire, Alfred Lunt and Lynn Fontanne, Marilyn Miller, Viola Tree, Clifton Webb and Hope Williams.

By combining romance and riches Ivor Novello, who is a young gentleman of considerable sensibility, has turned out a perfect matinée comedy . . . It is cute. If matronly hearts are hungry for romance while the businessmen are computing their losses downtown, *The Truth Game* should administer to one of the primary theatrical needs.

Brooks Atkinson
in the New York Times

The success of *The Truth Game*, which ran for over three months on Broadway followed by a long tour, led to Ivor's being offered a contract as both actor and scriptwriter by Metro-Goldwyn-Mayer. With the advent of talkies, the Hollywood studios were frantically signing up playwrights, novelists and journalists—anyone who could supply them with literate scenarios and intelligent dialogue; but, despite the financial rewards, not all of them found the working conditions congenial. Ivor's initial assignment was to write the screen-play of *The Truth Game*, but he arrived to find that this had already been completed by somebody else. He insisted on re-writing it himself and did so several times until very little was left of the original. Altogether his time in Hollywood was a period of disappointment and frustration,

only alleviated by the new friendships he made there. Joan Crawford and Douglas Fairbanks Jr, whom he had met in New York, were particularly kind, meeting the train on which he arrived in California and making sure that he was introduced to everyone of importance on the MGM lot. But he was missing London and the Theatre badly, and his homesickness was intensified when, after six months in Hollywood, he received news of the death of his father. None of the subjects to which he was assigned provided much outlet for his particular talents, and MGM failed to find him any acting rôles. The only film he made in Hollywood, at the suggestion of his friend, Ruth Chatterton, was *Once a Lady* at Paramount, an almost unqualified failure. Ivor finally went to Irving Thalberg, then in charge of production at MGM, and requested to be released from his two-year contract. Thalberg made him sit out the remaining three months of the first year and suggested he should fulfil the second year at a later date, but never called upon him to do so. Ivor returned to England in the spring of 1932.

Ethel Barrymore backstage with Ivor at the theatre named after her, during the run of *The Truth Game*. She sits between Phoebe Foster and Billie Burke, with Viola Tree at her feet.

April 23, 1974

Dear Sandy Wilson,

How wonderful you have been commissioned to do a book on Ivor.

I do wish I had some photographs, souvenirs and/or letters that I did save for some time, but I do not.

My memories of him are that he was a beautiful man, an enchanting actor, and had the great gift of being a friend. He felt, as I did and do - "In order to have a friend, you must be a friend."

Good luck on your book, and thank you for thinking of me.

Bless you,

Joan Crawford

The film of *The Truth Game* was released by MGM in 1932 under the title *But The Flesh Is Weak*. Robert Montgomery played Max, who had now been endowed with a rascally but lovable father, Florian Clement, played by C. Aubrey Smith. Rosine Browne was played by Nora Gregor, an Italian-born actress who had worked with Max Reinhardt in Vienna and whose previous Hollywood rôles had been in German-speaking versions of American films. She was to achieve celebrity some years after her career had ended when Renoir's *La Règle du Jeu*, in which she played the

Opposite: Ivor attends the première of Douglas Fairbanks Jr's film, *Union Station*, with Fairbanks and his wife, Joan Crawford, and Bill Haines.

Below: An unspecified Hollywood function, presided over by Laura Hope Crewes, at whose feet sit Ramon Novarro and Richard Rose (*right*), who was later to present several of Ivor's plays in London. The English film director, Edmund Goulding, sits behind Miss Crewes, and Dorothy Arzner, one of the few women ever to succeed as a director in Hollywood sits on the right. Ivor stands in the back row.

lead, was reassembled and shown in its original version. Heather Thatcher, who happened to be visiting Hollywood, was, on Ivor's suggestion, tested and cast for the part of Lady Joan Culver, played on stage by Viola Tree, but the rôle of Mrs Brandon, which was generally considered to be the most rewarding in the play, was, for some mysterious reason, eliminated altogether.

The publicity read: Cash or Kisses? It's Amusing What You Can Get Away With If You Have Technique! But the film failed to get away with anything. 'The Flesh is Weak, but the Plot is Weaker' was the verdict of the New York News, while the New York Times, whose theatre critic, Brooks Atkinson, had praised the play, used the film as a peg on which to hang a remarkably spiteful attack on Ivor:

Even if you had not been warned in advance that the new picture at the Capitol Theatre was supposed to be a screen version of Ivor Novello's play, *The Truth Game*, you would have been inclined to suspect that there was a trace of Novello about it. Certainly Robert Montgomery, its star, could never have made up, of his own accord, the imitation of the coyest actor that the increasingly whimsical Britain has yet sent us, unless there had been some sinister cause for the transformation.

A second film version of *The Truth Game*, entitled *Free and Easy*, was released in 1941 and was, if anything, more inept than the first. Max, now surnamed Clemington, was played by Robert Cummings, with Nigel Bruce as his father, while C. Aubrey Smith reappeared as a new character, the Duke. Rosine was played by Ruth Hussey and Lady Joan by Judith Anderson, the only one to emerge from the movie with any credit.

Doesn't Metro know that a war is going on, that the British bounder with an empty purse and a roving eye is quite as passé at present as half the homes in Mayfair?
The New York Times

If the original drama was a semi-lollipop, the present movie version is no more than a stale semi-lollipop . . . Judith Anderson, as Lady Joan, is about the only person in *Free and Easy* whom you would want to spend any time with.

The Herald Tribune

Opposite: Nora Gregor, Robert Montgomery and C. Aubrey Smith in *But The Flesh is Weak*.

Below: Reginald Owen, Ruth Hussey, Judith Anderson and Robert Cummings in *Free and Easy*.

While in Hollywood, Ivor also scripted *Lovers Courageous*, a film based on a Lonsdale play, and contributed dialogue to Greta Garbo's *Mata Hari*. But his most astonishing assignment was to write the screen-play of *Tarzan, the Ape Man*, the first of the enormously successful Tarzan series, starring Johnny Weismuller. Playing opposite him, as Jane, was Maureen O'Sullivan:

'My mother loved dancing, and she used to take me with her. I was about fourteen, I suppose. Ivor Novello came down to Brighton, where we were living, to judge a dance contest of some kind. We all danced by very politely, trying not to stare at him. He looked very handsome and very bored—no wonder! I never told him when we met up again in Hollywood. I didn't get to know him very well; I only loved the script he wrote for the first *Tarzan*, although I'm sure he was furious at having to do it. It was made because MGM had just filmed *Trader Horn* in Africa and they had a lot of footage left over which they didn't know what to do with. One of the big producers at MGM, Bernie Hayman, said "Let's make a Tarzan Film." They didn't expect anything of it, but when it came out it was such a smashing success that they went on and on. But Ivor's was the kick-off. I think his script brought a reality to the subject. It was lovely for me, because I hadn't been in Hollywood all that long and so I understood the girl I played—a very sophisticated English girl. It never seemed at all far-fetched, because, after all, who knows what lives in the jungle? And because the dialogue was so witty and charming, I loved doing it. In those days, once the script was written, one didn't see much of the writer: they were condemned to their cells to write from nine to five-thirty, with a break for lunch. But once Ivor came on the set and said to me, "I love the way you throw away lines." I was very new to acting and very bad at it and didn't know what he meant. "But just emphasise this and that a little more," he said. "You're throwing away *too much*." I always said it was probably my favourite film—that and *The Barretts of Wimpole Street*.'

The celebrated exchange between Tarzan and Jane, often misquoted, actually went as follows:

JANE: (*pointing to Tarzan*) Tarzan. (*pointing to herself*) Jane.

TARZAN: (*finally comprehending*) Tarzan—Jane ... Jane—Tarzan! Tarzan—Jane! Jane—Tarzan!

JANE: (*in desperation*) Listen, I can't stand this! Please let me go!

When a Man Picks his Mate!

Tarzan saw the White Body of Jane.

He lifted her in his arms and took her away.

Maybe Modern Marriages would be Happier,
if they were based on the infallible
Jungle Instinct of Mating!

Don't Miss the Bath of Love,
in the Crystal Clear Jungle Pool!

Girls!—Would you live like Eve—
If You Found the Right Adam?

Publicity quotes

Above: *Lovers Courageous*: Robert Montgomery and Madge Evans.

Opposite: *Tarzan, the Ape Man*: Johnny Weismuller and Maureen O'Sullivan.

Below: *Mata Hari*: Greta Garbo and Lionel Barrymore.

Ivor, on his return from America, is welcomed home by Benita Hume, Viola Tree and his mother.

I Lived with You (1932)

> It is pleasant to have Mr Novello home again; he is far too good to be exiled in the wastes of Beverly Hills.
>
> The Daily Mail

During this exile, Ivor had utilised some of his ample spare time to write two stage plays. The first of these, *I Lived with You*, opened at the Prince of Wales in the spring of 1932 and proved to be his most successful venture so far, and the part of Felix Lenieff the most rewarding he had written for himself since *The Rat*.

Felix, a destitute Russian prince, meets Glad Wallis in Hampton Court Maze. She takes pity on him and asks him to come and stay at 'Malmaison', her family's suburban villa. In no time at all Felix makes himself at home and

proceeds to exert his influence on the family—to disastrous effect. Mr Wallis takes a mistress, Mrs Wallis takes to vodka, Ada, Glad's sister, goes to live with her boss, a married man, and Glad herself breaks up with her steady boy friend and falls in love with Felix. Only Aunt Flossie, who is treated by the family as an unpaid maid-of-all-work, fails to respond to Felix's charms and, after a catastrophic tea-party, persuades him that he must leave 'Malmaison' before he does any more harm. Felix departs and the Wallises go back to normal. After the opening Ivor added a new ending, where Glad sets off for Hampton Court again to find Felix and share her life with him.

Minnie Rayner made her second appearance in a Novello play as Mrs Wallis; Mr Wallis was played by Eliot

Makeham, Ada Wallis by Thea Holme, and Matt, Glad's boy friend, by the still relatively unknown Robert Newton. The play, ostensibly just a domestic comedy, was unusual in that instead of changing the Wallises' life for the better, as one would expect, Felix's influence is almost wholly malign, although he imagines he is improving their lot.

Only Flossie, played by Cicely Oates, sees through both his and her family's pretensions and brings everyone back to their senses before it is too late. The tea-party scene, where Mrs Wallis attempts to show off her royal house-guest to her snobbish neighbours, is a delicious passage of cumulative chaos, as well as revealing an acute observation of the petty ambitions and jealousies that bedevil English suburban life.

Right: Glad (Ursula Jeans) finds Felix in the Hampton Court Maze.

Below: Mrs Wallis's tea-party ends in disaster: Minnie Rayner, Ivor and Ursula Jeans.

In *I Lived with You* Novello has for the first time found a substantial theme and sustained it without divagation from beginning to end. It is a clash between two violently contrasted ways of life. The Tartar aristocratic and autocratic authadeia, a doing-as-you-please ... impinges on the English lower middle-class respectability. The story is developed with grace and ease of appropriate invention ... To illustrate the playwright's resourcefulness in giving a 'twist' to the situation, I will relate that on the first night the tale was carried to its most austere conclusion, the adorable and intolerable Felix disappeared into the night for ever. This was too much for either author or audience to bear, and I was afraid he was going to sacrifice the logic of his play to a happy ending; but he found a solution which gives nothing away, and yet leaves Felix and Glad in each other's arms.

Edward Marsh, in an
introduction to Ivor's published plays

This is Mr Novello's best play to date and therefore worth tearing to pieces, which I could do with pleasure if it were not such an unhandsome return for an exceedingly jolly evening ... The piece was obviously written by Mr Novello for that good actor, Mr Novello, who, as Felix, walked delicately and adroitly, combining the wistfulness of Mr Francis Lederer with the chest-notes of Miss Constance Collier.

James Agate
in the Sunday Times

Mr Novello knows how to flavour the popular sweetmeat with an astringent sense of fun. His Fulham household is good company and sometimes authentic. Mr Novello acted the Dark Prince with all his nice desire and ability to please. His story is definitely a tall one, but its life may not be short.

Ivor Brown
in the Observer

It is a pretty idea for a comedy and, as long as it is treated as that and no more, it proves to be a very ingenious basis of entertainment ... Though Mr Novello, actor, is evidently having the time of his life, Mr Novello, dramatist, seems to be paying for it. In a word, the drama is built too high on too fanciful a foundation and, in spite of an admirably significant sketch by Miss Cicely Oates, its seriousness never wins us to a suspension of disbelief. For all that, the piece remains, even in its solemnities, a lively entertainment, for even its solemnities are decorated with a ready humour and sustained by a quick sense of theatre ... In the midst of all the activities Mr Novello continuously glitters. The prince has been over-romanticised by the author, who would have done better to ride his emotions more lightly, but the actor in Mr Novello knows how to control his mount and to give it the appearance, if not of a thoroughbred, at any rate of a winner in amusing company.

The Times

Left: Ivor with Ursula Jeans.

Opposite: With Ursula Jeans and Thea Holme.

STRAND THEATRE
"PARTY"
By IVOR NOVELLO

Produced May 23rd, 1932

The "party" is given by a popular young actress after a fashionable first night, when we hear the candid opinions of the various guests on the play they have just witnessed. It is all very cynical and very amusing. . . .

EVA PLUMER (NANCY PAWLEY): "You knew I'd wear this dress, and she swore she wouldn't copy it."

FAY STRUBE (JOAN SWINSTEAD): "Well, she has, and you're wearing the copy."

ROSIE faints at the Party.

LORD ELLERTON (MARTIN LEWIS): "Hadn't you better go home?"

ROSIE (MARGARET VINES): "Oh! no please! I'm quite alright."

Party (1932)

The second play Ivor wrote in Hollywood was to be 'tried out' at the Arts Theatre, but Leslie Henson came to a dress rehearsal and was so impressed that he phoned the impressario, Firth Shephard, on the spot and arranged for the two of them to present it at the Strand within a few days of its opening at the Arts, thus accomplishing what must be the swiftest transfer to the West End in the history of the London Theatre.

Opposite: Scenes from *Party* in Plays and Players.

Right: Hynes' caricature of Lilian Braithwaite as Mrs MacDonald.

Below: The full company of *Party*.
On the divan: Martin Lewis, Benita Hume, Lilian Braithwaite and Sebastian Shaw. Douglas Byng, who did a turn in the second act, stands at the right.

Ivor Novello Throws a Party
for "Party"!

A LITTLE LIGHT REFRESHMENT: THE BATHING-DRESS-CLAD GUESTS AT TEA.

THE HOST AND GUESTS: MR. IVOR NOVELLO, ACTOR AND AUTHOR, MISS HEATHER THATCHER, AND MISS LILIAN BRAITHWAITE.

"PARTY," Mr. Ivor Novello's play, which has just moved from the Strand Theatre to the Gaiety, is certainly a very good "party." The author, therefore, felt it would be a good move to "throw a party" for "Party" and the members of its cast. This gathering took place at Red Roofs, Littlewick Green, near Maidenhead, and was blessed with what was ideal weather for a swimming, tea, and tennis gathering. Miss Lilian Braithwaite plays Mrs. Macdonald in the play; Mme. Namara is herself, Namara; Miss Pamela Willins is Gloria Mumford, and Mr. Ivor Novello, the author of the piece, is now himself acting in it.——Mr. John van Druten is the successful young playwright, and author of "Young Woodley," "London Wall," etc. His latest play, "Behold, We Live," has just been produced at the St. James's, with Sir Gerald du Maurier and Miss Gertrude Lawrence in the leading rôles. Mr. Arthur McRae is the author of "Flat to Let."

A LITTLE SUN-BASKING: MISS DORIS GILMORE, MISS PAMELA WILLINS, MISS MAIDEE ANDREWS, MISS DOROTHY FENWICK, MISS ELISE LINDEN, MISS BINKIE MOSS, MISS NETTA WESTCOTT, AND MR. IVOR NOVELLO, THE HOST.

PHOTOGRAPHS

Party was exactly what its title implied: the entire action took place at a party given by the actress, Miranda Clayfoot (Benita Hume), after the first night of her new play. The guests were an easily recognisable cross-section of London theatrical society, headed by Mrs MacDonald (Lilian Braithwaite), an ageing and embittered actress, whose sweetly bitchy remarks reminded everyone irresistibly of Mrs Patrick Campbell. Miranda has also invited an ex-lover, Bay Clender, now happily married, with whom she intends to resume her affair. This and the success of her new play are a matter of life and death to Miranda, who is on the verge of becoming a drug addict.

Through the unexpected intervention of Mrs MacDonald Miranda is prevented from accomplishing her schemes. The play turns out to be a failure, Bay is reunited with his wife, and after the guests have departed Miranda and Mrs MacDonald, now the best of friends, settle down to have breakfast together.

In *Party* Ivor was dealing unashamedly with his favourite subject, the Theatre, and most of the play is an authentic and consistently entertaining exploitation of the foibles and failings of theatrical folk and their hangers-on. Only in the melodramatic conclusion does disbelief creep in—to take over completely in the final moments when Gerald du Maurier, of all people, rings up Miranda at three a.m. on the morning after her flop, offering her the lead in a new play in which there is also of course a 'divine part' for the unemployable Mrs MacDonald.

One trembles to think what would be said of Mr Novello's plays if anyone else had written them. But some writers, like some people, mean so well, and, like children, are so obviously happy when you are pleased with them, that one hasn't the heart to be anything else. Mr Novello is such a writer, and nothing is going to make me say that this is not a good play.

James Agate
in the Sunday Times

Left: Ivor gives a summer party at Redroofs.

Below: A page from the Redroofs Visitors' Book.

Ivor attempts to drown Lilian Braithwaite in the swimming pool at Redroofs. Bobbie Andrews and Richard Rose come to the rescue.

All that part of the play which lifts the shutters on theatrical 'shop' is grand fun, and, since the public who like to chatter about the politics and personalities of the stage is a large one, there should be eager support for this piece.
Ivor Brown
in the Observer

Now comes Ivor Novello, an author of plays so artificial that he was the last person to be suspected of painting life, with the novel idea of showing stage people as they really are . . . You believe in this crowd of stage people as you never believed before in stage people who had been characters of plays, and the result is a refreshing surprise.
The Sporting & Dramatic

I enjoyed it myself immensely, for I know this strange little corner of the London world almost as well as Mr Novello himself. And if it appeals to the general public, no one will be more delighted than myself.
The Daily Mail

Enormously amusing and a predestined success. But whether it is true to life or not I'm afraid I cannot tell you . . . He has hit off with wicked certainty that mixture of good nature and cattiness, of honest humanity and sham personality, which is the hall-mark which the theatre sets upon those who serve it.
The Daily Telegraph

Ivor sunbathes outside Redroofs with Richard Rose, Anthony Bushell and Benita Hume. 'Lloydie' reads the paper.

None can complain of the entertainment in *Party*. Visitors from Melton Mowbray or Chicago who know nothing of backstage manners and mannerisms will enjoy it. Mr Novello has not made the mistake of thinking that his own occupation must interest merely because it is the Theatre. He removed unwanted innards before cooking his theatrical chicken and he has served it with well-spiced sauce which is splendid for everyone's palate.

The Tatler

When you pass through the French windows from the garden of Redroofs into the large and comfortable living-room, gay with flowers and vivid curtains, you are in the room which expresses Ivor's personality and sums up his talents as well as his hobbies. It is in this room that he writes his plays, it is there he composes. It is on the deep fawn-coloured settee in front of the fine brick fire-place that he sits with a favourite book. It is in a corner by the window that he delights in his favourite game, Bridge, and it is in another corner near the window that you will find his amazing collection of gramophone records . . .

'In my opinion the public is always right,' he exclaims emphatically. 'I always have a test line early in my plays, and if that goes well, I know the audience will like the play. And if it doesn't, then I know my fate.'

Confessions of Ivor Novello
in the New London Magazine

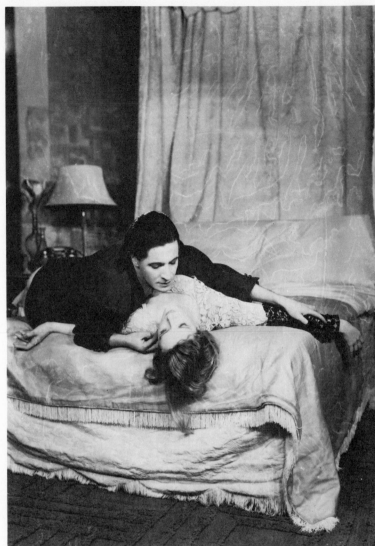

Above: Ivor and Glady Cooper.

Opposite top: Madame Clara in the drawing-room beside the wrought iron gates which came from the house of David Garrick.

Opposite bottom: Ivor's bedroom at Redroofs.

Flies in the Sun (*1933*)

'Jane Marquis, the rich but heartless beauty of the Riviera, getting tired of Seraphine, a film star known as the King of Lovers, casts her eye upon Bob Mitchell who, with his young wife, is sunning himself upon the private beach of the Hotel Splendide . . .'

Thus The Times critic parodied the story of *Flies in the Sun*, the play which Ivor wrote for himself and Gladys Cooper and which was an unwise—for him—venture into Somerset Maugham territory, a supposedly searing exposé of the rich and decadent denizens of the South of France, a milieu which was largely outside his experience and certainly beyond his capacity to re-create with any conviction.

That bedroom scene may fill the Playhouse for some time to come.

The Daily Mirror

One can but hope that, in his parade of presumably popular effects, the dramatist has had his tongue in his cheek . . . There is scenery and suicide and song; there is a lady's maid in hysterics, and there are little jokes of all sorts . . . and there is some extremely accomplished acting . . . Much of the furniture is decorative, and when anyone dives into the sea, one hears the hopeful splash. Unhappily they can all swim.

The Times

Everything possible has been provided to give this piece an air of smart and shocking modernity . . . but all the labour is in vain, for the plain reason that Mr Novello has not recognised that a demand to be interested, to care about the people on the stage, to understand them and to wish to understand them better, has returned to the theatre.

Charles Morgan
in the New York Times

Fresh Fields (1933)

Minnie Rayner was the cause of *Fresh Fields*. Ivor had said to her, 'Do come down to Redroofs,' and she did, one Sunday afternoon, without a by-your-leave, with twenty people—which sent Ivor straight to bed. And when he got there, he suddenly thought of the plot of *Fresh Fields*.

Peter Graves

Although Ivor himself was not in it, *Fresh Fields* was his most successful play and had the longest life, being performed by amateurs and repertory companies for many years after the West End run. It provided Lilian Braithwaite with one of her best and most typical parts: Lady Lilian Bedworthy, an impoverished aristocrat, who writes a newspaper column called 'Can I Help You?' The part of her widowed sister, Lady Mary Crabbe, with whom she shared their Belgravia home, was offered to Marie Tempest, who, after a good deal of shilly-shallying, turned it down on the grounds that the final scene had Lady Mary planning a world cruise in company with Mrs Pidgeon (Minnie Rayner). Miss Tempest considered such a situation beneath her dignity, and the part went instead to Ellis Jeffreys.

The plot concerned the efforts of Lady Mary to keep the household solvent by installing an Australian family, Mrs Pidgeon, her brother, Tom, and daughter, Una, as 'paying guests', part of the arrangement being that Una will 'come out' under the auspices of Lady Strawholme (Martita Hunt). Lady Lilian is kept in ignorance of the plan, which results in various misunderstandings, the most celebrated being the scene where, under the impression that Una is one of her correspondents, she assumes that the girl is discussing an unwanted pregnancy when she is in fact apologising for breaking an ornament. All ends happily when Una marries Lady Mary's son, Tim (Robert Andrews), and Lady Lilian succumbs to the advances of Tom.

This piece justifies the surprising originality of its title by refusing firmly, and with entertaining consequences, to see the wood for the trees. As wood, field or pasture, as a unity of any sort, it is flagrantly unpersuasive, but as an aggregate of absurdities it is rewardingly absurd. Mr Novello, in brief, having taken an irresponsible holiday, has had the wit to communicate his enjoyment of it.

The Times

Every time I see a play by Ivor Novello I find myself thinking the same thought—'How well this dramatist knows the theatre.' He never bothers his head about life. All his characters are, in one way and another, caricatures. Everything he says about them is artificial. And

Top: Robert Andrews, Lilian Braithwaite and Ellis Jeffreys.

Bottom: Lilian Braithwaite, Martita Hunt and Ellis Jeffreys.

yet what excellent entertainment he can provide. His latest comedy . . . is exactly true to type. I shall be very much surprised if you believe a word of it. But I shall be entirely astonished if you do not find it very funny.

The Daily Telegraph

Fresh Fields was so successful that one Saturday night, when Mam arrived at the Criterion expecting four complimentary tickets, she had to be turned away, which precipitated one of several petty rows between herself and Ivor. A New York production opened at the Empire Theatre at the beginning of 1936, with an American cast, headed by Margaret Anglin, a celebrated tragedienne who had been absent from Broadway for some years. She had played Lady Mary Crabbe successfully in several stock productions, but by the time she brought the play to New York tastes had changed and it was a failure. The World Telegram called it 'as haphazard a dish of hokum as Ivor Novello ever cooked up in an uninspired moment', while Brooks Atkinson referred to Ivor as 'the dancing-master of London fiddle-faddle . . . but it is to be feared he cannot turn the theatrical clock back'.

A party backstage at the Criterion to celebrate the two hundredth performance. Ivor is with Ellis Jeffreys, Bronson Albery, Lilian Braithwaite and 'Mam'. Minnie Rayner is in the background (*left*).

Ivor signed this photograph for Zena Dare: 'To my ravishing Mother'.

Ivor, looking very much like his own father, in make-up as Sir Geoffrey Bethel.

Proscenium (1933)

Ivor was dealing again with his favourite subject, but whereas *Party* was a comedy about the Theatre with a dramatic background, *Proscenium* was a romantic drama with a background of the Theatre. In the prologue, set in 1918, he appeared as Lt.-Col. Sir Geoffrey Bethel, who is in love with an actress, Norma Matthews (Fay Compton). But he is married and Norma refuses to have an affair with him, preferring to devote herself to the Theatre. Sir Geoffrey is killed in France. In the present day Norma is the successful manager of her own theatre and is loved by a man some years younger than herself, Gray Raynor, also played by Ivor. Meeting Gray's mother (Zena Dare), she discovers that Gray is the son of Sir Geoffrey by a previous marriage, but she is eventually persuaded to become his wife. Norma and Gray set up a successful theatrical partnership, but when Gray decides to play Romeo, Norma suggests that Juliet should be a younger actress, Eunice Manners (Joan Barry), who becomes infatuated with Gray. *Romeo and Juliet* is a success, while Norma finds her career going downhill. Gray is offered a theatre of his own, but, realising that his marriage means more to him, he resumes his partnership with Norma.

If ever Ivor wanted a thing, he got it—absolutely—and for some reason he seemed to think that I could be a comedienne, although I had never played comedy before. In *Proscenium* he wanted me to play a part he had written for Lilian Braithwaite, who was then his comedienne, but she was growing a little older and he saw in me something that would perhaps take her place. I said to him, 'Why do you think I'm funny? I'm not funny at all. I haven't got a funny face.' So he said, 'Oh, I don't know. You live so *desperately*: I think it's very funny.' He wrote the part so beautifully for the personality of someone who amused him, and it came off so successfully that, although nobody's indispensable, you were indispensable to Ivor, and if somebody else—your understudy—played it, it wasn't quite the same. I can't tell you why.

Zena Dare

Opposite: A cartoonist's impression of *Proscenium* in Theatre World.

ARMY MANOEUVRES AT THE DINNER-TABLE.
THE GALLANT WARRIOR — ABOUT TO PART PERMANENTLY FROM HIS ADORED ONE — CONTRIVES TO CAMOUFLAGE HIS REAL FEELINGS BY SPRAWLING "AT EASE."

MICHAELSON -33

ANDREA MALANDRINOS AS ANSELMO

FAY COMPTON AS NORMA MATTHEWS — AND — IVOR NOVELLO (BELIEVE IT OR NOT) — AS LIEUT-COL. SIR GEOFFREY BETHEL

"IT'S NEVER TOO LATE —"
THE SHREWD WIDOW BEGINS "GOLD-DIGGING OPERATIONS" ON THE WEALTHY AMERICAN WIDOWER.

ZENA DARE AS LADY RAYNOR

KENETH KENT AS MR HYMAN

AN UNREHEARSED "SCENE" BEHIND THE SCENES BY ROMEO AND JULIET!
JOAN BARRY AS EUNICE

IVOR NOVELLO AS GRAY RAYNOR

Fay Compton, as the actress, succeeds in giving to her part just that touch of simple reality which has escaped Mr Novello, and often achieves genuine, as well as theatrical, emotion . . . Zena Dare scores heavily in a comedy part. She is an actress to be reckoned with these days.

The Daily Telegraph

The strength of the play lies in the determination with which Mr Novello, as dramatist, has avoided commonplace variations on his central theme: though the young actor plays Romeo to the Juliet of a girl, Eunice, who loves him, his own love of his wife is unswerving, as is hers of him. The dramatic interest is in consequence not dissipated in giddy irrelevance, but concentrated in the relationship made difficult by age and ambition, of a man and woman who love each other.

The Times

This is a play of theatrical life, it should be explained. Some of it is very like *Party*, and those scenes, amusing

Opposite top: Norma (Fay Compton) learns the truth from Lady Raynor (Zena Dare).

Opposite bottom: Ivor, as Gray, visits Norma's dressing-room.

Below: Ivor as Romeo.

as they are, do not help the play. Still, I was thrilled to see Fay Compton in trousers. As for Ivor Novello himself, he proved in an unnecessary prologue that he will make a very presentable old man when the time unfortunately arrives. Otherwise he was again the Ivor Novello we know so well.

The News Chronicle

Proscenium is sentimental in its treatment and Mr Novello has the courage of his own emotions. He will attack us with the theatre's sentimental ordinance and end with slow music; he does it without shame or evasion, which is preferable to having sentimental conclusions propelled under a mask of cynicism. You may dub *Proscenium* as Ivor-Novelette, but at least you know where you are with Mr Novello.

The Observer

After *Proscenium* had opened, Ivor decided to interpolate a 'masque' of *Romeo and Juliet* for himself and Joan Barry, which was played without dialogue. He had had his eye on the part of Romeo for some time, but apart from performing the balcony scene with Jean Forbes-Robertson at a charity matinée in 1935, this was the nearest he got to it. In 1926 an item appeared in the papers announcing that he would play Romeo to the Juliet of Evelyn Laye, but nothing more was heard of it. In 1928 a production was actually planned and financed for Ivor and Fay Compton, but fell through when Miss Compton had to go to America.

Phyllis Monkman, Dorothy Dickson and Joan Clarkson.

The Sunshine Sisters (*1933*)

It is a wild, rough, uneven piece, but probably a success, and so establishing Mr Novello's West End hat-trick.

The Observer

The 'hat-trick'—three plays, *Fresh Fields*, *Proscenium* and *The Sunshine Sisters* running simultaneously in the West End—was not established for very long, since the latter closed after a few weeks and was one of Ivor's few failures. Billed as 'a musical comedy without music'—not in itself a very inviting proposition, one would have thought—it dealt with a music hall act, Pearl, Ruby and Emerald Sunshine, who are discovered, while down and out in Paris,

by George (Jack Hawkins) who takes them home to stay with his mother, the eccentric Duchess of Frynne (Irene Brown). The Duchess collects displaced people and George tells her the girls are reformed prostitutes. The resulting complications can be imagined.

There is only one joke in Ivor Novello's *The Sunshine Sisters* . . . It was not a very good joke to begin with, and by the time it had been thrust at me again and again for about an act and a half I was sick to death of it. Mr Novello has in fact written a thoroughly bad play.

The Daily Telegraph

Telephone 4686 Temple Bar.

11. ALDWYCH.
W.C.2

Darling Puffin —

You know all I'm feeling about tonight — thank you darling for your lovely performance, your unswerving loyalty and your sweet courageousness — and better luck next time! —

All love

Ivor

Ivor's letter to Phyllis Monkman on the last night.

Murder in Mayfair (1934)

This was the last play in which Ivor himself appeared before his career took an entirely new turn with the production of *Glamorous Night*. It was also the first time he had been associated with the German director, Leontine Sagan, who was later to direct all his Drury Lane shows. Sagan had made her reputation in Germany with the production of both the play and the film of *Children in Uniform* and repeated her success when the play was presented in London.

Murder in Mayfair was, as its title implies, a thriller, and the title itself, combined with the names of the stars: Ivor, Fay Compton, Edna Best, Zena Dare and Robert Andrews, was enough to ensure a respectable run in the West End in 1934.

Ivor again played a foreigner—this time a Frenchman, Jacques Clavel, complete with accent—and an internationally famous pianist. Failing to win the hand of Mary, Duchess of Ventyre (Fay Compton), because of her loyalty to the Duke, Jacques marries, on the rebound, Auriol Crannock (Edna Best), a drug-taking bad hat who proceeds to ruin him. Some years later Jacques again meets Mary, now a widow, and on the same evening Auriol is shot dead after a party. Suspicion falls on Jacques, but the murderer turns out to be Auriol's disappointed lover, Bill Sherry (Robert Andrews). Jacques and Mary are now free to marry.

Ivor as Jacques Clavel, surrounded by admiring ladies.

170

Whoever killed Auriol, Miss Edna Best, in a performance of discreetly edged depravity, did her honour while she lived. Mary and Jacques were free to marry, all obstructive spouses disposed of. Mr Novello with stern charm and Miss Fay Compton with vigorous attack had earned what bliss the coroner may leave them. Theirs was a difficult world to be happy in—one of those 'post-war' worlds in which life is all cocktails and courage.

The Times

Mr Andrews is always a much better actor than anybody supposes ... But the leopard cannot change his spots, and vice versa! What I mean is that this actor has bounced up and down with a tennis racket on too many of Marie Tempest's sofas to steep his hand in murder. And perhaps after all it didn't matter who killed the slut.

James Agate
in the Sunday Times

To say that (Ivor Novello) is not a first-class actor is just nonsense. See him in his present thriller, *Murder in Mayfair*. Note the consistency of his portraiture, his nervous sincerity and concentration, how he acts with every one of his fingers, how every mood of the temperamental foreign pianist works itself out to perfection, and how subordinate he can be when the situation calls for deference to the other player.

Sydney Carroll
in the Daily Telegraph

Jacques gives a concert at the house of Mrs Sherry (Zena Dare, *right*). Fay Compton stands in the doorway, Edna Best adorns a pillar, while Robert Andrews perches on the chaise longue. On the floor, *left*, sits Christopher Hassall, soon to become Ivor's lyric-writer.

with Edna Best.

site: Robert Andrews, Fay Compton, Zena Dare.

Ivor and Zena Dare.

There'd be a tap on my dressing-room door and I'd think, 'Oh, goodness, now what's coming?', and he'd give me a new line and I'd say, 'But, Ivor, I don't think that's really very funny.' And he'd say, 'But you will say it?'—he was rather pathetic about it! So I did, and of course there was a roar of laughter. Whether the critics liked it or not, I think he knew his audience. The plays were very much of their time, and they had that romantic sentimentality—which wasn't quite me! But they came to see *him*, and the women loved him. Waiting outside the Stage Door—that was dying then, but it didn't die for Ivor.

I was very lucky, because the big thing in my life happened when I was with Ivor. We were in Glasgow with *Murder in Mayfair*—before coming to London—and I was living in our home, only thirty miles away in Callender. My husband was out shooting one day, and he felt pretty ill. The chauffeur took him home, and he said, 'I think you ought to go to the doctor on the way,' but my husband said, 'No, it's nothing.' I was playing a matinée

and I thought he was coming to the theatre that night. He said to the chauffeur, 'I'm going to bed. Don't tell her ladyship (my mother-in-law), but call me for a cup of tea at six.' The butler went up to call him, and he'd died—just like that. They rang up to speak to Ivor and his secretary said, 'He can't speak. He's resting,' but they told him it was very important. So Ivor got up and they told him, and he said, 'I can't tell Zena now, because she'll be on in a minute.' So I was the person who didn't know, but everybody else did—imagine! He got everyone out of the way, and then when I came off, I was told, and I went home—and that was that. Then Ivor wrote to me, 'Come back as quickly as you can.' I did, after a fortnight, and he said, 'My home is your home until you're settled.' And so I lived at Redroofs for six or seven weeks until I had my new home. At that time in one's life one had one's greatest friend, that's all.

Zena Dare

173

THEATRE WORLD

OCTOBER, 1935

Vol. XXIV.—No. 129

THEATRE WORLD

SPECIAL SUPPLEMENT
"FULL HOUSE"

1'-

Heather Thatcher   Isabel Jeans   Lilian Braithwaite

Full House (1935)

Full House and Empty Heads.
Mr Leslie Henson as producer made a speech at the end and implied more with a single look than Mr Novello had said in three acts. The audience was brilliant.

The Observer

Ivor's next play, written while he was appearing in *Glamorous Night*, was little more than an excuse to cash in on Lilian Braithwaite's success in *Fresh Fields*. She was again a scatter-brained upper class lady, down on her luck, who attempts to salvage the family fortunes by turning her house into a casino. Again she had a sister, played by Isabel Jeans, a malade imaginaire who is separated from her husband and whose quarrels with her rival (Heather Thatcher) provide a sub-plot and included a ju-jitsu bout which ended in Miss Jeans putting Miss Thatcher across her knee and spanking her. Robert Andrews played the son once more, in this case Lilian Braithwaite's. From another play, *Party*, Ivor borrowed the 'gimmick' of two women turning up at a gathering in the same dress. Altogether *Full House* was a warming-over of an old recipe, but it managed to enjoy a fair run, and was later revived on tour, with Phyllis and Zena Dare as the two sisters.

I am quite prepared to believe that Mr Novello spent a couple of anguished years over the play, but the net impression it leaves on me is that it was noted down on the backs of envelopes, from his own and other people's random remarks, in a fortnight.

The Observer

Full House proves two things. One is that Mr Novello has it in him to write a true comedy of femininity. The other is that he has too easily satisfied his artistic conscience with a play that is mainly puerile.

The Daily Mail

It is very cheap stuff . . . Miss Braithwaite does all that is possible with the leading part. She brings her own brilliant sense of fun to the character. There is nothing else to say about her performance; we have seen it so often before.

The Daily Telegraph

THE ACES OF "FULL HOUSE," AT THE HAYMARKET.

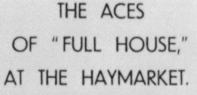

Duplicates! Full of enmity for Lady April Hannington for stealing her husband, Lola Leadenhall attacks her on a "vulnerable" point, and wears a duplicate dress at a party.

Opposite: The three leading ladies.

Left: An old 'gimmick' revived: Heather Thatcher and Isabel Jeans.

Below: Tom Titt's cartoon of the 'spanking' Scene.

EVOLUTION of a HYPOCRITE
(in which Ivor Novello becomes a very different person)

  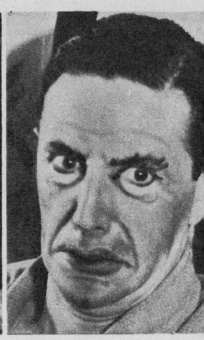

1 *Ivor Novello as he is. Now watch him change into Lord George Hell. . . .*

2 *. . . There goes twenty years on his face, just in a few lines. . . .*

3 *. . . Now he acquires loo sagging muscles, a deprav expression . . .*

Ivor makes up as Lord George Hell.

The Happy Hypocrite (1936)

An Easter Garland.

Mr Novello plays Lord George with great sincerity. His make-up for the first act is very effective and exactly gives the note of Caligula with a touch of Sir John Falstaff. He acts all the latter part of the play with a disarming simplicity; to have such a profile and pretend not to know it would write him down as an artist of enormous sensibility. It is a beautiful performance throughout.

James Agate
in the Sunday Times

Despite the enormous success of *Glamorous Night*, the Drury Lane management insisted on closing it at the end of 1935, to make way for the annual pantomime. They had asked Ivor to submit a show for the following year, but when he presented them with *Careless Rapture*, they turned it down. Hurt and disappointed, Ivor took a trip to America and on his return decided to present this adaptation, by Clemence Dane, of a story by Max Beerbohm.

He played Lord George Hell, a notorious debauchee of the Regency period, who is smitten with love for the innocent Jenny Mere. Realising that she will not look at him, owing to his repellent appearance, he visits a mask maker and emerges with the visage of a beautiful young man. Jenny falls in love with him and they retreat to a country cottage, but their idyll is interrupted by the arrival of Lord George's jealous mistress, La Gambogi. She tears the mask from his face, only to discover that true love has transformed him from a devil into an angel.

The play was mounted at great expense, with beautiful décor by the new designing team, Motley, and a score by Richard Addinsell. Isabel Jeans played La Gambogi, and for Jenny Ivor engaged Vivien Leigh, who had just made a striking West End début in *The Mask of Virtue*. The supporting cast included Marius Goring, Viola Tree, Carl Harbord and Stafford Hilliard. The director was Maurice Colbourne and the dances were arranged by Antony Tudor.

I never thought the day would come when Novello would demand serious consideration as an actor. Yet I here and now affirm that he plays Lord George Hell as no other actor could. His is a beautiful, restrained and sincere performance.

The Sunday Graphic

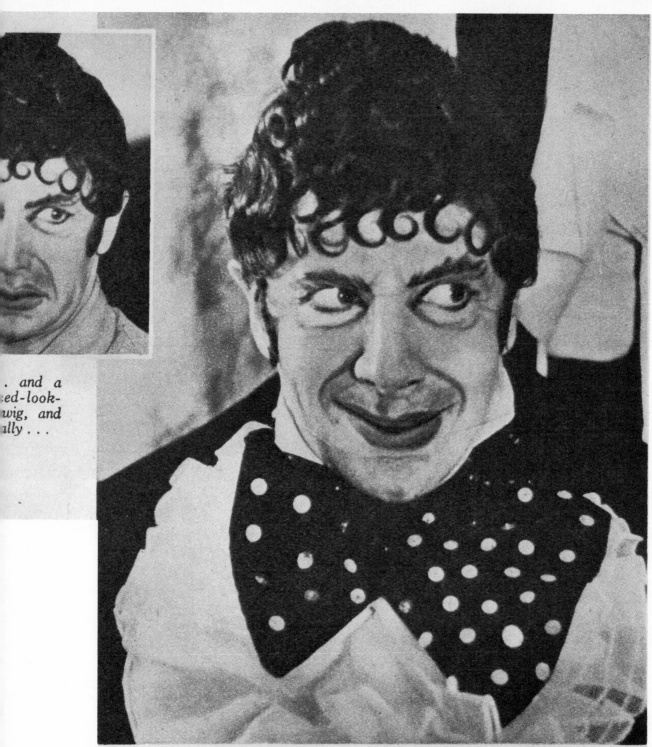

. and a
ed-look-
wig, and
lly . . .

5 . . . *nose-tubes make havoc of another famous Novello feature,
and his neckwear completes the transformation. Ivor Novello
has become wicked Lord George Hell.*

Ivor Novello broke with his own tradition last night . . . when he appeared in a make-up as ugly as Lord George Hell was conceived by Max Beerbohm. Mr Novello justified his courage, both in that respect and in tackling a rôle far from his normal field. His performance had a simple sincerity and is a personal triumph.

The Daily Mail

It is so much easier to imagine the saint-like mask of Lord George Hell than comfortably to observe its resemblance to Mr Ivor Novello or to any actor known in the flesh. And it is Mr Novello's triumph that he transcends this inescapable difficulty of the theatre and, after a brilliantly saturnine opening as George Hell, discreetly tempers with humour the miracle of his redemption . . . One of the gods said, in the third act, 'I have been here a month, and not for a moment have I been bored.' We had all shared his good fortune.

The Times

Above: Lord George admires his new face: the Mask-maker is Stafford Hilliard.

Opposite top: Lord George takes part in a duel: Isabel Jeans reclines on Ivor's chair, with Peter Graves behind her.

Opposite bottom: Cupid's Arrow finds its mark: onstage are Jenny Mere (Vivien Leigh) and Amor (Marius Goring).

Right: The Arcadian Idyll: Ivor with Vivien Leigh.

It is possible that his performance of George Hell will be the one whereby, as an actor, Mr Novello will be best remembered.

The Tatler

But the public were not prepared to accept Ivor in this strange guise, and *The Happy Hypocrite* closed after a few weeks.

It was the best thing he ever did, but it was frightfully expensive to run. The management asked everyone to take a cut and they all agreed—except the musicians. Just before it came off he and I went to see a matinée of the new musical at Drury Lane, *Rise and Shine*, and in the interval Ivor went out, and when he came back he whispered, 'Guess what! They've offered me the Lane for *Careless Rapture*.'

Robert Andrews

Kathleen Harrison and Lilian Braithwaite.

Ralph Michael and Lilian Braithwaite, with Alan Webb in the background (*left*).

Comedienne (1938)

This was the culmination of Ivor's association with Lilian Braithwaite and also gave her the opportunity to present in depth the character of a temperamental, ageing and unemployable actress which she had sketched in in *Party* and which was generally taken to be based on Mrs Patrick Campbell, with traces of Constance Collier. This time the name is Donna Lovelace and she is living in unwilling retirement in a friend's flat, attended by her faithful dresser, Winkie (Kathleen Harrison). Lord Bayfield (Barry Jones), an old admirer, introduces her to a young playwright, Owen Sands (Ralph Michael), who has written the lead in his new play for Donna. She agrees to play it, but behaves abominably throughout rehearsals and then discovers that she is incapable of learning the lines. The play opens to luke-warm reviews, but when an offer comes from America Owen insists that Donna should go too. But, realising that she is now past it, Donna withdraws, only to plan another come-back when a fresh admirer offers to finance her.

There is a melodramatic sub-plot by which Owen turns out to be the illegitimate son of Donna's former husband, who is also backing the play, but this only serves as an additional factor in Donna's disintegration. The point of the play is its presentation of a character who is both appalling and admirable, and, as such, it is something of a tour de force. The scenes where Donna, driven by an uncontrollable demon of malice, causes havoc among the company and then, in a burst of remorse, confesses to a rival actress that she is frightened to death have an almost unnerving ring of truth.

Mr Novello's study of Donna Lovelace herself is of genuine value both as entertainment and as illuminating comment on the theatre ... Mr Novello knows and loves his theatre—knows it well enough to perceive that an actress, who is an actress, is not and cannot be bound by the rules applicable to the classroom ... The play does not go far beneath the surface and would be a much better play if it did so instead of wasting time in the side-tracks which Mr Barry Jones, Miss Cecily Byrne and Mr Ivan Samson competently but unprofitably pursue. But the character of Donna Lovelace is much more than a piece of entertaining caricature, and Miss Braithwaite has seen and taken full advantage of its merits.

The Times

If he does not care to acknowledge the sources of his inspiration on the programme, he might ask the orchestra to play a certain tune about the coming of a certain clan as his overture ... Half the dialogue is as good as a feast. Not a little of the rest could be advantageously omitted.

The Observer

This product of Ivor Novello's is, I think, the best play he has written, certainly his best backstage piece. It may not prove his most financially successful one, but it represents decidedly the most artistic work of his career. *Comedienne* bristles throughout with genuine wit. It is practically a one part play, but it never allows us to tire of its principal character.

The Daily Telegraph

The playwright's fiancée, Vivian, was played by Betty Marsden. It was her first important West End rôle, and Ivor himself took her to Lillywhites to choose her dresses:

'We came out of the stage door and he took my hand, and all the way up the Haymarket I thought, "Please, God, let everyone look out of the windows and see me walking with this great star!" I don't think anybody did. When we came back to the theatre, he said, "The next time I write a play, if there's a part in it for you, your name will be on a poster on one of those pillars." I remember fighting back the tears. He was just a lovely, lovely man.'

Second Helping (1939)

When war broke out, Ivor was playing in *The Dancing Years*. In common with all other theatres, Drury Lane closed and later became the London Headquarters of ENSA. In October 1939 Ivor took out a tour of this light comedy, which came into London in the spring of 1940, retitled *Ladies into Action*, and with Lilli Palmer replacing Dorothy Dickson.

After his recent concern with very large-scale musical productions ... this little bedroom comedy must have seemed small beer; to Mr Novello it is a pleasant tipple none the less. It develops at times into something more exotic than beer, but never, however, becomes champagne.

The Daily Mail

Ivor with Isabel Jeans and Dorothy Dickson.

Above: Ivor with Mary Kerridge, in the Windsor production of *I Lived with You.*

Opposite top: Peter Graves and Olga Lindo in *Breakaway.*

Opposite bottom: Roma Beaumont as Alice, with Sybil Thorndike and Zena Dare, in Ivor's production of *Alice in Wonderland* at the Scala Theatre in 1943.

The Theatre Royal, Windsor, was Ivor's local playhouse when he was at Redroofs. In the summer of 1940 he suggested to the director, John Counsell, that he might appear there in a revival of *I Lived with You*. The dress rehearsal took place on the 17th of June.

> When the first act finished, I went to the pub next door to listen to the one o'clock news. What I heard made the rest of the rehearsal seem very unimportant. At its end I went on to the stage, ostensibly for notes. I had, however, none to give. All I had to say was, 'France has fallen.' There was a long silence, broken at last by Ivor. 'How terrible, terrible.' Another silence. Then, 'I suppose that means there won't be a soul in the house tonight.' I replied, 'My dear Ivor, if there was a German machine gun mounted in the foyer and others at every entrance to the theatre, your fans would somehow contrive to find a way in.' We were, I believe, the only theatre in England to be packed that night to suffocation.
>
> John Counsell,
> *Counsell's Opinion*

The success of *I Lived with You* prompted Ivor to offer John Counsell a try-out of his new play, *Breakaway*. Another of Ivor's vehicles for two star actresses, it had originally been written for Edith Evans and Marie Tempest. At Windsor the two leads were taken by Olga Lindo and Frances Rowe. The former's rôle was the one intended for Miss Tempest and was that of Liza Duffy, the director of a multiple store, who takes a 'break away' from her job to stay in the Venetian palazzo belonging to Princess Stasia Ottiano, the part intended for Edith Evans. Peter Graves played the juvenile, Clive Andover. As far as is known, the play never re-appeared after its Windsor try-out.

The Dancing Years returned to London in 1942 and stayed at the Adelphi Theatre for a further two years. Roma Beaumont continued to play the part of Grete:

> 'I was getting rather tired of being a little girl of fourteen——after all, I was nearly thirty by then——and one night I told Ivor so. He said he had something lovely in mind for me, and do you know what it turned out to be? *Alice in Wonderland!*'

First Reading of Novello's new play ends in Phyllis Monkman sitting on a table and explaining to Ivor and Ena Burrill how she will render her ex-star-turned-secretary role

NOVELLO PRESENTS

PHOTOGRAPHED BY ERICH AUERBACH

An ex-officer this week plunges into West End management with a play specially written for him

THE PROFILE has turned the back of his neck to the Gallery Girls and wonders if he need cover his ears with his hands to keep out the cat-calls, or do a quick turnabout and present a full face to watch their looks of admiration which have persisted for so many fruitful years. This time The Profile will not be silhouetted by the theatre lights; more likely the wings will hide the classic features.

The about-face has been made by Ivor Novello who, in between gathering the endless lilac bouquets at the

Author goes over the play with the cast while Produ[cer] Max Adrian sits on Ivor Novello's right and P[eter] Daubeny, for whom comedy was written, on his

Ivor at rehearsals.

We Proudly Present (1947)

Ivor's last straight play was written in fulfilment of a promise to Peter Daubeny, whom he had met during the war, to help launch his career in management. The story followed Daubeny's own: Bill Whittaker and John Pearson, war-time chums, decide to set up as producers and take a lease of the blitzed Pantheon Theatre. Assisted by a loyal secretary, ex-actress Phyl Perriman (Phyllis Monkman), they overcome successive difficulties, including the machinations of a temperamental leading lady (Ena Burrill), and their first play is a hit.

Mr Novello, having resolved, not for the first time, to grind stardom and pseudo-stardom to their dusty elements, does the job with relish, thoroughness and skill.

The Observer

Now and then some gossipy little joke will cleverly pretend to sting some person of importance, but only a moment's reflection is needed to show that it is quite harmless. On the morning after the first night Mr Novello could have lunched without the slightest embarrassment at the theatre's most fashionable restaurant.

The Tatler & Bystander

He relies most of all on his own flagrant and unblushing sense of theatre to protract a gossipy little sketch of backstage life into three acts. The aim is never very high, but it never misses.

The Daily Mail

MUSICALS

Glamorous Night (1935)

It was a completely new departure, because they hadn't had anything like that before, at Drury Lane or anywhere.

Mary Ellis

Glamorous Night was not, in fact, a musical—not, at least, in the sense in which the term is understood today. Part opera, part melodrama, part operetta, part musical comedy, it was Ivor's own invention: a Novello Show. And from then on, for the next fifteen years, any theatregoer, whether he liked them or not, would know what to expect from 'a Novello Show'. It meant, to begin with, that Ivor would be the hero; but a hero unique in 'musical' terms, because Ivor could not sing. Therefore this hero, although he was at the centre of the story, was a curiously detached figure who, at certain moments, would disappear while the singers took over. But it was around him, and because of him, that the story happened: it was him that the leading lady—or, sometimes, ladies—loved, and lost or won, as the case might be; and, whatever he did or whatever was done to him, you knew that, unless he was there, both onstage and off, none of it could possibly have happened.

The three architects of the Drury Lane shows: Ivor with his director, Leontine Sagan, and his lyricist, Christopher Hassall.

As if to emphasise this characteristic, Ivor would sometimes, at the climax of the show, appear deliberately detached from the rest of the company: in a plain blue suit against the pomp of a royal court, in sweat-stained shirt sleeves against the immaculate whiteness of a Chinese wedding, or, in the last show of all, alone in a vast cathedral, empty after the crowded Coronation ceremonial.

Musicals, as a rule, have three credits below the title: Book by . . ., Lyrics by . . ., Music by . . . A Novello show had one legend only: Devised, Written and Composed by Ivor Novello. And of these three functions, the 'devising' was the one that singled out a Novello Show from any other, because, starting with the theatre itself—the Theatre Royal, Drury Lane—he did in truth physically devise an experience for his audience which would exploit for their benefit the full resources of one of the most impressive and elaborately equipped stages in the world, in a way that they have never remotely been exploited since.

The Theatre Royal, Drury Lane, in 1935.

189

Cheers, shouts, yells and a tornado of clapping greeted Mr Ivor Novello's first entrance at Drury Lane last night ... Anthony Allan, the part he plays, is the young inventor of a new TV process who is given £500 by Lord Radio ... to keep quiet. The scene shifts to Krasnia, where backward English is spoken—as we can tell from the notice, ON GNIKOMS, in its opera house. King Stefan of Krasnia loves Militza, a Gypsy prima donna, whom we see and hear at a grand gala performance, ending in an attempt on her life. Here is Anthony's chance. He disarms the would-be assassin and is invited to the gypsy's boudoir. Then he has to return to his ship for the duration of the cruise, plus her cheque for £1,000. She follows. Gay scenes aboard ship end in a spectacular wreck. Our hero and his prima donna reach the shore where they are married gypsy fashion. But her country is in danger, and to save it she has to agree to become queen. He returns to England and witnesses her coronation by means of the TV he has invented. Beyond all doubt, *Glamorous Night* is wildly, inspiringly, intoxicatingly triumphant.

The Daily Mail

I frankly do think that, unless we had met, the Drury Lane thing would never have come about, because it was, just at that psychological moment, a most terrific combination.

Mary Ellis

Ivor first saw Mary Ellis in 1933 at His Majesty's Theatre in Jerome Kern's *Music in the Air*, in which she had the part of Frieda Hatzfeld, a temperamental prima donna. He sent her a box of lilies—'like a coffin', she describes it—with a message saying that he would like to write a show for her. But as she was under contract to Paramount in Hollywood for three films, the project had to be postponed. When Ivor first suggested the story of *Glamorous Night* to Harry Tennent, the manager of Drury Lane, it seems more than likely that he had Mary Ellis in mind: a prima donna, who is also a king's mistress, who is also a gypsy, the part could have been played by nobody else.

Opposite: Mary Ellis read the reviews of *Glamorous Night* at Redroofs.

Below: 'Hail, Her Majesty Militza!': the Royal Guard announce the King's Mistress.

The opera within the show: centre-stage, Trefor Jones, Mary Ellis and Olive Gilbert.

Mary Ellis—an artist, nay, I am bold to say, a great artist, in every sense of the word: infinitely versatile, vibrating with emotion, throwing heart, soul and brain, to say nothing of her magnificent voice, into her work.

The Sketch

Owing to her film commitments, Miss Ellis was unable to reach London until after rehearsals had begun. But a script was despatched to her in Hollywood, and as Ivor composed the melodies he recorded them—on disc, as it was before the days of tape—and sent them to her. She promised to have learned the first act, words and music, by the time she walked off the boat and into rehearsal—and did. Musically, the rôle was demanding, because Ivor had interpolated into

the first act a complete scene from an opera, *Glamorous Night*, the device of a 'show within a show', which he was to employ several times subsequently.

The Opera in *Glamorous Night* was nearly cut, and all I would have had was three lines in the Gypsy Wedding.

Olive Gilbert

Miss Gilbert, a lead singer with the Carl Rosa Company, auditioned for *Glamorous Night* on the suggestion of Madame Clara Novello Davies. She sang an operatic aria, and as soon as she had finished Ivor told the management he had found the voice he was looking for and the other candidates were dismissed. Thus began an association which was to last until his death.

The Assassination Foiled: Anthony saves Militza's life outside the
Opera House.

Miss Gilbert was engaged originally to sing in a mock-opera quartet, written in Italian by Viola Tree. Then Ivor composed the 'Glamorous Night' operatic sequence, which introduced *Shine Through My Dreams*, one of the most beautiful melodies in the score. Since the show threatened to be of inordinate length, Leontine Sagan decreed that the sequence should be cut, but Ivor made one of his rare scenes and it was kept in. During rehearsals Ivor said to Miss Gilbert, 'I'll write you some wonderful parts after this. You're going to be lucky to me, and I'm going to be lucky to you.' He was as good as his word, and she appeared in every show he wrote subsequently, with the exception of *Gay's the Word*.

Musically, *Glamorous Night* is something of a hotch-potch—but a hotch-potch full of good things. In the printed score, the opening number *Suburbia*—a musical mime to show Anthony Allan's humble background—has been cut, because, in the version of the script published for amateur production, the whole introductory episode of Anthony's transaction with Lord Radio has been removed—as has the finale in which he views Militza's marriage to King Stefan (Barry Jones) on a mammoth television screen. Thus the first number is the male chorus, *Hail, Her Majesty Militza*, ostensibly a stock operetta opening, but given fresh character by Christopher Hassall's sarcastic lyric. Why the King's mistress should be addressed as Her Majesty is never made clear, but in Krasnia anything is likely to happen. Mary Ellis suggests that Militza was inspired by Magda Lupescu, at that time the mistress of King Carol of Rumania.

In the first act there is not just one waltz, but two: the first, *Fold Your Wings*, was written as a duet for Mary Ellis and Trefor Jones to sing in the course of a scene where Militza is rehearsing for the night's opera performance; the second is the title number, *Glamorous Night*, and it was this melody which Ivor gave to Christopher Hassall to set, when he first had the notion of collaborating with Hassall as his lyricist. The musical centrepiece of the first act is the operatic sequence, where for the first time an audience heard the tremendous range Ivor had now discovered in himself as a composer.

The second act introduced the spectacular pièce de résistance, the shipwreck of the cruise-liner Silver Star, on which both Anthony and Militza are travelling and which is sabotaged by order of Prime Minister Lydyeff (Lyn Harding) in a further attempt to do away with Militza. The Drury Lane stage consists of a series of platforms built on hydraulic lifts, which can be raised and lowered independently or in combinations, and at varying speeds, and are controlled from machinery in the basement, which itself resembles a ship's engine room. Under the directions of the brilliant stage manager, William Abingdon, the structure of three decks of the Silver Star, complete with practical promenades and companionways, was built on one of the down-stage platforms. The wreck commenced with several explosions; smoke poured across the stage, as the passengers began to panic; then, to the accompaniment of bellowed orders from the crew, fog-horns blaring and the screams of women and children, the whole ship lurched to one side and began to sink inexorably into the ocean. The curtain fell and rose again on a scene of total chaos; the audience, shattered and delighted, needed the interval to recover.

Previous to the wreck, the Silver Star had been the scene of a cabaret on-deck, during which dancers performed both a rhumba and, surprisingly, a skaters' waltz. Militza is prevailed upon to contribute and obliges with a 'haunting melody' remembered from her Romany childhood, *When the Gypsy Played*. As a final diversion, Ivor introduced a totally extraneous character, a black stowaway called Cleo Wellington, played by Elisabeth Welch, whom he had seen stopping the show with *Solomon* in Cole Porter's *Nymph Errant*:

Ivor and Mary Ellis on board before the wreck.

'I was just there because he wanted this song sung. I was a stowaway, but no-one ever discovered where I stowed away from! They just found me during the cabaret and dragged me on. There I was, with a darkened stage and all the company, including Ivor, Mary and the dancing girls, listening to me. So how could I fail?'

The song, of quite a different character from the rest of the score, was called *Shanty Town*, a lilting 'blues'-type tune which Miss Welch performed memorably.

Opposite: The wreck of the S.S. Silver Star.

Above: Anthony and Militza cast ashore.   Opposite: Two moments in the Gypsy Wedding.

Musically, the third act of *Glamorous Night* is almost completely operetta. Militza and Anthony, having been warned of the impending disaster, manage to escape from the ship and are cast ashore, like Viola, upon the sea-coast of Krasnia, which is really a latter-day Illyria. There the gypsies discover them, and Militza and Anthony, who have somehow found time to fall in love, are united in a gypsy wedding ceremony to full choral accompaniment. Lilian Braithwaite, on Ivor's appearing at the luncheon-table at Redroofs in a state of disarray, cried out, 'You little gypsy! Go away and wash!', and the gypsy theme was a recurring one in Ivor's career. In two of his silent films, *Miarka* and *The Bohemian Girl*, he was a member, either through inheritance or adoption, of a gypsy clan, and, after a uniform, gypsy costume seems to have been his favourite stage attire. Both he and Mary Ellis had the black hair and flashing eyes of the idealised Romany, and provided a striking focus for a stage picture crammed with life and colour.

Meanwhile, back at the Palace, all is not well. Baron Lydyeff has brought about his revolution and King Stefan is threatened with execution unless he agrees to abdicate. News comes to the gypsies' encampment and, headed by Militza singing the Krasnian National Anthem, they march on the capital. At this point, out of limbo and frankly to cover a scene change, Elisabeth Welch reappeard in a Victor Stiebel suit to sing *The Girl I Knew*. Cleo Wellington's success in cabaret has apparently been her downfall, and this is a wry lament for her lost innocence. The song has, sadly, vanished from the score, but survives in Miss Welch's recording.

Anthony arrives just in time to prevent the King's execution and shoot Lydyeff dead. He and Militza plan to return to England together, but Stefan tells her that he cannot carry on without her: unless she marries him, he must abdicate. Putting her country before her heart, Militza renounces Anthony.

Highbrow authors ... may pettishly suggest that the whole thing is punk. It may be so, but it is inspired punk, and it is given to few to write it.

The Bystander

Mr Ivor Novello has devised an entertainment so excellent in its fripperies that it is a pity he bothered about a story that is both steep and flat.

James Agate
in the Sunday Times

I lift my hat to Mr Novello. He can wade through tosh with the straightest face: the tongue never visibly approaches the cheek. Both as actor and as author he can pursue adventures too preposterous even for the films and do it with that solemn fixity of purpose which romantic melodrama inexorably demands.

Ivor Brown
in the Observer

In contriving this show Mr Novello has brought off the biggest achievement of his career. It is not an easy task, now that the talkies have been brought to technical perfection, to invent a big-scale stage entertainment that will rival them in popular appeal. Only a superb theatrical craftsman could bring it off—and that is exactly what Mr Novello is ... Superior persons will no doubt scoff at the show, and dismiss it as a lot of nonsense ... If it is nonsense, it is glamorous nonsense, and for those who are ready to be entertained, it is the best show of its kind Drury Lane has had for years.

The Daily Telegraph

Farewell to Militza: Anthony is honoured for bravery at the court of Krasnia.

THE KING AND QUEEN AT DRURY LANE

A "Daily Mail" photograph of the King and Queen and the Duke and Duchess of Kent watching last night's performance of Mr. Ivor Novello's musical play, "Glamorous Night," at Drury Lane Theatre. The visit took the audience by surprise, and there was great cheering when the royal party entered their box.

The Royal Visit to Drury Lane.

A week after the King and Queen had seen *Glamorous Night*, Ivor and his mother received an invitation to a Royal Garden Party at Buckingham Palace. When Ivor was introduced, George the Fifth is reported to have said, 'And you write the story and music and act the principal part yourself! Don't you find it very tiring in this hot weather?', to which Ivor gave the inspired reply, 'Not when *you're* in front, Sir.' The King then went on, 'Well, I can tell you this. We enjoyed ourselves enormously, with one reservation—we could have wished a different ending. We found it a little sad, the Queen and I; in fact you made the Queen cry. Make the next one with a happy ending please.'

Ivor complied with the royal request, but by the time the 'next one', *Careless Rapture*, reached the stage, King George had died. But Queen Mary remained an inveterate theatregoer for the rest of her life.

It was the custom of the Drury Lane Management to present a Christmas pantomime annually, and, despite the great success of *Glamorous Night*, they stuck to this tradition and Ivor was informed that his show must close in November after only six months' run. Considering the theatre had been on the verge of bankruptcy before Ivor brought them *Glamorous Night*, the management's behaviour seems ungrateful as well as short-sighted. However, Ivor offered them a financial guarantee of £8,000 as the equivalent of what they would make on the pantomime,

if they would keep *Glamorous Night* on. They countered with a demand for £10,000, which was beyond Ivor's resources. As some sort of consolation, they then offered him the theatre in the spring of 1936 for his next show, which he had already written. He took the script along to read to them, but it was coolly received and a few days later Harry Tennent rang Ivor and told him that the new show had been turned down. Instead the management planned to follow the pantomime with a musical called *Rise and Shine*, written by Harry Graham and Desmond Carter, with a score by Robert Stolz and a cast headed by Binnie Hale, Jack Whiting and Syd Walker.

In a funny way Ivor was a terribly unsophisticated person—not that he didn't know everything, do everything, see everything! He was mischievous and naughty and everything under the sun, but his saving grace was that he was utterly sincere. He wanted *Glamorous Night* to be as good as possible and he was so close with me and Leontine that there was not a night that we didn't meet and talk over the next day's scenes. I would spend my wits and my spirit on a scene which, if it had been done less well, would have been ghastly. If it had been done badly or cheaply, it would never have worked. There are certain shows that create a magic that you can never repeat.

Mary Ellis

Right: The dedication Ivor wrote on the script which he sent to Mary Ellis in Hollywood: he had it bound for her in green leather.

Below: Nerman's cartoon of Ivor and Mary Ellis.

The screen rights of *Glamorous Night* were bought by Associated British, but the film did not appear until 1937. Mary Ellis was cast as Militza, but there is no record of Ivor's having been asked to play opposite her, and the rôle of Anthony went to a moderately well-known juvenile, Barry McKay. Two minor Hollywood names, Otto Kruger and Victor Jory, were imported to play King Stefan and the villain—now called Lyadeff. Olive Gilbert appeared briefly in the opera sequence, but the part of Militza's dresser, Phoebe, played on stage by Minnie Rayner, was given to Maire O'Neill. The story was updated to include much talk of Dictators and Abdication, and at one point there was even a reference to a Concentration Camp. Anthony has now become an oil prospector investigating a hidden oil field in Krasnia, which turns out to be under a forest in 'Gypsy Land'. Militza wishes to keep this a secret from Lyadeff, who plans to trade the oil for arms in order to overthrow the monarchy, and at a crucial moment she utters the prophetic words, 'Oil means War!' Otherwise the story follows the lines of the show, except that, surprisingly for a film, there is no shipwreck, Militza and Anthony merely commandeering a life-boat to return to Krasnia when they hear the King's Abdication speech on the radio. The romance between them is underplayed and, when King Stefan claims Militza for his bride, Anthony announces, with some relief, that he is off to South America 'where there are only republics!' The film is creakingly directed (by Brian Desmond Hurst) and shoddily produced with inadequate resources; in fact one would estimate that the theatre company probably outnumbered that employed on the screen. Without the presence and singing of Mary Ellis, it would be just another second-grade melodrama with music.

It is about as bogus as a film could be, but . . . it has the advantage of Mary Ellis's daemonic good looks.

Graham Greene
in the Spectator

Opposite top: Mary Ellis and Trefor Jones in front of the cameras during the filming of *Glamorous Night*.

Opposite bottom: Mary Ellis with Barry McKay.

Right: Mam continues to occupy her share of the limelight.

ENTERTAINMENTS
à la CARTE

By ALAN BOTT

RAPTURE AND RUPTURE: (FROM TOP) PRIEST IN SPECTACLES, GEORGE ELTON; DINKY DEVIL-DANCER, WALTER CRISHAM; IN CHAYNESE COSTUME, DOROTHY DICKSON; IN SKINS AND PROFILE, IVOR NOVELLO; IN WHAYTE TAYE, IVAN SAMSON

THE tale, children, is of a glamorous girl named Penelope, an impetuous young man named Michael, and a nasty piece of work named Sir Rodney. Unfortunately it was Sir Rodney, and not Michael, to whom Penelope was engaged. Was Michael downhearted? You bet he was not. He chased Penelope into beauty parlours and singing classes (for Penelope was a golden-voiced actress). He leaped, clean-limbed, through windows; he hid himself under rugs in Penelope's dressing-room while Sir Rodney was saying, in a cold and snobbish manner, "Ay love you." He was so impetuous that he made Penelope—"Penny" for short—forget her Savoy supper with Sir Rodney and accompany him to Hampstead Heath, which was decorated for the occasion with lovely colours, luscious merry-go-rounds, and costers dressed in pearlies like they had before the Great War. So Michael and Penny danced in careless rapture with the costers and then went to sleep on a merry-go-round.

When they woke up from their glamorous night Michael was on a wooden horse and Penny on a mournful ostrich, which they christened Garbo. Soon Sir Rodney broke in upon their merriment, grinding his teeth with rage. He told Penny that Michael only pretended to love her so as to be revenged. For Michael, it appeared, was half-brother to Sir Rodney; only Sir Rodney's father forgot to marry Michael's mother, and left a Will saying that if Michael came to England for more than a month, his money was to go to the legitimate son (Sir R.). So Penny was hurt and spurned Michael—this sort of thing is known as a Misunderstanding—and to make matters worse, Michael had remained a day too long in England, so Sir Rodney was able to take his money and leave him penniless.

But Michael stayed smiling, for he was a happy bastard. He was also a dauntless one. He followed Penny and Rodney to China, where they were to be married; and though Sir Rodney ordered that he was to be shot at sight, he again met her by climbing through windows. He saved her from an earthquake, and they ran away to a big temple where they met a priest in spectacles, who told them a legend about a priestess who was slain because she loved a prince. So Michael and Penny slept in the temple, a suitable distance apart, and in their dreams Penny was the priestess in flowing robes and Michael the prince in spotted skins and handsome profile.

Next morning they were being arch with each other when they were

Careless Rapture (1936)

There is always rapture at these Drury Lane first nights-
—at least upstairs. The gallery hysterically applauds anything and everything; besides, Miss Dietrich was present
in the stalls, a cause for rapture in the pit ... Mr Novello
personally and charmingly conducted the whole party on
this simple-minded escapade on whose splendours the
stage staff must be congratulated.

The Observer

There is a story, perhaps apocryphal, that Mam, seated in
splendour in the Royal Box, was so put out by the attention
accorded to Marlene that she pushed her chocolates over
the edge to create a diversion—successfully.

If *Glamorous Night* was largely operetta, *Careless
Rapture* was more nearly akin to musical comedy—as
indicated by the respective heroines' professions. Mary Ellis
had played a prima donna; Dorothy Dickson was cast as
Penelope Lee, star of *The Rose Girl*, who is about to retire
from the stage to marry Sir Rodney Alderney (Ivan
Samson). To her consternation, she finds herself pursued by
a young man—rather as Rosine Browne was pursued by
Max in *The Truth Game*—from whom she takes refuge, first
in a beauty parlour run by her friend, Phyllida Frame (Zena
Dare), and then in the studio of her singing teacher, Mme
Simonetti (Olive Gilbert). The young man, played by Ivor,
turns out to be Sir Rodney's illegitimate brother, Michael,

Opposite: Tom Titt's cartoon in the Tatler.

Below: Dietrich arrives at Drury Lane with Douglas Fairbanks Jr.

Above: Dorothy Dickson and the Boys sing *Wait For Me*.

Left: Zena Dare with 'David Davies' (Ivor in disguise as Prince Meiling).

Opposite top: Michael interrupts Penny's singing lesson.

Opposite bottom: Ivor with Dorothy Dickson in the scene on Hampstead Heath.

who lives abroad on an allowance. He turns up again in Penny's dressing-room after her farewell performance and, overcoming her misgivings, persuades her to ditch Sir Rodney and come with him to the Fair on Hampstead Heath. Sir Rodney follows them, reveals Michael's identity to Penny and informs his brother that he has overstayed his allotted time in England and forfeited his inheritance. The scene changes, in the second act, to the town of Fu-Chin in China, where Sir Rodney is organising an International Exhibition. As part of the celebrations, Phyllida is producing an amateur version of *The Rose Girl*, with Penny in the lead, and has also brought along one of her most intractable clients, Mrs Ripple (Minnie Rayner). Michael, having

worked his passage to China on a cargo boat, reappears in disguise as Prince Meiling, offering some Chinese objets d'art for inclusion in the exhibition. Penny recognises him and faints in the middle of a rehearsal. Sir Rodney sets the police on to Michael, but he manages to reach Penny and inform her of an impending earthquake. With Phyllida's help, she and Michael leave Fu-Chin, which is devastated. Finding refuge in a ruined temple, they fall asleep and dream of the legendary Priestess and her Lover, sacrificed to the Temple's Idol. On waking, they are surprised by rebels and taken captive; but Rodney ransoms Penny, who agrees to marry him immediately, if he will ransom Michael as well. The plot then thickens to an almost impenetrable consistency with the introduction of a troop of bandits and much double-crossing and turning of the tables between Sir Rodney and Michael; but the upshot is that the former is left in captivity in the bandits' cave, while Michael returns to Fu-Chin, arriving just in time to marry Penny on the Bridge of Lovers.

Ivor said, 'Can you come down at ten o'clock on Thursday morning? They're delivering the earthquake.' So there it was, all collapsed—it was magnificent, and we passed out laughing! In the scene that I had on one of those Chinese balconies, when the rumbling started, I had to say, 'My maid says it's earthquake weather.' And that was in our dialogue from then on.

Dorothy Dickson

Miss Dickson had first met Ivor in New York in the 1920s, and they later became friends when she came over to London with Jerome Kern's *Sally*. She first appeared for him in his play, *The Sunshine Sisters*, which was a failure, and at the time he was producing *Careless Rapture* she was starring at the Saville, with Ivy St Helier and Nelson Keys, in Herbert Farjeon's revue, *Spread It Abroad*, in which she created the song, *These Foolish Things*, dancing with another American emigré, Walter Crisham. She and Crisham both left to go into *Careless Rapture*, their rôles being taken over by Madge Elliott and Cyril Ritchard. This operation was facilitated by the assistance of Bill Newman, stage manager at the Saville, who, with his wife, Winifred, later went to work for Ivor. Dorothy Dickson was primarily a dancer and comedienne, and Ivor adjusted the range of her numbers to suit this, entrusting the more demanding parts of the score to Olive Gilbert, Sybil Crawley and Eric Starling. Zena Dare's was a non-singing rôle and, as Phyllida Frame, she was simply required to look chic and react in her own inimitable way to the extravagant and alarming events occurring in her vicinity. The opening chorus, *Thanks to Phyllida Frame*, takes place in her establishment and is a very 'period' comment on the beauty parlour vogue. Dorothy Dickson's first song, *Music in May*, is introduced dur-

ing her singing lesson, as is *Why is There Ever Good-bye?*, one of the most luscious melodies Ivor ever wrote—sung at this point by Olive Gilbert and reprised at Penny's farewell performance. The 'show within a show' is now *The Rose Girl*, a typical musical comedy hybrid, whose numbers range from Penny's ultra-modern *Wait For Me* through the Rose Ballet to the semi-operatic duet (sung by Sybil Crawley and Eric Starling) *Love Made the Song*, while for the Fair Scene Ivor composed a set of pastiche Cockney ballads, which were sung by the ensemble as a musical background to the spectacle. In the second act, during the rehearsals of *The Rose Girl*, a novelty dance, *The Manchuko*, was performed by Dorothy Dickson and Walter Crisham. A kind of Oriental version of the Continental or the Piccolino, it was perhaps intended to cash in on the current success of such numbers on the dance floor, but there is no record of its having done so. In *Careless Rapture*, for the first and last time, Ivor sang in one of his own shows. During the run of *Glamorous Night* he had been taking singing lessons from Lawrence Leonard, without marked effect, and he composed a 'cod' opera duet for himself and Dorothy Dickson to perform in Mme Simonetti's studio. This was curtailed later in the run, but was recorded in full. Also curtailed and finally dropped altogether was Ivor's one and only appearance as a dancer, in the Dream Ballet that takes place in the ruined temple. Such—fortunately rare—errors of judgement were a source of embarrassment to most of his friends.

Running round Drury Lane stage with those heavy boots on—how could he? In the end I invented a formula for going round after anything like that had happened. I would open his dressing-room door, pop my head in, give a big smile and say 'Ivor!' And he would look up and say *immediately*, 'I *knew* you'd love it!'

Cyril Ritchard

To me the most attractive moment that he ever had was at the music rehearsal, sitting in the stalls when the whole orchestra was there, the stage-hands and everything. You would have thought that he couldn't be in command of the whole of Drury Lane, but he was! If people had seen him at that moment, they would have seen all his talents come together at once.

Dorothy Dickson

Opposite: Ivor dances the Temple Ballet with Dorothy Dickson.

Mr Novello has succeeded in imposing a unity rare in musical plays. The story skilfully assists the spectacle and yet is not without a certain suspense of plot. This suspense may be in great part due to Mr Novello's persistent hold on the note of sincerity in the midst of choral interruptions, and to the dainty but definite personality with which Miss Dickson endows the heroine.

The Times

It is gratifying that Mr Novello should find time to be witty and musical among so much scenery and plot. His acting, which might have been in the nature of an afterthought, is, on the other hand, full of the most careful rapture.

The Sunday Times

Michael reunited with Penny on the Bridge of Lovers.

Mr Novello must be one of the happiest men in London at the moment. He must be happy because Drury Lane is notoriously an exacting theatre to write for, and this he has now done successfully not merely once (like Noël Coward) but actually twice. Easy enough, no doubt, to say, as Mr Novello says, 'Let there be roundabouts on Hampstead Heath.' Easy enough to add, as Mr Novello adds, 'Let there be an earthquake outside the palace in Fu-Chin'. But not so easy to concoct the mammoth jokes and to pump up the mammoth emotions that will keep the feet of the audience from shuffling during the mammoth spectacles.

Herbert Farjeon
in the Bystander

The best of its kind ever conceived.

Variety

Crest of the Wave (1937)

An impoverished but romantic young man, Don Gantry, Duke of Cheviot, having rejected the determined advances of a millionairess, is very rudely shot by her four times in the back. Her unladylike conduct is explained by her being the daughter of a gangster, but she seems not to have inherited the paternal marksmanship, for Mr Novello survives without a single scratch. Thus Don Gantry is free to become, on his merits, a film star, to retrieve the family fortunes by the sweat of his profile and to become engaged to Honey Wortle and to shake the dust of Hollywood from his feet. So home to Gantry Castle. Snow, Christmas, tenants' ball, lights out, electric Christmas tree, the old carol, and, behold, the young Duchess, invalided by a villainous train crash, tottering in to receive the feudal cheers. How bare the narrative seems! How richly Drury Lane has clothed it! ... The train crash of tradition is perhaps the best of all ... A boyish and simple evening.

The Times

If the story of *Crest of the Wave* sounds more preposterous than its predecessors, the answer is that it was, even by the standards of a Novello Show. The script gives every indication of having been run up in a hurry to fulfil a commitment, and even the score is sparse in comparison with Ivor's previous efforts. 1937 was Coronation Year, patriotism was again in fashion, and *Rose of England*, sung by Edgar Elmes and the chorus as the spirits of Gantry Castle's past, struck exactly the right note and has survived as a sort of musical comedy *Land of Hope and Glory*. Ivor's own rôle was also topical: the Earl of Warwick had gone to Hollywood for a lark, and was now being groomed for stardom—unsuccessfully, as it turned out. But the hit of the show was Dorothy Dickson's Honey Wortle, a Cockney extra girl who makes it both on the screen, as June May, and off, as a Duchess.

Below: The Gantry family at breakfast: Ivor, Marie Lohr and Peter Graves.

Opposite: Tom Titt's cartoon in the Tatler.

ENTERTAINMENTS à la CARTE

By
ALAN BOTT

AN ODD LIFE ON THE OCEAN WAVE: IVOR NOVELLO, DOROTHY DICKSON

ROLLING ROUND IN RIO: DOROTHY DICKSON, WALTER CRISHAM

IN the first place, Ivor Novello has again rung the bell with a resonant clang. Time rolls on, and he continues to fill Drury Lane with a consistency that no other author, actor or manager has been able to achieve. Once a year he delivers the formula, the story, the script, the tunes, the ideas for spectacle, the personality, the profile, the archness, the attitudes and the variegated goods ; and that once is enough to fill London's Largest Theatre until half-way through the next year. He draws to the Lane thousands who enter a theatre hardly ever. As for his formula, it has given pleasure to a million or two ; and as for the queer doings which it involves, they can be enjoyed even by the minority, as ho-hum or the stuff of luscious day-dreams. There is no malice in my memories of *Crest of the Wave*.

The moon shone bright on Gantry Castle when a procession of ghostly Knights and Ladies, Barons and Dukes entered to chant about the Rose of England. But the rats gnawed deep in Gantry Castle since Lord Snowden's Budgets, so that the reigning Duke (Ivor Himself) had to buy his riding-breeches and breakfast kidneys with the shillings charged to sightseers. When the sightseers strolled through the Morning Room at breakfast-time, the impoverished family left their bacon and kidneys unspeared while they pretended to be noble waxworks. Some £500,000 was needed to restore Gantry Castle ; and after breakfast a young woman arrived to offer exactly £500,000 for the Castle, on behalf of Helen Winter, American gangster's daughter and owner of Colossal Pictures, Inc. It seemed likely that Helen Winter would want to buy the Duke with the Castle ; so the Duke was inclined to spurn the half-million (he was good at spurning), because he didn't want to be a gangster's moll.

Meanwhile, at a film-centre near London, a Cockney extra named Honey Wortle was on top of the world because her Uncle Bob (or Aunt Ethel) had left her a mere £10,000. Otto Fresch, an ageing but conceited film-star, tried to seduce her, but she quickly put him in his place, because at this point the Formula now needed a bit of Spectacle. So they did a movie director's very pink, very gilt and grandiose version of Versailles, where the girl-extra, being Dorothy Dickson, joined a Freddie (Walter Crisham) in a graceful mazurka before she booked the royal suite for a cruise to Hollywood.

It happened that the gangster's daughter was travelling by the same stupendous liner, and so were the Duke and his sister-in-law. Already at the gangway, Honey and the Duke fell in love ; and since H. W. could stand for Helen Winter as for Honey Wortle, here was the usual Mistake in Identity. So the Duke felt he could honestly marry

Olive Gilbert had no part in the script this time, but sang *The Haven of My Heart* in 'the show within a show'—a film sequence entitled *Versailles in Tinsel* in which Dorothy Dickson and Walter Crisham danced a Mazurka arranged by Lydia Sokolova. Minnie Rayner, on the other hand, had a larger rôle than before, as Honey Wortle's omnipresent mother, and Peter Graves was promoted from playing secretaries and ADCs to the second male lead, Lord William Gantry. New members of the troupe were the majestic Marie Lohr as the Dowager Duchess and Ena Burrill as the 'heavy', Leonora Hayden. Having masqueraded briefly as a Chinese prince in *Careless Rapture*, Ivor now went further and essayed a dual rôle: the hero *and* the villain, Otto Fresch, an embittered film star who, out of jealousy for his

rival, engineers the train crash which provided this year's disaster at Drury Lane. Ironically the most effective number was a little song and dance done in front of the tabs by Dorothy Dickson and Walter Crisham, called *Why Isn't It You?*

Opposite top: The Chorus sing *Nautical*: the cruise liner . . .

Opposite centre: . . . becomes a battleship in the best MGM tradition.

Opposite bottom: The Ghosts of Gantry Castle.

Below: Dorothy Dickson and Walter Crisham dance the Mazurka: Olive Gilbert is enthroned in the background.

MUSICALS

First honours, without any sort of doubt, go to Miss Dorothy Dickson, who ... dances as divinely as ever, contrives to give an acting performance in a part which can scarcely have existed on paper, and looks like June sunshine and peach-blossom and milk all rolled into one.
The Sunday Express

One staggers out sated and a trifle stunned, observing, with a bloated species of relief, as one does at the end of a long Christmas dinner with the family, that this occasion is over for another year.
The Observer

As for Dorothy Dickson, she is as humorous as she is beautiful, which says much for her in both capacities. Her Cockney affords us so much amusement that our hearts inevitably sink at the announcement that she proposes to take elocution lessons. But heroines are like that.

The Bystander

Walter Crisham dances *The Venezuela*.

Crest of the Wave closed at the end of February 1938 after only six months' run, and Ivor decided to send it out on tour with Esmond Knight playing Don Gantry. For Dorothy Dickson's part he auditioned, on the suggestion of Peter Graves, a young dancer called Roma Beaumont:

'I was convinced I hadn't got it, and I went to the dressing-room to change. Then I was called onstage, and I went down—very reluctantly. Ivor just said to me, "Do you want to play this part?" I said, "Oh, yes!" And he said, "Then you shall."'

Ivor returned to the show in Birmingham, as *Henry V* had failed at Drury Lane. He went in on the Monday night, without rehearsal, and Miss Beaumont was understandably nervous. At the final curtain he led her forward and announced to the audience: 'Tonight I have found my new star. I shall write my next play for her.'

Right: Ivor as Otto Fresch.

Below: Honey prepares to board the fatal train: *left to right*, Dorothy Dickson, Peter Graves, Marie Lohr.

Above: Punch's view of the train crash.

Below: The ceremony of the Baddeley Cake, backstage at Drury Lane: the trustee, C. M. Lowne, cuts it, watched by Marie Lohr, Ivor, Dorothy Dickson, Walter Crisham and Ena Burrill.

Henry V (1938)

It was Ivor's idea—he always wanted to play it and he and Lewis were great friends, and Ivor realised that Lewis knew his Shakespeare hind-side-before and had played Henry the Fifth himself. And he knew that Lewis was musical and would never give him any dull intonations. He was so humble, like a little beginner! Lewis said he was wonderful about it, and I thought he played it beautifully. But the public didn't want him in anything but really sloppy romanticism—an awful frustration for him, but it meant his money. He was such a sensitive actor; I think he could have done big things—he would have been a lovely Hamlet! And Dorothy was awfully good as the Princess, and it was such a wonderful production—that ship going off to France, wasn't it spectacular? I'm sure Ivor was upset about it, but he realised that it wasn't the time to do a war play. I think it's a tragedy that it was lost.

Sybil Thorndike

Why Lewis Casson picked on me to play the Chorus, as a boy, I have yet to know! But it was a thrilling experience, because Ivor was so dedicated, so modest and sincere, and worked so hard. He couldn't be told enough, he couldn't rehearse long enough hours. After the rest of the company had gone, he would work with Lewis. But it was the disastrous time of the Munich Crisis, and no one wanted to know about militarism. The thing that impressed me was that Ivor never let out a squeak of disappointment, and it was not only his money; it was his most cherished ambition to make a success as a serious actor. It was very, very important to him, and he did indeed give a very creditable, touching performance.

Gwen Ffrangcon-Davies

'Upon the King . . .': Ivor as Henry V.

Gwen Ffrangcon-Davies as Chorus.

Does there hang about the stage the faint suggestion that the piece should have been called *Sanders of the Channel*? For the life of me I can't see why not ... Mr Novello has a voice and, though a little light in timbre, it will do ... He has fire where fire should be; the prayer before battle and the reading of the list of the dead are beautifully done, and the soliloquy beginning 'Upon the King ...' has an entirely admirable cogency.

James Agate
in the Sunday Times

In the midst of this extremely good-looking and well-valeted warfare Mr Ivor Novello gives a modest and careful and well-graced performance ... His best speeches are his quiet ones, the reflections on ceremony and the conversations with the private soldiers.

Ivor Brown
in the Observer

The Battle of Agincourt.

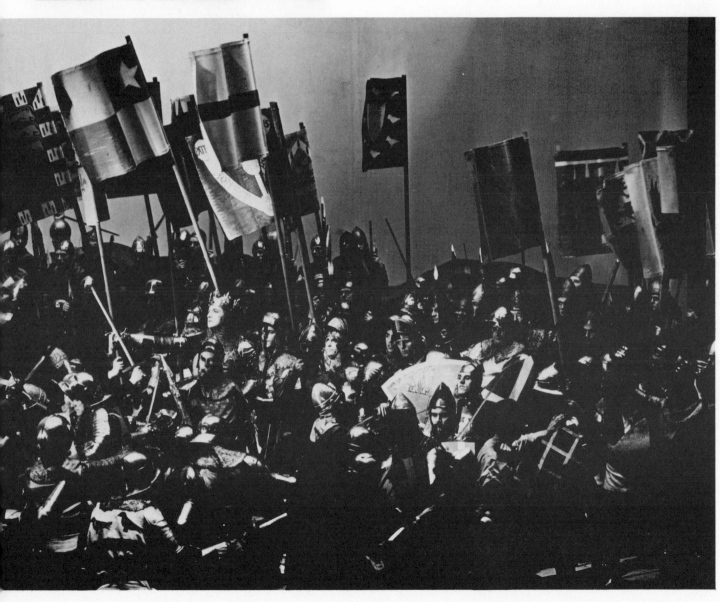

There are two possible motives behind Mr Novello's production of *Henry V*. Either he was inflamed with the desire to play a genuine as distinct from a musical hero, or he audaciously set out, as if for a wager, to prove that his vast public would come to gaze upon him even in Shakespeare. The two motives may, of course, have combined themselves. Whatever the cause, the effect is stirring and vivid. Mr Novello plays the king with far more zest and poetry than his more serious admirers could have anticipated.

Alan Dent
in the Manchester Guardian

Above: Ivor with Dorothy Dickson as the French Princess.

Right: The final curtain.

The Dancing Years (1939)

It began one morning in Liverpool, on the tour of *Crest of the Wave*. Viola Tree had just died and it was in the papers. I rang Ivor at the Adelphi to tell him, and he was terribly sad. So I went down to the hall and asked the porter if there were any trade shows of films on that morning, and he said, 'Yes. There's one at the Trocadero: *The Great Waltz*, with Militza Korjus.' So I rang Ivor and said, 'Come on, get up. Militza Korjus is at the Trocadero.' He said, 'I'll be down in ten minutes,' and down he came, dark glasses on, unshaved, and we got into a taxi and off we went. When we came out of the cinema, he said, 'I've got an idea. Do you think Roma Beaumont can look twelve?' And I said, 'She's only twenty. I'm sure she could.' So he said, 'Ring her up and ask her to lunch, and I'll fiddle with her hair.' And he did. And then he said, 'I'm going to start writing this afternoon.' And that was the first scene of *The Dancing Years*.

Peter Graves

Perhaps Mr Novello's best achievement of all this lovely, colourful production is his discovery of Roma Beaumont, in whom unquestionably a star is born ... In every way *The Dancing Years* is Ivor Novello's best work for the theatre.

The Daily Sketch

It was a more solid piece—less beautiful to look at, but a more serious story. I've never heard such a first night. The applause for *The Wings of Sleep* kept going until the scene had changed.

Mary Ellis

Opposite: Ivor and Mary Ellis dance to the Music of Time.

Below: Ivor with Roma Beaumont in the opening scene.

The opening scene: Rudi's first meeting with Maria.

Of all Ivor's shows, *The Dancing Years* is probably the best loved and certainly the most durable. This is due, to a large extent, to the excellence of the music: every song, from the soaring *Waltz of my Heart* to the tender *My Dearest Dear*, is both memorable in itself and a harmonious component of the score as a whole. But what also marks it out from the others is that for once Ivor was attempting, perhaps in a small way but none the less significant, to say something to his audience: that music has the power to survive both the conflicts of human nature and the wickedness of the world at large, that there is something in a man's aspirations that will rise above the tragedy of life and be remembered after him. In 1939 this was hardly a negligible statement, and could perhaps be applied, with even greater benefit, to the world of today.

Ivor's original intention was to harness the story quite firmly to a current situation: Hitler's persecution of the Jews, and the rehearsal script opens with a prologue in which the composer, Rudi Kleber, now an old man, is condemned to death by the Nazis for his complicity in the escape of Jews from Austria. The management were nervous about introducing anything political into a musical play, and tried to excise this element altogether. But Ivor

stood his ground and in the version as presented at Drury Lane the scene came at the end; but Maria, through the influence of her husband, Prince Metterling, obtains a reprieve and, in the final moments, assures Rudi that her son by him is free from any taint of Nazism. Even so, the German uniforms were deliberately made non-committal and there was no overt reference to the Hitler régime. Unfortunately in recent revivals even this scene is usually removed, thus nullifying Ivor's express purpose in writing the show and reducing *The Dancing Years* to the level of just another operetta.

Mary Ellis, returning triumphantly to Drury Lane, played another prima donna, Maria Ziegler. of the Vienna Opera, who discovers the struggling young composer, Rudi Kleber, in a country inn, brings him to the city to write her new operetta and, after breaking off with her protector, Prince Charles Metterling, instals him as her lover. Rudi intends to marry her, but has made a secret promise to Grete, the innkeeper's niece, that she will have first refusal of his hand when she grows up. Grete returns from England, where she has become a musical comedy actress, and Rudi fulfils his promise. Maria, who is pregnant, overhears his proposal and in a fit of jealous temper returns to Prince Charles and

226

marries him. The years pass and Rudi, now an internationally successful composer, meets Maria again by chance. They both admit that they are still in love, but Maria requests a rendezvous in a week's time at the Inn. She arrives with her—and Rudi's—son, Otto, and Rudi realises that he cannot ask her to abandon her marriage and her home. She tells him that his music 'has made the whole world dance', and they part. In modern productions the story normally ends here, eliminating the epilogue already described.

The part of Grete was written for Roma Beaumont, who stopped the show on the first night with her performance of *Primrose*, a pastiche of a soubrette number in an Edwardian musical comedy. Olive Gilbert had the small but important part of Cäcilie Kurt, Maria's singing teacher, who also takes part in the 'show within a show', an excerpt from Rudi's opera, *Lorelei*, which was the most ambitious piece of continuous composition that Ivor had so far attempted. Minnie Rayner, relegated to service again, was Hattie, the maid at the Inn, and Peter Graves, once more in uniform, played Franzl, who becomes a car salesman in the impoverished Vienna of the Twenties and, one assumes, marries Grete. Prince Charles was played by Anthony Nicholls, whom Ivor had met during the tour of *Crest of the Wave* when Nicholls was appearing in Noël Coward's *Operette* in Birmingham:

'Peggy Wood introduced me to Tyrone Guthrie, and I went to the Old Vic to do five plays. Then one day Guthrie sent for me and said, "I've had a letter from Ivor, who wants you to play in *The Dancing Years*." So I said,

"But I'm under contract to you,"—and I didn't really want to do it. But Guthrie said, "No, that would be ridiculous. It's too good an opportunity to miss." So I went and it was a wonderful experience, from several points of view. *The Dancing Years* was a *very good* musical—all right, it was conventional, but he was trying to say something. And it was a marvellous score. We were a hit from the word go, and we were doing very good business right up to the War. Roma Beaumont had an extraordinary quality—very difficult to define, unlike anyone I've ever seen. I can never understand why she chucked it up!'

Mr Ivor Novello's success was suggested earlier in the evening with his first waltz song, promised by the interval, and assured by the deafening cheers at curtain-call, cheers which deafened even the still, small voice inside me which I keep trained to remind me that these musical spectacles are all nonsense. This nonsense, at all events, is like the Mad Hatter's butter, the best ... And when, in the last scene of all, in the captured Vienna of 1938, Mr Novello, now artistically decrepit, defies the conquerors ... and brings the house down—why, this is only to show that Mr Novello is astute enough to make the best of both worlds, the tinkles of 1911 and the tragedies of our own day.

The News Chronicle

He knows his audience so well indeed that, although we may quibble over details, we are forced to admit that in *The Dancing Years* he has given it a most vivid and glamorous entertainment—perhaps the most vivid and glamorous he has ever accomplished ... Mr Novello, as Rudi, strikes romantic poses, plays the piano better than he conducts and shows himself the incomparable stage architect in every scene. Miss Mary Ellis has never been better: a tender, passionate and utterly lovely performance. And Miss Roma Beaumont, as Grete, captured our hearts from the moment she took the stage.

The Evening Standard

Rouson's cartoon in the Bystander: Roma Beaumont dances *Primrose* and Ivor conducts the orchestra for *Lorelei*.

The little girl who grew up: Grete (Roma Beaumont)

Conducting in intervals of singing, dancing, acting and piano-playing: writer-composer Ivor Novello as Rudi Kleber

Sketches by Rouson

Quint Act III Scene 2 (Page 19)

✗ *We shall see great changes*
& feel it here—Times
unrest and anger & hated
in the world - and then they
are strong - we shall almost
forget to laugh and make
music - but we shant
quite forget and someday
will wake up a. form
an evil dream and the
world will smile again
and forget to hate and the
sweetness of music well
and friendliness will once more
be important - Keep me in your
heart darling & I will keep
you in mine

Ivor Novello certainly has the Drury Lane touch. Almost alone among our theatre men he is able to devise shows that will fill that enormous playhouse, and he seems to be able to do it at will. *The Dancing Years*, which began its run last night, is likely to be even more successful than its predecessors ... If Mr Novello is Drury Lane's ideal author, Mary Ellis is its ideal leading lady ... She takes a great share in the play's success, and so does Roma Beaumont, whose grace and charm earned her thunders of applause. Leontine Sagan's work as producer is as thorough as can be, and the Masque of Vienna arranged by Suria Magito makes an attractive interlude. Indeed the whole affair is a triumph of craftsmanship.

The Daily Telegraph

A speech inserted by Ivor, during rehearsals, into the scene of Rudi's parting from Maria:

'We shall see great changes and feel it here—times of unrest and anger and hatred in the world—and these things are strong. We shall almost forget to laugh and make music, but we shan't quite forget, and some day we'll wake up, as from an evil dream, and the world will smile again and forget to hate, and the sweetness of music and friendliness will once more be important ...

Keep me in your heart, darling, as I will keep you in mine.'

Opposite: Maria overhears Rudi proposing to Grete.

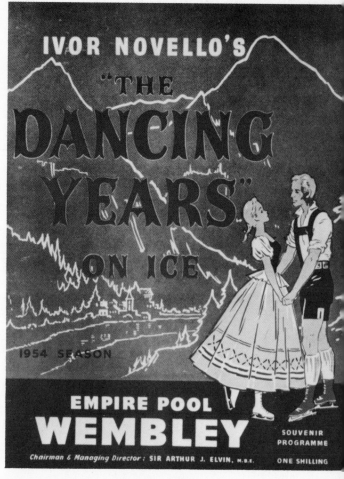

The Dancing Years in a new form, 1954.

Dennis Price and Patricia Dainton in the film version of *The Dancing Years*, 1950.

The Dancing Years, perhaps because of its comparatively simple settings, in contrast to the elaborate spectacle of the previous Drury Lane shows, is often revived in touring productions and by amateurs, and is, at the time of writing, again on tour, with John Hanson in the lead. In 1968 a revival was presented by Tom Arnold at the Saville Theatre, with David Knight as Rudi and June Brönhill as Maria, but shoddy décor and lack of style in the production made it a pale shadow of the original and it only ran a few weeks. Apart from the obvious necessity of giving it a decent presentation, the problem with *The Dancing Years*, as with all Ivor's shows, is finding the right actor to play his rôle—even more so in this case, as he not only acted the composer, he *was* the composer.

The film version of *The Dancing Years* was a good deal better, in production values at least, than the film of *Glamorous Night*. It was made in Technicolor, with attractive backgrounds and costumes, the music was arranged by Louis Levy, and the ballets were choreographed by Frank Staff. A French actress, Gisèle Préville, played Maria effectively, but her singing voice was dubbed in by Vanessa Lee. The film was moderately well received by the Press:

On the whole I thoroughly enjoyed it, though I'm afraid Dennis Price, in the Novello rôle, is no Novello.

The Observer

In subjecting his greatest work, *The Dancing Years*, to the camera lens, ... the producer seems to me to be taking a shocking risk of melting the sugar.

The News Chronicle

The Dancing Years, which had been playing to full houses until a few nights before, closed on Thursday, August 31st 1939, three days before war was declared. The house was reduced to a scattering of patrons, and Ivor came on in the first interval and asked those sitting in the circles and gallery to come down and join those in the stalls. In the first scene, where Rudi plays *The Waltz of my Heart* on the piano, he played instead *Glamorous Night*, as a reminder to the company and the audience of the beginning of an era at Drury Lane which was now about to end, possibly for ever.

On the outbreak of war, all places of entertainment were closed throughout the country, but provincial theatres opened again in October and Ivor took out a tour of a new play, *Second Helping*, starring himself, Isabel Jeans and Dorothy Dickson. The programme included *Song Parade* in which, to Ivor's accompaniment, Olive Gilbert, Muriel Barron (Mary Ellis's understudy in *The Dancing Years*), Wolsey Charles and Anthony Fones gave a pot-pourri of songs from the Drury Lane shows, supplemented, in Ivor's words, 'by the introduction of a completely new song, *We'll Remember the Meadows*, which people tell me, and I hope they're right, is another *Keep The Home Fires Burning*.' The lyric, written by Collie Knox and himself, was printed on slips inserted in the theatre programme and the audience were encouraged to join in. Unfortunately, unlike the audience on that famous night in 1914, they failed to do so—at least with much enthusiasm, and the song, along with *Song Parade*, had vanished by the time the play reached London.

The Dancing Years however was far from dead. Drury Lane was taken over by ENSA early in the War and was no longer available, but in the autumn of 1940 Ivor and Tom Arnold decided to take the show out on a tour of the provinces. Originally intended to last a few months, it was so successful that it was extended and extended and finally continued for a year and a half. The hazards of taking a full-scale musical, complete with scenery and costumes, round war-time Britain, when many cities were under attack from the Luftwaffe and transport, accommodation and every other facility were at a premium, were daunting; but the show went on, often under appalling conditions, and despite the fact that members of the company were constantly being called up and replacements had to be found at short notice. In the spring of 1942 it was decided to bring *The Dancing Years* back to London, to the Adelphi Theatre, for a limited season. The season, like the tour, was prolonged and prolonged and lasted, in the end, for over two years. Mary Ellis had taken up hospital work at the

'WE'LL REMEMBER'

Words by
COLLIE KNOX and IVOR NOVELLO

Music by IVOR NOVELLO

(Composer of "KEEP THE HOME FIRES BURNING.")

REFRAIN

We'll remember the meadows
And the fields of waving corn
We'll remember the music
Of the land where we were born
We'll remember the laughter
And the sunshine after rain
And we'll grin, grin, grin
Till we win, win, win,
And they come back again.

Copyright MCMXXXIX by Chappell & Co., Ltd.

Price **2/-** *of all Music Dealers or*

ASCHERBERG, HOPWOOD & CREW, Ltd.
16, Mortimer Street, London, W.1.

and CHAPPELL & CO., Ltd.
50, New Bond Street, London, W.1.

The song sheet of Ivor's new war-time number.

beginning of the War, and the part of Maria was played by Muriel Barron; but Roma Beaumont, who had gone into a revue, *Black Velvet*, at the Hippodrome, returned, as did Olive Gilbert and many of the supporting cast. *The Dancing Years* became in fact to the Second World War what *Chu Chin Chow* had been to the First.

Arc de Triomphe (1944)

In 1943 Ivor was seriously ill for the first time in his life, with bronchial pneumonia, and had to leave the cast of *The Dancing Years* for five weeks. His place was taken by Barry Sinclair, who had been understudying him since *Glamorous Night*, and had to be released from the Air Force to do so on this occasion. While convalescing at Redroofs, Ivor received a letter from Mary Ellis, telling him that she was contemplating returning to the theatre in a new musical about Lola Montez by Eric Maschwitz, which Tom Arnold was planning to present. The letter arrived at a time when she was much in Ivor's thoughts, and he replied enthusiastically, saying that she must certainly do the show. 'You've been away nearly three years,' he wrote, 'and it's too long . . . Get the beloved Jock (her husband) to wangle a delicious appointment in London and *appear*.' Miss Ellis had also been approached by Tennents to play Regina in *The Little Foxes*, but Ivor felt a musical would be more appropriate for her return. He went on to tell her that he had written a new show himself, but there was no suitable rôle for her (this was to become *Perchance To Dream*), and in any case there was no sign of what he referred to as *The Advancing Years* closing.

He signed himself 'Ivor—the Rudiest Boy in Krasnia.'

When he returned to London, he was given the script of *Lola Montez* by Tom Arnold, and, after reading it, told Arnold that in his opinion it needed extensive re-writing,

Ivor's letter to Mary Ellis telling her that he has an idea for a new show to bring her back to the West End.

and offered to do the job. Tom Arnold's answer was, 'If you're going to do that, why not write a complete Mary Ellis show yourself?'—'to which,' Ivor wrote to her, 'I had no reply—until today, when I really think I have got a *superb* idea.' The idea became *Arc de Triomphe*, a treatment of the life of Mary Garden, the American prima donna. Ivor made her a French-woman, Marie Forêt, who is studying singing in Paris in the 1900s and has an affair with a struggling young actor, Pierre Bachelet (Peter Graves). He goes to America and becomes a film star, while Marie, under the protection of the impresario, Adhémar de Jonzé, becomes a prima donna of the Paris Opera. Pierre returns to claim her, but, on learning of her relationship with de Jonzé, breaks off the affair. War is declared, Pierre is called to the colours and is killed on the Western Front. The climax was again a 'show within a show': a scene from an opera about Joan of Arc, in which Marie sings a patriotic aria, *France Will Rise Again*. This had, of course, a topical relevance, since France was at the time still occupied by the Germans. *Arc de Triomphe* was presented at the Phoenix Theatre towards the end of 1943 and enjoyed a moderately successful run. It had to contend with renewed air-raids on London, including the 'doodle-bugs', and the fact that, good as Peter Graves was in the part, the public expected a Novello Show to star Ivor Novello. Elisabeth Welch was recruited to play another peripheral part, a cabaret artist called Josie, who sings two numbers: *Josephine* and the strangely haunting *Dark Music*. Although Olive Gilbert was still appearing in *The Dancing Years*, Ivor contrived to have her in *Arc de Triomphe* as well by persuading her to come across to the Phoenix from the Adelphi every night to sing the part of Agnes Sorel in the opera sequence:

'I did it for six weeks, until one night my car didn't turn up and I had to walk through the streets in a tin helmet. So I said to him after that, "You can get back that walking tent (Ivor's description of the actress she had replaced at short notice). I'm not doing it any more." And he said, "I just wanted you to be in every musical I do."'

The rehearsal of *Arc de Triomphe* this morning was *most* delightful. The music sounded *most* lovely, and it was a pleasure to watch Ivor smiling with joy. He was in a good vein of wit—at one moment Mary went out, and he asked the conductor to wait until she came back. When she did, he told her he had said, 'Oh, Harry, Miss Ellis has gone to the telephone, but was too shy to say so.' And before the last number he announced to the audience that it was to be *France Will Rise Again*, and then, sotto voce, to us, '—unless we're very careful.'

Edward Marsh

Above: Peter Graves and Mary Ellis sing *Easy to Live With*.

Ivor said, 'I've written you a lead with Mary, and I've got a place for a number for you. What sort of thing would you like to do?' Then he described the story, and I said, 'It must have something to do with Paris, mustn't it? And can I have some girls?' And he said, 'Then I think you must be in a top hat. And I think Cyril Ritchard must set it.' My part was quite small: I was dead at the end of the second act. Then after sixteen weeks Ivor decided to bring me back—in the trenches. There I was, dressed as a Zouave, and he put in another number called *The Mayor of Perpignan*, which he eventually used in *King's Rhapsody*. Mary sang it, in a hospital. We kissed goodbye, and off I went, to be killed. But the business went down, and it wasn't helped by Ivor having to go to prison.

Peter Graves

Right: *Paris Reminds Me of You*: Peter Graves and the Girls.

A singer of genius chooses between love and a career, and chooses wrongly. She has a brilliant success in opera; but her poor young lover has a brilliant success in Hollywood and, as is the way, will not listen when she tries to explain that the cynical impresario has never succeeded in making her anything but a mistress in name. After the war it is too late, and that is why the final scene, for all its brilliance of colour, has nothing to do with the story. But it is a melodious declaration of faith in the power of France to rise again ... Even those who delight in Mr Novello's sense of a stage picture may feel on this occasion that the pictures somehow fail to get going any particular strain of sentiment. The story is at once elaborate and perfunctory. But it allows Mary Ellis to sing of young and happy love, of regret for joys that might have been, of faith in love beyond the grave, and that is perhaps enough.

The Times

Right: Elisabeth Welch sings *Dark Music*.

Below: The Opera Finale.

I can conceive of several reasons why Mr Novello's *Arc de Triomphe* may not wildly succeed. It is not at any time vulgar. Nobody croons. Nobody uses a microphone. No classical composers are jazzed. Nothing is swung . . . On the contrary the piece has many negative virtues. It is well-mannered. It has a reasonable, if sentimental, plot which actually hangs together. Miss Mary Ellis sings quite a number of songs without adventitious aid; moreover she is an extremely accomplished singer. To conclude, Mr Novello's music possesses the last quality lovers of musical plays want to be concerned with—that of being musicianly.

James Agate
in the Sunday Times

There is no composer for the theatre nowadays who can give us such pleasant music as can Mr Novello. Although his scene from an opera about Joan of Arc . . . comes too late in the programme, it proved both tuneful and tender.
The Daily Mail

Left: Mary Ellis as Joan of Arc.

8 WEEKS' SENTENCE ON IVOR NOVELLO

By Your Special Correspondent

SOBBING into a handkerchief, and with a handbag covering her face, thirty-five-year-old, plump Miss Dora Grace Constable, of Mayfield-avenue, North Finchley, left Bow-street Police Court, London, yesterday, after hearing that Ivor Novello, the actor and composer, had been sentenced to eight weeks' imprisonment.

He was also ordered to pay £25 costs. Notice of appeal was given. Bail was allowed in his own surety of £20.

Novello was summoned for conspiring with Miss Constable—who was fined £50, with £25 costs—to commit offences against the Motor Vehicles Order.

Miss Constable, self-confessed admirer of Novello, with whom she declared she was "infatuated," sat in the court the whole day saying hardly a word.

She seldom looked at Novello, even when he sat only a foot or so away from her in the dock.

Mr. H. A. K. Morgan, prosecuting, said that Novello, in November 1942, applied for a permit to use his producer-gas-driven Rolls-Royce between his Berkshire home and London.

It was refused, and this apparently upset the actor, Mr. Morgan continued. One night he mentioned the fact in his dressing-room.

Miss Constable, then a clerk to the Electric and General Industrial Trusts, Ltd., London, was in the dressing-room with other people.

According to her statement said Mr. Morgan, she conceived the idea of transferring the car to the company and applying for a permit in their name for work of national importance.

Company Did Not Know

"Mr. Novello"— her story continued—"fell in with this scheme and the car was duly transferred and a permit obtained.

"The company had no knowledge of this transaction. Mr. Novello, when he received the permit, was tremendously elated and declared I could have anything in the world I wanted."

But she refused everything except a pair of earrings belonging to Mr. Novello's late mother worth about 25s.

The permit, she added, stated that the car must be used only for work of national importance but Mr Novello had used it for numerous week-end visits to his home.

Actor's Explanation

His explanation was that he thought that the transfer was bona fide and that he believed Miss Constable's assurance that he could have a lift at any time when the car was going to the company's branch at Reading.

Mr. Morgan said that Mr. Novello's story was "incredible," and added that the actor knew that the arrangement was a "subterfuge to get round the permit."

Even assuming that Novello knew the transfer was a genuine transaction he must have realised that it was being used in a flagrant breach of conditions of the permit.

Mr. Morgan said that when served with the summons, Miss Constable said: "He is trying to put all the blame on me. That is grossly unfair. He was willing to do anything crooked so long as he had the use of the car."

She told a Fuel Inspector that if she could not do anything to assist Mr. Novello it would go "far towards losing his friendship which I so deeply value"

Novello, in the witness box, said that Miss Constable used to wait outside his stage door with several others to say good-night.

She frequently appeared at the theatres where he was playing and had been admitted to his dressing-room. She had never been to his flat while he was there.

Asked if this sort of conduct was a nuisance he said, "No. We appreciate our fans very much."

When in Edinburgh in 1938 she wrote to him: "Only one thing compensates me for the dreary prospect of spending Christmas Day alone and that is the fact that you are playing.

"Can I come round and see you for a moment? I have managed to procure a seat. C21. if you can see that far. As ever Grace."

Novello said that socially he was well acquainted with Miss Constable as with many others."

Miss Constable, he said, was persistent and had the gift of the gab.

He would agree with the opinion that she was an inveterate liar.

Mr. McKenna, the magistrate, said it was obvious Miss Constable was not a truthful woman.

Whoever originated the scheme, he thought, it was one into which they both went with their eyes open, to get round what Novello thought was a harsh decision in refusing him a licence.

Ivor Novello does not think fans are a 'nuisance'

Centre Piece
★
By Your Special Correspondent

MARRYING in haste—parting at speed. The Divorce Mills of London ran in top gear in eight Courts at once yesterday; eight Judges intoning "decree granted" after counsel, instructed to keep it short, had told their trite tales of truancy, forgiveness, bickering, hopelessness; romance gone to seed, then thrown on to the dump of decayed marriages

It was the busiest day of putting asunder the Law Courts have had since the war started. More than 120 "cases" came along on the conveyor belt

People go gaily into matrimony; it is not yet the fashion here to go gaily into divorce, and parting is not always such sweet sorrow.

Some of the cases took only five or six minutes

For seventy minutes, in No 3 Appeal Court, I heard Mr. Justice Hodson cancel the marriages of five men and one woman

Shortest case I heard was that of soldier Henry Saville. At 11.7 he took the stand and read the oath in a firm voice. At 11.7½ his counsel, claiming divorce on the grounds of desertion by the wife, was questioning him.

11.8—Henry Saville tells how unhappy he was. How he had been driven from his home by his mother-in-law

11.9—He describes the efforts to patch things up

11.10—Documents handed to Mr Justice Hodson

11.12—Saville's mother takes the stand and reads the oath

11.12½—Her son lived with her, but all efforts to fix things up with his wife had failed

11.13—His mother leaves box

11.13½—Justice Hodson grants decree nisi

And at 11.14 the next case is being heard

So it went on—in panelled rooms all over the dusty, grey Law Courts building

Emergency Courts had to be held in temporary buildings in the courtyard.

But the story was always the same. Only the names changed.

Lion turns 'doctor' to terrier he injured

By Your Special Correspondent

MOWGLI, the three-year-old lion at Chester Zoo, has put paid to the circus legend that a lion is all right to live with till he tastes blood.

Since he was a cub he has lived with Peter, a Sealyham terrier who strolled into his cage three years ago when Mowgli was disconsolate at the death of a baby brother.

Peter has bossed Mowgli, hung on to his whiskers, ridden on his back, teased him and gnawed his tail.

"Ah," they all said. "Wait till he's tasted blood!" Meaning that all that would be left of Peter would be his epitaph.

Now it's happened. As they romped, Mowgli set his great foot on Peter's paw and tore it. "Ah," they said. "Poor Peter."

But all the lion did was to lift the Sealyham between his paws, cuddle him, and lick the wound clean. For the rest of the day he stayed close, just stirring now and then to renew his clinical attentions with his tongue.

A lion is lion-hearted—if you get on his right side.

Mowgli, the lion, with his pal Peter in their cage.

ARCHDEACON, 76, TO WED TEACHER, 40

A 76-year-old Archdeacon—a widower—is to marry a 40-year-old ex-teacher of the school where he is chairman of the Governors.

He is the Venerable Archdeacon Joseph William Coulter, Vicar of Calne, Wilts, and Archdeacon of Wilts.

His bride is Miss Evelyn Delabere Prior, of Ridge End, Virginia Water, Surrey.

They will be married by the Bishop of Salisbury at Virginia Water tomorrow.

Dora Constable photographed yesterday

FOOD FACTS

NAMCO
To the Under-Eighteens

Are you having Namco, the National Milk-Cocoa, at the office or factory or shop where you work? If not you are missing a good thing. Namco is an 'Extra-special' which provides the extra first-class protein you need to be fighting-fit. It is a delicious blend of cocoa, sugar and milk. Choose it in place of the usual cup of tea or coffee.

PRESERVES AND SUGAR

From April 30th you will have six coupons every four weeks to buy either preserves or sugar. They will be the four sugar coupons and the coupon marked P (as at present) plus the coupon marked R, all of which are in the sugar section of coupons. Each of these six coupons will be worth either 1 lb. preserves or ½ lb. sugar. This means that you will be able to buy as much as 6 lbs. preserves (6 x 1 lb.) or as much as 3 lbs. sugar (6 x ½ lb.). But as you will probably want both preserves and sugar, remember that you use one coupon for every 1 lb. of jam, and two coupons for every 1 lb. of sugar. This is an excellent chance to fill the jam shelf in your store cupboard. Take advantage of it.

THIS IS WEEK 40 — THE LAST WEEK OF RATION PERIOD No. 10

THE MINISTRY OF FOOD, LONDON, W.1. FOOD FACTS

BREAKFAST CEREALS

Some people don't understand why they cannot get the kind of breakfast cereals they have. This is the explanation. No corn flakes are being made owing to the shortage of maize. Wheat flakes are being manufactured instead. Again, owing to the need to save shipping breakfast food distribution had to be "zoned" which restricts the choice. The Ministry of Food have ever arranged with the manufacturers that at least one puffed or granular cereal and a biscuit type are distributed in each area.

WELFARE FOODS

There are over 10,000 distributing points spread over the country where you can get ORANGE JUICE AND COD LIVER OIL for your child. Don't risk your child's health by forgetting or not bothering to get it.

Your child needs orange juice in summer as well as winter. Every time you see your Green Ration Book think—orange juice and cod liver oil!

In December 1942 Ivor applied to the Ministry of War Transport for a petrol allowance in order to be able to drive his Rolls down to Redroofs at the week-ends. The application was turned down and, at Christmas time, in his dressing-room at the Adelphi, he jokingly offered to give the car away as he had no further use for it. Grace Walton, a passionate fan of Ivor's since before the War, heard the remark and suggested to him that the company for which she worked, Electrical and General Trusts Ltd, could take on the Rolls for business purposes, and as their offices were situated in the vicinity he could continue to use it to drive to Redroofs on Saturday night and back to London on Monday morning. Ivor, without informing his associates, agreed, the transaction was made, and he used the car as arranged. In October of 1943 he discovered that the firm involved knew nothing of any transaction with Miss Walton, and that she simply worked for them as a clerk under the name of Dora Constable. Ivor informed the Petrol Board, further inquiries were made, and on March 24th 1944 he was summonsed for conspiring with Dora Constable to commit an offence against the Motor Vehicles Order of 1942. On April 24th he appeared at Bow Street with Miss Constable, and both pleaded 'Not Guilty'. Constable was dismissed with a fine of £50, but Ivor was sentenced to two months' imprisonment. His attempt to shift the blame on to Miss Constable, whether justified or not, told against him, and his demeanour on the witness stand gave a bad impression. An appeal was lodged and came up for hearing at Newington Butts on May 16th. Sybil Thorndike, Lewis Casson and Sir Edward Marsh were called as witnesses to Ivor's character, and it was confidently expected that the prison sentence would be commuted to a fine. Instead it was halved, and Ivor was sent to Wormwood Scrubs.

It's the most monstrous miscarriage of justice, and till it actually happened I could never believe that it would. All the evidence seemed to go in his favour, and his counsel made a most magnificent and convincing speech, and then the grotesque old judge, who looks as if he came out of Punch and Judy, went out with the other four or five members of the committee, the sort of people no doubt who think of actors as rogues and vagabonds, and after about two minutes came back and said, 'Four weeks.' That was all. Not a word about his reasons. It was an incredible shock.

Edward Marsh

Everyone, even the police, said what a ghastly man the judge was, and he died soon afterwards, so we were all rather pleased.

Maidie Andrews

Ivor's letter to Mary Ellis, commiserating with her on the closing of *Arc de Triomphe*, written while he was waiting for the appeal. The last line reads, 'Pray for me on the 16th (even if it is your matinée).'

IVOR NOVELLO
APPEAL: WOMEN PACK COURT

COUNSEL MENTIONS A "ROMANCING GIRL"

IT was a "packed house" with standing room only when Ivor Novello's appeal against a entence of eight weeks' imprisonment on a fuel conspiracy charge was heard at London Sessions to-day.

Most of the audience were women, but a lot of Ivor Novello's friends from the stage world were there, too.

"Number 49—Ivor Novello!" called the Clerk of the Court.

Novello reached for a carafe on the solicitor's table, poured himself a glass of water, took a sip, and settled down to listen to the evidence.

It concerned the transfer of his car to Electrical and General Industrial Trust, Ltd.

"No Authority"

The transfer was arranged by Dora Constable, a clerk with the firm, without the firm's knowledge. She was fined £50 with £25 costs, but did not appeal, and was not present in court.

Ivor Novello's case is that he did not know that Dora Constable, writing as "Grace Walton, secretary of the firm," had applied for, and got, a licence to run the car.

Mr. Charles Heywood, managing director of E.G.I.T., gave evidence.

Mr. G. D. Roberts, K.C. (for Ivor Novello) asked him: Had Miss Constable any authority to describe herself as secretary of the company?—None whatever.

The last thing I want to do is to attack a lady who is not here, but you now know that this lady has been romancing to you?—Very much so.

Romancing to you for a good many years?—Yes.

Mr. Roberts then read extracts from a statement which, it was alleged, had been made by Miss Constable. Some of the lines in it he did not read aloud. He said: "I will give time for the justices to read it themselves."

"Never Engaged"

One portion of the alleged statement which Mr. Roberts did read, but from which he omitted a name, was: "I have never been engaged to ⟵, and I have never had any play accepted or produced."

Turning to Mr. Heywood, Mr. Roberts said: "Had she told you that she had been engaged and had had a play produced?"

Mr. Heywood: She had told the staff and the secretary of the company, and of course I had heard it from them.

Mr. Roberts now read a statement alleged to have been made by Miss Constable to Novello, which said:

"I wish to confess that I have constantly lied to you about my position with Mr. Heywood. I have never travelled about with

---

OFFICERS AND MEN
MUST GO ON SALUTING

'AS IN MOSCOW': PREMIER

MR. CHURCHILL refused in the Commons to-day to consider making an order by which failure to salute officers when off duty would cease to be a breach of discipline.

"The salute is an acknowledgment of the King's Commission and a courtesy to Allied officers, and I do not think it desirable to attempt to make the distinction suggested," he said.

Mr. J. J. Tinker (Lab., Leigh), who previously said that all ranks in the Services thought saluting in the streets was "honoured more in the breach than by observance," suggested that unless the rule was respected by the majority, it soon fell into disuse. Walking down Whitehall it was possible to see everybody—officers and men—trying to avoid the salute.

IVOR NOVELLO photographed to-day. A special "Evening News" picture.

NOVELLO'S "GOOD-BYE" AS HE GOES TO PRISON

By 'Daily Sketch' Correspondent

DARK - HAIRED smartly tailored Ivor Novello turned to the public benches, almost entirely filled by actors and actresses, at London Sessions yesterday, and in almost a whisper said "Good-bye."

He had just heard that his appeal against sentence of eight weeks' imprisonment imposed at Bow-street, for conspiring to commit an offence against a motor vehicles control Order, had been dismissed—but the prison sentence was reduced from eight to four weeks.

With A Bow

With a bow to the chairman of the Appeals Committee, Mr. Eustace Fulton, he walked to the dock and formally surrendered to two warders.

Dame Sybil Thorndike, who gave evidence, was allowed to interview Mr. Novello in the cells afterwards.

Several people from the theatrical world gave evidence of the generosity of Mr. Novello to his fellow workers in the profession.

Mr. Barry Sinclair, who for the past year has understudied Mr. Novello in "The Dancing Years" at the Adelphi Theatre and appeared in his place at matinée performances, will take his place at all performances.

The ordeal of imprisonment was considerably alleviated by the kindness and concern of the prison chaplain, the Rev. Meredith Williams, and his wife. Ivor was given the job of cataloguing books in the prison library and was also asked to make a plan for the prison theatre. He was released just after midnight on June 12th in order to avoid meeting the Press at the prison gates. On June 20th he returned to the cast of *The Dancing Years* and the reception on his first entrance lasted nearly three minutes. At the end he said to the audience, 'This has been the most exciting and wonderful thing that has ever happened to me. I've always known your kindness to me as a player, but tonight I feel it's kindness to me as a person. If I've been in any way enriched by the experience of these last weeks, I shall try to hand it on to you.' Afterwards he told Eddie Marsh that, while his first reception was going on, he was thinking, 'Now you know, I haven't come back from Normandy with a VC; I've merely been doing a spot of time.' Some months later Marsh asked him how he felt about the whole experience, and Ivor said that it had made no difference to him: he had neither gained nor lost by it, and now felt that it was unjust and absurd, but entirely a thing of the past.

I don't think he ever was a strong man after going to prison. He lost weight and he never put it on again.
Zena Dare

He had a great sense of humour about it, but how much it affected him I don't know. People say now, and I often wonder if they're right, that it was the beginning of his health deteriorating—that it meant more to him than we realised.
Robert Andrews

My own feeling was that it left a very deep scar. I don't know who told me, but I heard that he had a vision, that Mam came to him one night—that she was with him.
Gwen Ffrangcon-Davies

We were driving down to Redroofs, and I said, 'Ivor, the Rolls looks marvellous. Is it a new one?' And he said, 'No. I've just had the arrows painted out!'
Heather Thatcher

Novello Misses a Four-Girl "Gallery"

Several people who waited at Wormwood Scrubs to-day to meet Ivor Novello on his release found he had left the prison some time earlier.

After a few days' rest Mr. Novello is expected to resume his part in "The Dancing Years" at the Adelphi Theatre.

He was sentenced at Bow-street on April 24 to two months' imprisonment for conspiracy to commit an offence against the Motor Vehicles (Restriction of Use) Order, 1942, and the sentence was reduced on appeal at London Sessions on May 16 to four weeks.

Mr. Novello completed his sentence at midnight.

He is staying with friends, one of whom told a reporter: "It was arranged that West End stars and other friends would not wait at Wormwood Scrubs for Mr. Novello."

Four girls, on their way to work, waited for some time at the prison in the hope of seeing him. That was the extent of the "gallery."

But they did not get a glimpse of him.

Love from a Stranger (1944)

Apart from the effect on his health and spirits, the most tragic result of the prison sentence was not known until some years later. When D-Day was being planned, Winston Churchill suggested that a song should be written as a theme for the Invasion. Several composers were asked to submit melodies anonymously and a panel of fourteen, drawn from the Allied Commissions in this country, were asked to choose the winner after hearing each one twice. They unanimously decided on Number Three, Ivor's song. But when he was sent to prison, the whole idea was dropped. Churchill later confided to Eddie Marsh that he considered the sentence was ridiculous and that a fine would have been quite sufficient.

On the suggestion of Basil Dean, head of ENSA, Ivor decided to tour the Invasion front in the summer of 1944 with a production of Frank Vosper's thriller, *Love from a Stranger*, playing Bruce Lovell, a homicidal maniac who marries Cecily Harrington (Diana Wynyard) for her money.

At the climax Cecily, realising his intentions, outwits him by persuading him that she is a murderess too and has poisoned him.

Margaret Rutherford played Cecily's Aunt Louise and Robert Andrews was her former boy-friend, Nigel, who comes to the rescue. In her gossipy memoirs, *Myself Among Others*, Ruth Gordon repeats a malicious remark of Arthur Macrae's: 'You do know that the ENSA tour was responsible for the break-through at Caen. The chaps saw Ivor and Diana in *Love from a Stranger*. That did it.'

After the play was finished, he would go down to the piano and say to the boys, 'I wrote a song which your fathers seemed to like very much,' which went like this,' and he would play *Keep the Home Fires Burning*. And then he would say, 'And now I've written a new one,' and he would play *We'll Gather Lilacs*.

Robert Andrews

The cast of *Love from a Stranger* at Redroofs: back row, Ivor, Robert Andrews and ENSA officer; front row, Esma Cannon, Margaret Rutherford, Diana Wynyard, Daphne Rye, Joan Benham.

The climax of the play.

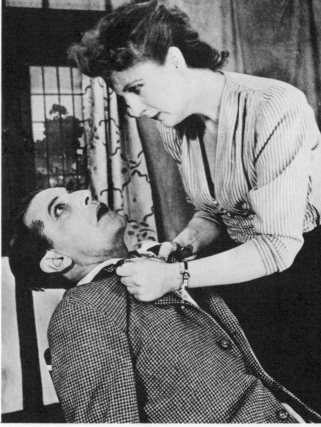

The last performance of *The Dancing Years*, the Opera House, Blackpool, 1945.

We were playing *The Dancing Years* in Morecambe with the Lane scenery—two thirds of it was left at the station of course—and we opened on the Tuesday night, and the stage-hands were all RAF trainees from the local camp, and it was a shambles. The ticket to the theatre included admission to the dance hall, and when the band had a rest all the people decided to clump down from upstairs to the gallery, to find out what was going on. Not having seen the first two acts of the play, they took one look at Ivor in costume, emoting in the moonlight, said '——!' and clumped out. We had to cut two scenes in the last act completely, because they couldn't get the scenery on, but he put up with it extremely well. But one night he said, 'I've got a cold coming on and I wouldn't be at all surprised if I were off.' And he was, and I played for the next fortnight—to packed houses! I would come home flushed with success, and he would say, 'Shut up, I don't want to hear about that. Now I'll read you what I've

written this afternoon'—and it was *Perchance to Dream*. He wrote it all on that tour.

He spent most of his time in bed—there's nothing to get up for in Morecambe even in peace-time—and scribbled and scribbled away. That was how he worked. He was an extremely lazy person—he admitted it himself—and he wouldn't start writing a new show until the current one was on its last legs. Then he'd suddenly get the 'fluence and off he'd go. It was remarkable how few alterations were made after the first draft. He would suddenly say, 'I'm stuck for a line—for Zena. She's just arrived at the house by train.' So I would suggest something, and in it would go—without the slightest compunction! If you saw the original scripts, you'd find that there is practically no comedy whatsoever. That would creep in as soon as Ivor got the first inklings of boredom —and he was awfully easily bored.

Barry Sinclair

241

Perchance to Dream (1945)

Perchance I dreamed at the first night of Mr Novello's new Hippodrome show. Anyhow the following is what the lighter stage's most popular magician induced me to believe I saw. A Regency buck, who is also a highwayman. A cad who will wager £5,000 that he will seduce an unknown cousin within twenty-four hours of her stay under his roof, doubled with a verray parfit gentil knight prepared to lay wager and a hundred thousand pound pearl necklace at the feet of Purity Unsullied. A cut-purse who dies babbling of reincarnation. Did I spend the rest of the Dream-time watching what gross and vulgar spirits would call subsequent developments? Yes. Was time punctuated by aeons and aeons of Ballet? Yes. Was there a very, very great deal of lush romantic music, scored principally for harp after the manner of that popular composer, Herr Mittel Europa? Yes. Or so these things seemed; I vouch for none of them . . .

Is the foregoing a trifle grudging, even bordering on the ungenerous? I think it may be, and I hasten to say that the curtain, when it went up, took with it the entire audience, which remained in seventh heaven until, after three hours and a half, the curtain descended and automatically brought the audience down with it.

James Agate
in the Sunday Times

Miss Olive Gilbert is the principal singer, and her prettiest song would seem to be *We'll Gather Lilacs*, but all the songs gain much from the rapture with which Mr Novello listens to them . . .

The Times

Below: With Muriel Barron.

Opposite top: With Roma Beaumont.

Opposite bottom: The Drawing-room of 'Huntersmoon': Margaret Rutherford is seated left, Ivor stands centre with Roma Beaumont, Muriel Barron and Olive Gilbert are seated right and Robert Andrews stands behind them.

Below: Ivor, in his first incarnation as Sir Graham Rodney.

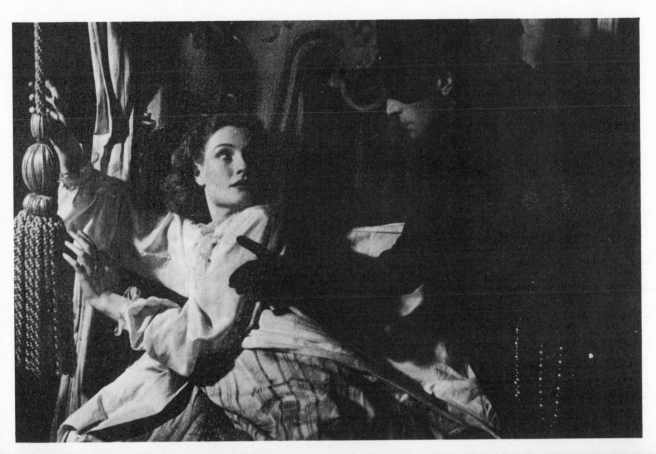

Above: Muriel Barron and Olive Gilbert sing *We'll Gather Lilacs* to Ivor, accompanied by Anne Pinder.

Right Ivor with Alfred Lunt and Lynn Fontanne.

Opposite: The cover of *We'll Gather Lilacs*, drawn by Anne Pinder and used in the production.

Legend has it that Ivor was inspired to write this, one of his best-known songs, by the sight of Lynn Fontanne, in a white dress, standing by a lilac tree in the garden of Redroofs. Whatever the truth of this, the melody which she may have inspired was lost on Miss Fontanne, who confesses to being tone-deaf. As was the case with *Home Fires*, the song was first called by its last line, *Till You Come Home Again*, but was always known as *We'll Gather Lilacs*, although, strictly, 'lilac' has no plural. As Christopher Hassall was in the Army, Ivor, for the first time, wrote all the lyrics for this show himself.

244

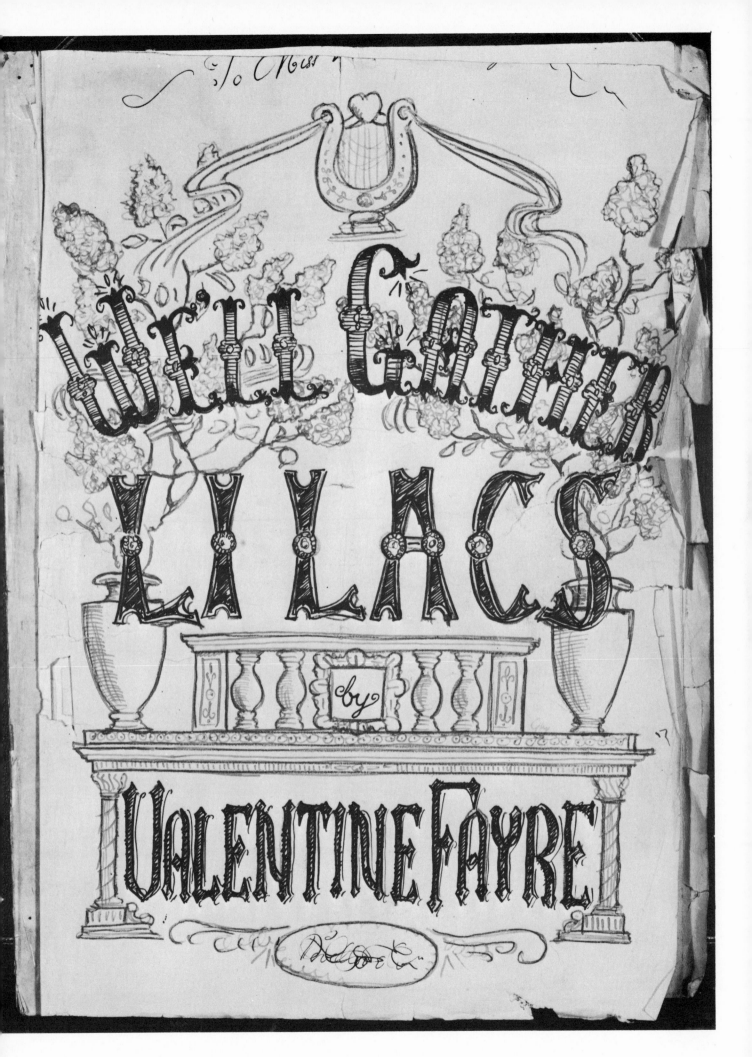

Although the critical reception was mixed—one notice was headed 'No, No, Novello!'—*Perchance to Dream* achieved the longest run of all Ivor's shows at the same theatre—1,020 performances, and was playing when the War ended. Margaret Rutherford left the cast to make a film and was replaced by Zena Dare. During the run, *The Dancing Years* went out on tour once more, with Barry Sinclair in the lead. The 'walking' understudy was a young singer called Ruby Moule, and when the production was brought into London to the Casino Theatre, she sang the part of Maria offstage at a dress rehearsal, because the leading lady had a cold. Ivor was watching and asked to meet her afterwards. He invited her to give him an extensive audition at the Hippodrome and as a result gave her the lead in the continuing tour of *The Dancing Years*, but later changed his mind and cast Muriel Barron. Miss Moule decided to forget about it, but was suddenly summoned by Ivor and offered the part of Lydia in *Perchance to Dream* which he was taking to South Africa. But he suggested she should change her name, and asked her to go away and think of some alternatives:

'He sent for me a couple of days later and said, "Have a look at the mirror," and on it was written "Vanessa, Virginia." I felt a little strange, and he said, "Don't you like them?" "Yes, very much." "Which would you prefer?" "Vanessa, because I've read Swift." Then he said, "I persuaded Vivien to change her name to Leigh, and it brought her luck. So I'll give you the same name, but we'll spell it L–E–E." And then, as I was going, he said, "There's only one other name that I think would have suited you. Sharon." And I thought, "This has gone too far. I really must tell him." I opened my bag and gave him a piece of paper. On it I had written, "Vanessa, Virginia, Sharon."'

Top: Ivor meets Zena Dare on her arrival in Johannesburg for the tour of *Perchance to Dream*.

Left: Ivor watches the Mine Dancing with Vanessa Lee and Roma Beaumont.

Opposite top: A visit backstage in Cape Town: *left to right*, Ivor, Laurence Olivier, Zena Dare, Olive Gilbert, Gwen Ffrangcon-Davies, Vivien Leigh, Robert Andrews.

Opposite bottom: Ivor with the leads of a touring production of *Careless Rapture*, 1949: Muriel Barron, Nicolette Roeg, Barry Sinclair.

Romance and court intrigue set to music in Murania with Countess Vera Lemainken (Olive Gilbert), Prime Minister Vanescu (Robert Andrews), Ivor Novello as Nikki with his enchanting Princess Christiane (Vanessa Lee), Phyllis Dare, the faithful mistress, and Zena Dare, the queen-mother

Anthony Cookman

[Illustration by Tom Titt]

At the Theatre

"King's Rhapsody" (Palace)

THERE is an element of uncertainty in everything but in an Ivor Novello first night.

As a great liner glides down the slipway we cannot help wondering for one wild moment if she will, after all, float. To indulge a similar doubt at the launching of a new Novello musical romance would be childish, and nobody does.

Her name—*King's Rhapsody* for instance—may not be a particularly fetching one, and personally you may dislike her lines from stem to stern, but the certainty that she will float is absolute.

All concerned, from the captain-owner to the humblest hand, are cheerfully confident that they are in for years of golden voyagings, and this air of confidence—exuberant and unstrained—makes an Ivor Novello first night unlike any other.

ONLY the critics—or those of them whose youth, in Stevenson's famous phrase, has been depressed by exceptional aesthetic surroundings—wear long faces. It is the business of these unfortunates to explain with good grace why something which they may well regard as a brazen absurdity should be an assured success, and their lot is not a happy one.

Still, even they must live, and Mr. Novello at the outset makes things reasonably easy for them. It is the coming of age of a Scandinavian princess, and the scene of birthday greetings and dances would have an innocent, Hans Andersenish charm if only the stage were not so wilfully crowded with loyal villagers and major and minor royalties.

THE princess learns in the end that she is to marry the disreputable monarch of Murania, who is returning to his throne after twenty years of exile with his beautiful mistress. The innocent charm of the scene is preserved, for she has already fallen in love with the romantic rascal through her ardent study of a collection of Press cuttings.

Then the romantic rascal himself—Mr. Novello, unshaven in a Paris hotel, managing with much skill to convey that Nikki, for all his long raffishness, is not without kingly ambitions. This scene introduces Miss Zena Dare, as a queen-mother with the delightful characteristics of a pantomime Dame, and Miss Phyllis Dare, as a mistress with the walk of a queen.

How much relief from first to last do these sisters bring to the unsympathetic critic! They use dissimilar methods, but both methods are used with style.

The rest of the story is increasingly tiresome, not because it is improbable, but because it is so transparently resolved to have everything both ways. The king, mistaking the Snow Princess for one of her maids, is seduced by her and after he has married her he returns to his mistress's villa where the magnanimous queen can help him to quell a rebellion and the equally magnanimous mistress can resign him to the queen. He has no sooner fallen in love with the queen than it is necessary for him to abdicate once more so that he may eat out his heart by his mistress's side at the Paris opera and in due course be left, white flower in hand, kneeling at his son's coronation. Miss Vanessa Lee and Miss Olive Gilbert help to sing him on his romantic way.

NO more than a pantomime is this piece to be judged by its fable. Nor can it be judged by its music, which is rather mild, nor by its dancing, which is rather massive than distinguished, nor by its décor, which is never less than grandiose. But the combination of these things is irresistible. Colour and crowd movement, music and romance—there is excess of each, and "nothing succeeds like excess." One glance at the show suffices to justify the programme's description of Mr. Novello as "the mainstay of the British musical stage."

King's Rhapsody (1949)

Ivor was so impressed by Vanessa Lee's performance in *Perchance to Dream* that he began to write a show specially for her during the South African tour. He called it *Lily of the Valley*, and it was to be about the Welsh National Eisteddfod; there was also to be a prominent rôle for Olive Gilbert. One night in Johannesburg he sent her a message, asking her to come to his hotel room:

'I went down and he said, "Let's have some coffee. I want to read you something I've written . . . You're sitting with two princesses at your feet, and you're going to sing a lovely operatic aria." And I said, "What's this got to do with the Welsh National Eisteddfod?" "Oh no," he said, "I got as far as the Eisteddfod and I couldn't carry on. So I'm writing a new show and I'm going to call it *The Legend of the Snow Princess.*" '

On the company's return to this country, they went on a national tour with *Perchance to Dream*, in the course of which Ivor worked on the score of his new show. The tradition is that *Someday My Heart Will Awake*, Vanessa Lee's opening song, was composed onstage when the character Ivor was playing, Valentine Fayre, was supposed to be improvising on the piano. But Vanessa Lee maintains that she and Ivor had already worked on the number and he was merely using the scene as a chance to try out the melody on his audience. When the tour reached Liverpool, he had the orchestra come onstage and play his new score to the company. 'Then the following night,' Miss Lee relates, 'when I was standing in the wings waiting to sing *A Woman's Heart*, he suddenly whispered to me, "Sing *Someday My Heart Will Awake*." So off we launched into the whole thing. Olive came on, and he made her sing *Fly Home, Little Heart*. Then he went down to the footlights and told the audience, "These are two songs from my next show." And of course they went raving mad.'

The show, now called *King's Rhapsody*, was intended by Ivor as a last salute to the land of Ruritania with which he had been so long—and a little unjustly—identified.

He also felt that it might be the last time he would play the lead in his own musical, and this time the part, Crown Prince Nikki of Murania, would be nearer his own age—fifty-six. Another purpose in writing it was to have two of the idols of his youth, Phyllis and Zena Dare, together in the same show. Zena was to play his mother, Queen Elena, and Phyllis his mistress, Marta Karillos, for whose sake Nikki has gone into exile. With the impending death of the King, he is prevailed upon by his mother to contract a diplomatic marriage with Princess Cristiane of Norseland. He returns to Murania with Marta but, when Cristiane arrives, ignores her and spends all his time at Marta's villa. But he meets

Opposite: Tom Titt's cartoon in the Tatler.

Ivor as Nikki with Vanessa Lee as Cristiane.

Cristiane by chance in the Palace and, mistaking her for a maid, seduces her. Cristiane attempts to ingratiate herself with Nikki, with whom she has fallen in love, by inviting Marta to the betrothal Ball, but it has the opposite effect. She gives birth to a son, and Nikki is finally drawn to her after they have both been involved in a peasant uprising. He attempts to bring about some liberal reforms in Murania, but is opposed by the reactionary Prime Minister, Vanescu (Robert Andrews), who arranges the kidnapping of the infant Crown Prince and, in return for his safety, demands Nikki's abdication. Nikki returns into exile with Marta, but after the coronation of the boy king appears incognito in the Cathedral and picks up a white rose left for him by Cristiane on the altar steps.

Above: With Phyllis Dare and Vanessa Lee.   Opposite: Ivor's manuscript for *The Violin Began to Play*.

King's Rhapsody opened in August 1949 at the Palace Theatre in Manchester and was an obvious hit from the very first performance. But one song, a duet for Vanessa Lee and Dennis Martin as Count Egon, seemed out of place in implying that the two were having an affair. Ivor told Miss Lee that he would write her a new song and two days later invited her to hear *The Violin Began to Play*, for which, since Christopher Hassall was not on hand, he had written the lyric as well as the music. She learned it and it was introduced into the show at the Palace Theatre in London, at the first dress rehearsal with audience. It was destined to be the last song written by Ivor for a 'Novello Show'.

Mr Novello, author, composer and actor, can with his tranquillity stand up to all the bounding Oklahomans and Brigadooners in the world. He is far the biggest box-office attraction of our native stage and he has earned his victories by honest service of the public's appetite. Sweet tooth is sweetly served, and, what is more, abundantly. He hands out no trivial fable but lashings of plot with plentiful changes of scene. His tunes and Christopher Hassall's lyrics, at once simple and dulcet, make no pretence. When Oive Gilbert sings *Fly Home, Little Heart*, a myriad homes will be emptied by little hearts flying out to hear her. It is the kind of thing, I suppose, that New Yorkers would not endure, but our greater tolerance can give the Gun-Getting Annie and her kind a three-year run and yet will now award Mr Novello and his colleagues a four or five years' term for this very different confection . . . Ivor Novello himself sadly rules and gladly deserts Murania, looking half Hamlet, half-Antony, and wholly the darling of the public.

The Observer

A New Success by an Old Master came to the Palace Theatre last night ... The master touch was stronger than ever, for Novello not only wrote the words and composed the music but took the leading part of a Ruritanian king himself. The Novello recipe? A stronger than usual musical comedy plot, mixed with light-hearted wit, tuneful numbers, a dash of melodrama and an occasional drop of sentiment. It should run for years.

The Daily Mirror

The show will probably prove Novello's biggest hit of all. If so, it will do it not by new tricks but by the simple, infallible formula of lavish spectacle, Ruritanian pomp, lush, if faintly familiar, music, well sung, and a story that gives them every excuse. As Novello himself admits, it is very much the mixture as before, just the desired blend of champagne and sugar.

The Daily Mail

Opposite: Ivor with Zena Dare as the Queen Mother.

Below: With Vanessa Lee.

```
                "KING'S RHAPSODY"                    17
                Property Plot                        '7

Act 1 Sc 1    Norseland

On stage :    1 chest containing Scrap book
              1 tall table, on it scarf, bible, cake, 2 pouch.
              3 wooden chairs
              1    do   armchair
              2 large square cushions
              2 blue matresses
              8 decorative wall plates on flats and stove.
Off right :   3 dolls
              6 parcels
              5 fir tree branches
              4 bunches flowers
Off left :    Nil
Personal Properties
     King Peter : 1 Necklace in case
     Trontzen   : 1 large period watch and fob

Act 1 Sc 2    Paris Hotel

On stage :    4 Mahogany chairs
              1 Armchair
              1 Table with plush cover
Off right :   1 towel and period shaving mug
Off centre :  1 small table set with coffee pot, (practical
                 coffe, hot) 3 cups and saucers, tray
                 and table cloth, 3 coffee spoons.
Personal Properties
     Prime Minister : 1 Despatch case containing 6 documents

Act 1 Sc 4&5  Boudoir

On stage :    1 prop piano          1 fire screen
              1 piano stool         1 cabinet - containing
              1 circular table        1 bottle Tokay
              1 oval table (louis)        (cold tea)
              2 oval back armchairs   2 wine glasses
              1 Louis settee         1 corkscrew
              2 square back armchairs to match
              1 carpet
              1 mantle fireplace
              2 decorative photo frames, containing Nikki's
                 and Cristiane's portraits.
              2 piles manuscript music on piano
              3 bowls flowers, 1 white roses and 1 mixed for
                 scene 4 and 1 pink roses for scene 5
              1 paper mache clock on mantlepiece
              3 cushions on settee to match upholstery.
```

A page from the property list.

No wonder the audience cheered, for there was so much—
—almost too much—to cheer. There was Vanessa Lee's
sweet singing, the grace and beauty of Phyllis Dare, the
humorous point with which her sister played the Queen
Mother, the brilliant pageantry of the court scenes, the
dancing of the ballet, and of course the handsome and
romantic air with which Novello played the King.

The Star

A romantic confection which employs every imaginable
stand-by of the light musical stage and which ends with
Mr Ivor Novello kneeling alone upon the altar steps might
be supposed to embody the ultimate in saccharine banality. Perhaps it does, but the result is an uncommonly
pleasant evening in the theatre.

The Sunday Times

There is no doubt about it: where Ruritanian romance
with music is concerned, Ivor Novello knows how to deal

himself a full hand of trumps every time. He has done it
again with *King's Rhapsody* at the Palace, and I take it
that the management of that enormous theatre can now
settle down to a couple of years or more of happy inertia.
The whole affair, though slightly preposterous, is aston-
ishingly efficient: romantic story, neat dialogue, easy
music, attractive settings, busy dancing—rather too busy
at times—are all there, directed with skill by Murray
MacDonald and all testifying alike to Mr Novello's
unrivalled supply of trumps.

The Daily Telegraph

Not all the reviews of *King's Rhapsody* were so amiable.
Milton Shulman headed his notice in the Evening Standard:

Novello does it again—but why?

There are certain pleasures which millions constantly
enjoy but which I have never been able to appreciate.
They include standing at football games, jellied eels,
transformation scenes and Ivor Novello musicals ...
Critics are realists and most of them have given up the
unrewarding experience of stubbing their pens tilting at
sugar-cake windmills and firing arrows at the loop-holes
in the Ivor Tower. To complain that *King's Rhapsody*
drips with cloying sentiment, that its situations are contrived and ludicrous, and that it is practically empty of wit
would only unnecessarily raise one's blood pressure and
make one vulnerable to early stomach ulcers. Therefore
let us concentrate on the more positive aspects of Mr
Novello's latest offering. The story has the advantage of
admitting that Mr Novello has at last reached middle age
by casting him as King Nikki of Murania, a monarch who
has already had a twenty-year liaison with his loyal
mistress when the curtain rises. The music is lilting and
languorous and will no doubt be whistled furiously by
whatever is the modern equivalent of butcher boys. Mr
Novello plays the king with all the assurance of a man
who has gauged public taste down to the last emotional
millimetre: he never puts a wrong inflection forward nor
pulls a facial muscle to no effect. Miss Vanessa Lee, the
Snow Princess, has poise, looks and a sweet voice that
could not fail to stop the show each time she allowed it
to explode in melody.

This notice, not unexpectedly, brought a stream of pro-
testing letters from loyal Novello fans, of which the following
is typical:

After reading Milton Shulman's attack on *King's
Rhapsody*, my family and I have determined not to buy
the Evening Standard while he is on your staff.

Opposite top: The set for Marta's Boudoir.

Opposite bottom: Phyllis Dare, as Marta, sings *The Mayor of
Perpignan.*

Above: Olive Gilbert sings *Take Your Girl*.   Opposite: The Coronation Scene.

Punch referred to *King's Rhapsody* as a 'vast, insipid musical in which Mr Ivor Novello has pulled out most of the known stops in the organ of easy sentiment', while the critic of Reynolds News complained that its efficiency had 'the sort of fascination a snake has for a rabbit', and wished that Ivor would 'attempt something more, even if he achieved less'. Writing in Time and Tide, Philip Hope-Wallace described it as 'mounted with much flunkery and balletry and with little mellifluous restaurant tunes which suggest a self-taught pianist vamping in F major on a Sunday after-noon', and also wanted Ivor to extend his range. But, speaking on the BBC Critics' programme, he changed his tune: 'Ivor Novello is a master of the shameless cliché, and if I were Sarah Bernhardt, I would ask him to write all my plays for me . . . I don't say that Massenet and Puccini didn't do it

better. The point is that Mr Novello does it very, very well, and keeps alive a whole part of the theatre which is, to my vulgar mind, very valuable and enjoyable. He also does what few poets seem to be able to do nowadays. He provides a real poetry for the masses.'

On the same programme, C. A. Lejeune, the film critic, who had never seen a Novello show, and went to this one with the worst apprehensions, found, to her surprise, that Ivor 'came through as the most tremendous stage person-ality, a really great theatrical tradition, and the like of which I have not seen for a very long time.'

The public, as usual, ignored the critics and came to the Palace Theatre in their thousands. *King's Rhapsody* was, as Ivor had anticipated in Manchester, the most commercially successful show he had ever written.

The recording session for *King's Rhapsody*: *left to right*, Vanessa Lee, Harry Acres (musical director), Ivor, Phyllis Dare, Olive Gilbert, Denis Martin.

In *King's Rhapsody* Ivor's music was, perhaps because of the subject, re-stating old themes rather than breaking fresh ground and, in this respect, the complaints of some critics that he was repeating himself were partially justified. But, taken as a valedictory to his 'operetta' days, the score is hardly to be faulted, and melodies such as *Someday My Heart Will Awake*, *The Gates of Paradise* and *If This Were Love* are fine examples of his accomplishment in this field, while *Fly Home, Little Heart* and *The Violin Began to Play* are admirable by any standard. This time he wrote no 'show within the show', but in the third act there is a prolonged vocal and choreographic sequence entitled *The Muranian Rhapsody*, for which Ivor concocted a kind of pastiche mélange of Borodin, Liszt and Delibes to illustrate a 'traditional' legend. In the theatre the sequence, probably because of hackneyed staging, seemed rather laborious and top-heavy, but on paper it is a good example of a neglected

side of Ivor's talent: his remarkable facility for composing incidental music, as opposed to straightforward 'numbers'. The Masques of Vienna in *The Dancing Years*, the Victorian Wedding scene in *Perchance to Dream* and numerous passages in his other shows are full of charm and invention and contain a plethora of themes which deserve to be recorded along with the better-known melodies. Unlike most other composers of the genre, who leave it to the choreographer and orchestrator to arrange such passages from the existing score, Ivor preferred to treat them as pieces of independent composition.

The film of *King's Rhapsody* was first announced by Associated British, the company which had produced the films of *Glamorous Night* and *The Dancing Years*, and the director was to be Brian Desmond Hurst who had directed the former in 1937. For the part of Nikki both Ronald Colman, Tyrone Power and Douglas Fairbanks Jr were mentioned at one time or another, but the film was never produced, and the rights were eventually bought by Herbert

Wilcox as a vehicle for his wife, Anna Neagle. Wilcox had just put a new male star under contract, the ageing and unreliable Errol Flynn, whose Hollywood career had foundered but whom Wilcox hoped to resuscitate with a series of films in Britain. The first was a film version of a stage extravaganza, *The Glorious Days*, in which Miss Neagle had starred during Coronation Year. It was called *Lilacs in the Spring* and she sang Ivor's song over the credit titles. The second was *King's Rhapsody* and was released in 1955. Errol Flynn played the King to Miss Neagle's Marta and the Cristiane of his wife, Patrice Wymore.

The film opened at the Warner Cinema in Leicester Square and was the first première to be televised. Vanessa Lee generously appeared onstage before the screening to sing *Some-day My Heart Will Awake* and the whole occasion was laden with pomp and nostalgia. Unfortunately the film did not live up to the launching ceremony, and Mr Flynn's contract with the Wilcoxes lapsed soon afterwards. His King was described in the Financial Times as a 'wastrel footballer bringing shame on his father's meat-packing firm', Miss Neagle's Marta as 'the most daring lady in Eastbourne' and watching the film as 'facing a blizzard of candy-floss whipped up by a wind machine'. 'The décor may be Ruritania,' wrote Alan Brien in the Evening Standard, 'but the emotions were pure West Kensington.'

Anna Neagle, Errol Flynn and Martita Hunt in the film of *King's Rhapsody*.

259

Above: Ivor on the verandah of his house in Jamaica.

Right: On his last holiday, with Phyllis Monkman.

Gay's the Word (1951)

During the run of *King's Rhapsody*, Cicely Courtneidge, whose show, *Her Excellency*, had just folded, called on Ivor at the Palace to ask him if he had a job for an actress in her company. 'Oh dear,' he said to her, 'I am disappointed. I hoped you were coming to see me about doing the music for your new show.' The show, based on an idea by her husband, Jack Hulbert—Cicely Courtneidge as a retired musical comedy star who opens a drama school—was being written by Arthur Macrae, and the three of them jumped at the idea of Ivor's composing the score. Then Macrae was obliged to bow out, owing to a previous commitment, but, to the Hulberts' delight and surprise, Ivor offered to take on the book as well. As lyric-writer they engaged a man who had made his reputation during the War writing the *Sweet and Low* revues for Hermione Gingold, Alan Melville:

'I thought, after all these years, he will naturally want to do the music first—which he did with Christopher Hassall—but he said, "No, no, not at all." I was very flattered, and what was fascinating was that we used to travel down to Redroofs together on Saturday night and on Sunday we would foregather round the piano and I would present a lyric to him; he would put his specs on, run his fingers up and down the keyboard, and then go into a melody that in nine cases out of ten was very nearly the finished article! Apart from bursting at the seams with tunes, he seemed to sense exactly where the stresses were. There was only one snag about him as a collaborator: he adored sneezing—he was absolutely kinky about it, and once Mr Novello started sneezing he was a very difficult man to stop. ''It flushes out the system,'' he said, and the poor old lyricist had to stand by until the LP was over.'

Gay's the Word opened in Manchester at the end of 1949 and played a ten-week season to capacity business, and then went on an extended tour prior to the West End.

Ivor was, of course, still appearing in London at the Palace Theatre and was, as a result, unable to concern himself to any degree with the re-writings and alterations which were felt necessary by the Hulberts in order to make the show a suitable vehicle for Miss Courtneidge's particular brand of humour. For Christmas 1950 Ivor took a leave of absence from *King's Rhapsody* and flew to Jamaica with a group of friends, including Phyllis Monkman, Beatrice Lillie, Olive Gilbert and Bobbie Andrews. After Christmas he gave Phyllis Monkman a trip to New York, which she had never seen, and returned to London in February in time for the opening of *Gay's the Word* at the Saville Theatre. He was feeling unwell, but, against his doctor's advice, went to the first night—the first of a show of his that he had attended since *Fresh Fields* in 1933. At the curtain he acknowledged the applause from his box and then, indicating Cicely Courtneidge, said, 'Give it all to her!'

A dinner party in New York: *left to right*, Richard Halliday, Rex Harrison, Beatrice Lillie, Olive Gilbert, Lilli Palmer, Mary Martin, Gordon Duttson (Ivor's secretary after the death of Lloyd Williams), Phyllis Monkman.

MARGOT BRYANT

Ivor Novello has done it again, but this time it is different. He has turned his back on Ivornovania, where Rhapsodic Kings spent their Glamorous Nights in Careless Rapture ... But if he is not careful, he will be putting his satirists out of work, for—whisper it—Novello has started guying himself.

The Daily Herald

How long can Ivor Novello keep turning out theatre-hugging hits? Last night Britain's top showman gave the answer. Novello knows better than anyone that if you keep on doing over an old hit, what you get is old hat. A new trick was wanted: the old dog has learned one. How long can he go on? As long as he can do as well as this.

The Daily Express

Cicely Courtneidge enters into the spirit of the fling at her author with gusto, and for the opening scene we have a Novello musical romance as it might be if he knew how to write one that would not succeed ... We gather that he regards underplaying with horror, that the antics of stage-struck amateurs fill him with wicked glee, and that he is at one with Mr Melville in proclaiming that in the light theatre Vitality is more than Originality. Vitality is indeed the special quality of this show. How could it not be, when Miss Courtneidge is never off the stage and rarely far from its centre.

The Times

Once more Ivor Novello proves that he is immortal without being divine. No Richard Rodgers, Cole Porter or Irving Berlin can dethrone him ... It is time that some official recognition were shown of his achievement in keeping the British flag flying over Ruritania.

The Evening Standard

If I do not enjoy this, it is probably because I have memories of an aunt who did much the same thing at church socials.

Ken Tynan
in the Spectator

Ivor was due to go back into the cast of *King's Rhapsody* the following week, but was persuaded to rest a few days longer and returned on the night of February 26th. The following week-end he spent at Redroofs, as usual, and on the Sunday afternoon complained of a pain in his chest and went upstairs to rest. Alan Melville was staying with him, and Ivor sent down word that he would like to see him:

'I sat on the end of his bed and he said, "We're going to do another one. I'm coming out of *King's Rhapsody* and we're going back to Montego Bay, just the pair of us," and he outlined the story. I was thrilled.'

Opposite: Scenes from *Gay's the Word.*

The show was *Lily of the Valley*, which he had abandoned for *King's Rhapsody*. After Ivor's death it was completed by Christopher Hassall, with additional music by Ronald Hamer, and called *Valley of Song*.

The last photograph, taken in the garden of Redroofs by Lady Juliet Duff: *left to right*, Ivor, Alan Melville, Tom Gill, Robert Andrews.

Tuesday, March 6, 1951

THE STAR

No 19,549   One Penny

Latest Prices—Page Two

Ivor Novello Dies 4 Hours After Show

Ivor Novello as he appeared in "King's Rhapsody." The brilliant-studded star he was wearing was owned previously by Sir Henry Irving and the great Edmund Keen.

"Star" Reporter

IVOR NOVELLO died early today in his flat above the Strand Theatre, Aldwych. He was 58. Death was due to coronary thrombosis.

Four hours earlier he had been playing the lead in his own production "King's Rhapsody" at the Palace Theatre. Tonight's performance of the show has been cancelled. It will be resumed tomorrow night with Mr Novello's understudy, John Palmer, taking the lead. [See Star Man's Diary and life story by A. E. Wilson on Page Five.]

On leaving the Palace Theatre after the performance Mr Novello went back to his flat with Mr Tom Arnold, the impresario, for supper.

After the meal he complained of a pain in his side. Mr Arnold suggested that a doctor should be sent for. Novello declined the offer and began to get ready for bed.

Found Him Dazed

Mr Arnold then left. Shortly afterwards Mr Novello collapsed.

The actor Robert Andrews, a lifelong friend who shared the flat with him, returned there to find him almost unconscious. Mr Novello died before a doctor arrived.

Today Mr Arnold and Mr Macqueen Pope, theatre historian and one of Mr Novello's closest friends, met at the flat and conferred on the immediate future of the Novello shows.

It was afterwards announced that "King's Rhapsody" would close down for one night and that "Gay's the Word" at the Saville Theatre would not be affected.

The New Play

Mr Novello was well advanced on another musical play when he died.

It was to have been called "Lily of the Valley" and based on Welsh music and the National Eisteddfod.

Some of the music had been written and the composer had sketched out the plot to Mr MacQueen Pope.

Among callers at the Novello flat today was Miss Phyllis Monkman who came back from America recently on the same ship as the actor.

While Mr Novello was in Jamaica on holiday his part in "King's Rhapsody" was taken by Barry Sinclair. He is now rehearsing for another play and could not resume the part. John Palmer was accordingly chosen for it.

Ivor died in the small hours of March 6th 1951, in the bedroom of The Flat. Two of the people who had been closest to him in life, Bobbie Andrews and Olive Gilbert, were with him.

Bobbie rang me at about two a.m. and said, 'Ivor's dead.' I didn't turn out the light again. I just lay there and looked at the wall. I couldn't take it in.

Phyllis Monkman

I knew at seven o'clock in the morning, when I heard it over the radio. We didn't play that night—but we did the next, with somebody else in his clothes. It was ghastly.

Zena Dare

I've never seen such a reaction. I walked down Berkeley Street and saw the placards, and the people were saying, 'Oh, my God! Ivor Novello...!'

Heather Thatcher

When I heard, I put on a coat and took a taxi to The Flat immediately. He looked beautiful...

Roma Beaumont

Phyl Monkman brought Olive and Bobbie round to me, to get them out of The Flat. I was having my furniture moved down to Brighton, and Ivor's body was being collected by the undertakers to be taken to Harrods Mortuary. After a drink or two, Bobbie's sense of humour got the better of him and he said, 'Wouldn't it be dreadful if they got muddled, and Alan's furniture went to Harrods and Ivor got carried down to Brighton!'

Alan Melville

The funeral was like a Coronation—the streets were lined with crowds all the way. I looked out of the car window and said, 'Look who's standing there!' It was Lady Churchill.

Phyllis Monkman

I suppose one could say he was a Golden Lad, and he died a Golden Lad. I love to think that he wouldn't have liked being an Elderly Gentleman, getting a bit stiff in the limbs. To go out literally on the crest of the wave ... although for us—I couldn't believe it. But people like him, and Gertie and Vivien—people who had been a symbol in their day for all that was beautiful and kind and glamorous and lovely—sometimes it seems right that they should never descend from that. For everybody who ever knew him, he's enshrined in our hearts.

Gwen Ffrangcon-Davies

God knows what magic it was, but, whatever it was, he had it.

Phyllis Monkman

On the first night of *Careless Rapture* everyone else was nervous. But Ivor came and kissed me on both cheeks and said, 'Can't wait to get out there, can you?'

And I said, 'No!'

That was the spirit we had . . .

Dorothy Dickson

APPENDIXES

The Songs

Lyricist in brackets, unless otherwise indicated

† Indicates publication

1910

† *The Spring of the Year* (Novello)

1911

† *Little One* (Bailey)
† *Slumber Tree* (Bailey)

1912

† *Blue Eyes* (Bailey)
† *If* (Teschemaker)
† *In the Clouds*, Two Step
† *Lament* (Douthitt)
† *The Little Damozel* (Teschemaker)
† *Our Help in Ages Past* (Watts)
† *Up There* (Teschemaker)

1913

† *The Haven of Memory* (Thomas)
† *Hindu Lullaby* (Teschemaker)
† *Not Really* (Novello)
† *The Valley* (Teschemaker)
† *Why Hurry, Little River?* (Scott)

1914

† *Bravo Bristol* (Weatherly)
† *Carnival Time* (Novello)
† *Gamin*, Piano Solo
† *The King of Love* (Baker)
† *Lagoon*, Piano Solo
† *Megan* (Weatherly)
† *Soldiering* (Weatherly)
† *The Vallery of Rainbows*, Set of Songs (Weatherly)
  1. *The Valley of Rainbows*
  2. *Feiyen*
  3. *Crimson Leaves*
  4. *Moon of the Cherry Garden*
† *Till The Boys Come Home (Keep The Home Fires Burning)* (Lena Guilbert Ford)

1915

† *From Distant Lands*, Set of Syrian Songs (Lockton)
  1. *Son of the Mountain*
  2. *The Pool of Solan*
  3. *Gold from Ophir*
  4. *Song of Exile*
  5. *Karna of the Sea*
† *Laddie In Khaki* (Novello)
† *When the Great Day Comes* (Teschemaker)
† *Just a Jack or Tommy* (Huggins)
† *Radiance of Your Eyes* (Novello)

1916

† *The Garden of England* (Grey)

Theodore and Co

Presented by Grossmith & Laurillard at the Gaiety, September 14th.
Book by H. M. Harwood and George Grossmith, from the French of P. Gavault.
Music by Jerome Kern and Ivor Novello.
Additional music by Philip Braham, Melville Gideon and Paul A. Rubens.
Lyrics by Adrian Ross and Clifford Grey.
Cast: George Grossmith*, Leslie Henson, Peggy Kurton, Adrah Fair, Davy Burnaby, Gladys Humphrey, Jameson Thomas, Madge Saunders, Julia James, Fred Leslie.
Numbers by Novello:
Isn't There a Crowd Everywhere? (Ross & Grey)
† *What a Duke Should Be* (Grey)
I'll Make Myself at Home (Ross)
The Candy Girls (Ross)
You'd Better Not Wait for Him (Grey)
He's Going to Call on Baby Grand (Ross)
We Are Theodore and Co (Ross)
† *My Friend John* (Grey)
Valse Saracenne
† *Every Little Girl Can Teach Me Something New* (Ross)
† *Any Old Where* (Grey)
Walk a Little (Ross)
Lazy Dancing Man (Grey)

Welcome Home (Grey)

See-Saw, a Revue

Presented by André Charlot at the Comedy, December 14th.
Book by Arthur E. Eliot, Herbert Sargent and Arthur Weigall.
Lyrics by A. B. Mills, Arthur Weigall and others.
Music by Philip Braham, Ivor Novello, Harold Montague and others.
Cast: Ruby Miller, Phyllis Monkman, Winnie Melville, Doris Barrington, Billy Danvers, Percy Carr, Norman Bowyer, Jimmie Leslie, Jack Hulbert.
Numbers by Novello:
† *Risk It* (Mills)
† *On the Tiles*—Dance
† *Rude Questions* (Mills and Weigall)
† *Dream Boat* (Novello)

*George Grossmith joined up shortly after the opening night and was replaced by Austin Melford.

1917

Arlette, a Musical Comedy
Presented by Grossmith & Laurillard at the Shaftesbury, September 6th.
Book by Claude Ronald and L. Buvet, tr. by José Levy.
Adaptation by Austen Hurgon and George Arthurs.
Lyrics by Adrian Ross and Clifford Grey.
Music by Jane Vieu, Guy le Feuvre and Ivor Novello.
Cast: Winifred Barnes, Joseph Coyne, Stanley Lupino, Adrah Fair, Mary Robson, Leonard Mackay, Madge Melbourne, Johnnie Fields, Blanche Stocker, A. G. Poulton.
Numbers by Novello:
† **Hail, All Hail** (Grey)
† **On the Staff** (Grey)
  A Man of Forty (Grey)
† **Cousinly Love** (Grey)
† **Didn't Know the Way To** (Grey)
† **Just a Memory** (Grey)
† **The People's King** (Grey)

1918

Tabs, a Revue
Presented by André Charlot at the Vaudeville, May 15th.
Book and Lyrics by Ronald Jeans.
Additional lyrics by Douglas Furber, Adrian Ross, Walter Donaldson, Hugh E. Wright.
Music by Ivor Novello.
Additional music by Guy le Feuvre, Bob Adams, Muriel Lillie, Herman Darewski, Walter Donaldson, Pat Thayer.
Cast: Beatrice Lillie, Odette Myrtil, Ethel Baird, Vera Lennox, Guy le Feuvre, Vivian Foster, Hal Bert, Margaret Campbell, Walter Williams.
Numbers by Novello:
† **Mr Pau-Puk-Keewis** (Jeans)
  Feed the Brute (Jeans)
† **Think Again** (Jeans)
† **When I Said Goodbye to You** (Jeans)
† **Something Doing Over the Way** (Jeans)
† **I Hate to Give Trouble** (Jeans)
† **Goblin Golliwog Trees** (Jeans)
  Have You Ever Noticed? (Jeans)
  Come Out, Little Boy (Jeans)
† **Lost** (Jeans)

† **Any Little Thing (Anything I Can Do for You)** (Burnaby and Jeans)
Sung by Phyllis Monkman and Jack Buchanan in André Charlot's **Tails Up** at the Comedy.

† **Mother, Teach Me How to Live** (Furber)

† **The Bridge Across the Stream** (McManus)

1919

† **Make Him Forget He's Ever Been Away** (Jeans and Novello)

Who's Hooper?, a Musical Comedy
Presented by Alfred Butt at the Adelphi, September 13th.

Book by Fred Thompson, based on **In Chancery** by A. W. Pinero.
Lyrics by Cliffor Grey.
Music by Howard Talbot and Ivor Novello.
Cast: W. H. Berry, Robert Michaelis, Marjorie Gordon, Cicely Debenham, Paul Plunket, Edward Rigby, Arthur Wellesley, Madeline Seymour, Violet Blythe, Fred Winn.
Numbers by Novello:
† **My London Town**
† **There's an Angel Watching Over Me**
† **Wonderful Love**
† **Wedding Jazz**
† **When No-one's Looking**
  Come, Landlord, Fill the Flowing Bowl
† **A Ladies' Man**
† **If You Were King in Babylon** (Novello)
  Who's Hooper?
† **The Garden of My Dreams**
† **Each Day in Passing**

1920

A Southern Maid, an Operetta
Presented by George Edwardes at Daly's, May 15th.
Book by Dion Clayton Calthrop and Harry Graham.
Lyrics by Harry Graham.
Additional lyrics by Adrian Ross and Douglas Furber.
Music by Harold Fraser-Simpson.
Additional music by Ivor Novello.
Cast: José Collins, Bertram Wallis, Jessie Fraser, Therese Mills, Jean Stirling, Dorothy Monkman, Lionel Victor.
Numbers by Novello:
† **Every Bit of Loving in the World** (Furber)
  I Want the Sun and the Moon (Furber)

† **Thoughts of You** (Grey and Novello)

1921

The Golden Moth, a Musical Play
Presented by Thomas F. Dawe and Austen Hurgon at the Adelphi, October 5th.
Book by Fred Thompson and P. G. Wodehouse.
Lyrics by P. G. Wodehouse and Adrian Ross.
Music by Ivor Novello.
Cast: W. H. Berry, Robert Michaelis, Thorpe Bates, Cicely Debenham, Nancie Lovat, Pitt Chatham, Fred Maguire, Bobbie Comber, Marjorie Mars, Beryl Harrison.
Numbers:
  We've Had a Busy Day (Wodehouse)
† **Fairy Prince** (Wodehouse)
† **Romance is Calling** (Wodehouse)
† **Lonely Soldier** (Wodehouse)
  Round the Corner (Ross)
† **Dartmoor Days** (Wodehouse and Ross)
† **Dear Eyes that Shine** (Wodehouse)
† **My Girl** (Wodehouse)
† **Nuts in May** (Wodehouse)
† **If I Ever Lost You** (Wodehouse)
  Song of Welcome (Ross)
  At the Servants' Ball (Ross)
† **The Island of Never-Mind-Where** (Ross)
† **Give Me a Thought Now and Then** (Wodehouse)

† **Bless You** (Furber)

A to Z, a Revue
  Presented by André Charlot at the Prince of Wales, October
    21st.
  Book by Ronald Jeans, Dion Titheradge and Helen Trix.
  Lyrics by Ronald Jeans, Dion Titheradge, Collie Knox.
  Music by Ivor Novello, Philip Braham.
  Cast: Jack Buchanan, Gertrude Lawrence, the Trix Sisters,
    Teddie Gerard, Marcel de Haes, Herbert Mundin, Elizabeth
    Pollock, Isabelita Ruiz, Enid Stamp-Taylor, Frederick Ross,
    Douglas Furber, Phyllis Haye.
  Numbers by Novello.
  † **Think of All the Fun You're Missing** (Titheradge)
  † **My Kind of Boy** (Titheradge)
  † **And Her Mother Came Too** (Titheradge)
  † **The Oldest Game in the World** (Jeans)
  † **Night May Have its Sadness** (Knox)
  † **Rough Stuff** (Jeans, Knox)
  † **I've Never Been Kept Waiting** (Jeans)
  † **I Hate That Tune** (Titheradge)
    There Are Times (Knox)
    A to Z (Titheradge)
  † **When I'm Dressed in Blue** (Jeans)
    I Don't Believe a Word of It (Titheradge)
    Chez Patou (Titheradge)
    Tears (Knox)

1922

† **Dusky Nipper** (Travers)
  Sung by Binnie Hale in The Dippers at the Criterion.

1924

Puppets, a Revue
  Presented by André Charlot at the Vaudeville, January 2nd.
  Book and Lyrics by Dion Titheradge.
  Additional material by Ronald Jeans and others.
  Music by Ivor Novello.
  Cast: Stanley Lupino, Binnie Hale, Arthur Chesney, Connie
    Emerald, Paul England, Neta Underwood, Frank Lawton,
    Rex Caldwell, Fay Cole, Josephine Dent.
  Numbers:
  † **And That's Not All** (Titheradge)
  † **April's Lady** (Titheradge)
  † **What Do You Mean?** (Titheradge)
  † **Same Old Moon** (Titheradge)
  † **Raggedy Doll** (Titheradge)
  † **Penelope** (Jeans)
  † **Barbary** (Titheradge)
  † **Old Acquaintance Blues** (Titheradge)
  † **She Needs Another Now** (Titheradge)

Our Nell, a Musical Play
  Presented by Robert Evett at the Gaiety, April 16th.
  Book by Louis N. Parker and Reginald Arkell.
  Lyrics by Harry Graham and Reginald Arkell.
  Music by H. Fraser-Simpson and Ivor Novello.
  Cast: José Collins, Arthur Wontner, Robert Michaelis, Muriel
    Pope, Miles Malleson, Faith Bevan, Walter Passmore.

Numbers by Novello:
† **Our England** (Arkell)
† **The Kingdom I'll Build for You** (Arkell)
† **The Land of Might-Have-Been** ('Edward Moore')

† **The Rat Step**—Dance
  Featured in The Rat.

1925

† **Quality Street** (Jeans)
† **Baby Blues** (Jeans)
  Featured in Charlot's 1925 Revue.

† **First Up** (Wimperis)
  Featured in Still Dancing at the London Pavilion.

1926

† **Odile (Lily of Montmartre)** (Novello)
  for the film of The Rat.

1929

† **Give Me Back My Heart** (Novello)
  Featured in Symphony in Two Flats.

The House That Jack Built, a Revue
  Presented by Jack Hulbert and Paul Murray at the Adelphi,
    November 8th.
  Book by Ronald Jeans and Douglas Furber.
  Lyrics by Donovan Parsons and Douglas Furber.
  Music by Ivor Novello, Vivian Ellis, Arthur Shwartz, Sydney
    Baynes.
  Cast: Jack Hulbert, Cicely Courtneidge, Helen Burnell,
    Bobbie Comber, Vera Sherburn, Irene Russell, Ivor
    McLaren, Robert Naylor, Lawrence Green.
  Numbers by Novello:
  † **The House We'd Build** (Parsons)
    At the Circus (Parsons)
  † **Teardrops from Her Eyes** (Parsons)
    The Dowager Fairy Queen (Furber)
  † **The Thought Never Entered My Head** (Parsons)
    Playing the Game (Parsons)
  † **Ever So** (Parsons)
  † **There Must Be Something on My Mind** (Parsons)

1930

† **Who Shall Say That Heaven** (Nichols)
  Featured in Cochran's 1930 Revue at the London Pavilion.

1933

† **Hold on to Love** (Novello)
  Sung by Gertrude Lawrence in This Inconstancy at
    Wyndhams.
† **Lend Me a Dream** (Novello)
  Featured in The Sunshine Sisters at the Queen's.

1935

†*Forest Echoes* (Novello)
†*Keep The Peace Fires Burning* (Clara Novello Davies)

1936

†*When Love Awakens* (Hassall)

1937

1018†*We're One Big Family* (Pyrke)

1939

†*We'll Remember* (Knox)

1944

†*Clear the Road to Glory* (Novello)
    March for the Liberation of Europe.

1950

1033†*Among the Hills of Wales* (Evans)

1951

†*Pray For Me* (Hassall)

Films

The Call of the Blood (*L'Appel du Sang*)
Mercanton/Stoll 1920.
Dir: Louis Mercanton.
Script: Louis Mercanton, from the novel by Robert Hichens.
Cast: Ivor Novello (Maurice Delarey), Phyllis Neilson Terry (Hermione Lester), Desdemona Mazza (Maddelena), Le Bargy, Lo Turco, de Gravone.

Miarka: Daughter of the Bear (*Miarka, Fille de L'Ourse*)
Mercanton 1920.
Dir: Louis Mercanton.
Scr: Louis Richepin, from his own novel.
Cast: Ivor Novello (Ivor), Réjane (Kate), Desdemona Mazza (Miarka), Charles Vanel, Louis Richepin.

Carnival
Alliance 1921.
Dir: Harley Knoles.
Scr: Adrian Johnson and Rosina Henley, from the play by Matheson Lang and H. C. M. Hardinge.
Cast: Matheson Lang (Silvio Steno), Hilda Bayley (Simonetta), Ivor Novello (Count Andrea Scipione), Maria de Bernaldo, 'Twinkles'.

The Bohemian Girl
Alliance 1922.
Dir: Harley Knoles.
Scr: Harley Knoles and Rosina Henley, based on Balfe's opera.
Cast: Gladys Cooper (Arline), Ivor Novello (Count Thaddeus), Constance Collier (Queen of the Gypsies), Ellen Terry (Buda), C. Aubrey Smith, Henry Vibart, Gibb McLaughlin.

The Man Without Desire (*The Man Without a Soul*)
Atlas Biocraft 1923.
Dir: Adrian Brunel.
Scr: Frank Powell, from a story by Monckton Hoffe.
Cast: Ivor Novello (Vittorio), Nina Vanna (Leonora/Ginevra), Sergio Mario (Almoro), Adrian Brunel, Dorothy Warren, Jane Dryden, Christopher Wallace.

The White Rose
Ideal/United Artists 1923.
Dir: D. W. Griffith.
Scr: Irene Sinclair (D. W. Griffith).
Cast: Mae Marsh (Bessie Williams), Ivor Novello (Joseph Beaugarde), Neil Hamilton (John White), Carol Dempster (Marie Carrington), Lucille laVerne, Peter Strong, Kate Bruce, Irville Anderson, Herbert Sutch.

Bonnie Prince Charlie
Gaumont 1923.
Dir: C. C. Calvert.
Scr: Alicia Ramsay.
Cast: Ivor Novello (Prince Charles Stuart), Gladys Cooper (Flora MacDonald), Hugh Miller, Sydney Seaward, Benson Kleve, A. B. Imeson, Lewis Gilbert, Bromley Davenport, Adeline Hayden-Coffin.

The Rat
Gainsborough 1925.
Dir: Graham Cutts.
Scr: Graham Cutts, from the play by 'David L'Estrange'.
Cast: Ivor Novello (Pierre Boucheron), Mae Marsh (Odile), Isabel Jeans (Zélie de Chaumet), Robert Scholtz, Julie Suedo, James Lindsay, Marie Ault, Iris Gray, Althea Lambert Glasby and Chorus of the Folies Bergère.

The Triumph of The Rat

Gainsborough 1926.

Dir: Graham Cutts.

Scr: Graham Cutts and Reginald Fogwell.

Cast: Ivor Novello (Pierre Boucheron), Isabel Jeans (Zélie de Chaumet), Nina Vanna (Madeline de l'Orme), Marie Ault, Lenore Hayden-Coffin, Charles Dormer, Julie Suedo, Mickey Brantford, Gabriel Rosca.

The Lodger

Gainsborough 1926.

Dir: Alfred Hitchcock.

Scr: Alfred Hitchcock and Eliot Stannard, from the novel by Marie Belloc Lowndes and the play, *Who Is He?*, by H. A. Vachell, based on the same.

Cast: Ivor Novello (Jonathan Drew), June (Daisy), Malcolm Keen (Joe), Arthur Chesney (Mr Bunting), Marie Ault (Mrs Bunting).

Downhill

Gainsborough 1927.

Dir: Alfred Hitchock.

Scr: Eliot Stannard, from the play by 'David L'Estrange'.

Cast: Ivor Novello (Roddy Berwick), Isabel Jeans (Julia Fotheringale), Robert Irvine (Tim Wakeley), Lilian Braithwaite (Mrs Berwick), Annette Benson (Mabel), Ian Hunter, Hannah Jones, Violet Farebrother.

The Vortex

Gainsborough 1928.

Dir: Adrian Brunel.

Scr: Eliot Stannard, from the play by Noël Coward.

Cast: Ivor Novello (Nicky Lancaster), Willette Kershaw (Florence Lancaster), Frances Doble (Bunty Mainwaring), Alan Hollis, Dorothy Fane, Julie Suedo, Kinsey Peile, Sir Simeon Stewart.

The Constant Nymph

Gainsborough 1928.

Dir: Adrian Brunel (supervised by Basil Dean).

Scr: Alma Reville, based on the play by Margaret Kennedy and Basil Dean, adapted from Miss Kennedy's novel.

Cast: Ivor Novello (Lewis Dodd), Mabel Poulton (Tessa Sanger), Frances Doble (Florence), J. H. Roberts, Tony de Lungo, Mary Clare, Benita Hume, Dorothy Boyd, Harold Scott, Clifford Heatherly, Elsa Lanchester.

The Gallant Hussar

Gainsborough 1928.

Dir: Geza von Bolvary.

Scr: ?

Cast: Ivor Novello (Lt. Alrik), Evelyn Holt, Ernst Verebes, Ibolya Szekely, Paul Otto.

South Sea Bubble

Gainsborough 1928.

Dir: T. Hayes Hunter.

Scr: Alma Reville and Angus McPhail, from the novel by Roland Pertwee.

Cast: Ivor Novello (Vernon Winslowe), Averil Rochester (Benita Hume), Annette Benson (Lydia laRue), S. J. Warmington, Ben Field, Sydney Seaward, Robert Holmes, Mary Dibley, John Hamilton, Harold Huth.

The Return of The Rat

Gainsborough 1928.

Dir: Graham Cutts.

Scr: Graham Cutts and Angus McPhail.

Cast: Ivor Novello (Pierre Boucheron), Isabel Jeans (Zélie de Chaumet), Mabel Poulton (Lisette), Gordon Harker, Bernard Nedell, Marie Ault, Hazel Terry, Scotch Kelly, Gladys Frazin.

Symphony in Two Flats

Gainsborough 1930.

Dir: Gareth Gundry.

Scr: Gareth Gundry, from the play by Ivor Novello.

Cast: Ivor Novello (David Kennard), Benita Hume (Lesley Kennard), Jacqueline Logan (Lesley in US version), Cyril Ritchard (Leo Chavasse), Minnie Rayner, Maidie Andrews, Clifford Heatherly, Ernest Dagnell and Jack Payne and his Orchestra.

Once a Lady

Paramount (USA) 1931.

Dir: Guthrie McLintic.

Scr: Zoe Atkins and Samuel Hoffenstein, from the play, *The Second Life*, by Rudolf Bernauer and Rudolph Osterreicher.

Cast: Ruth Chatterton (Anna), Ivor Novello (Bennett Cloud), Geoffrey Kerr, Jill Esmond, Doris Lloyd, Bramwell Fletcher, Ethel Griffies.

The Lodger

Twickenham 1932.

Dir: Maurice Elvey.

Scr: H. Fowler Mear, from the novel by Marie Belloc Lowndes.

Cast: Ivor Novello (Angeloff), Elizabeth Allan (Daisy), Jack Hawkins (Joe Martin), A. W. Baskcomb (Mr Bunting), Barbara Everest (Mrs Bunting), Shayle Gardner, Peter Gawthorne, P. Kynaston Reeves.

I Lived With You

Twickenham 1933.

Dir: Maurice Elvey.

Scr: George A. Cooper and H. Fowler Mear, from the play by Ivor Novello.

Cast: Ivor Novello (Felix Lenieff), Ursula Jeans (Glad Wallis), Eliot Makeham (Mr Wallis), Minnie Rayner (Mrs Wallis), Cicely Oates (Aunt Flossie), Ida Lupino (Ada), Jack Hawkins (Mort), Victor Boggetti, Beryl Harrison, Davina Craig, Hannah Jones.

Sleeping Car

Gaumont 1933.

Dir: Anatole Litvak.

Scr: ?

Cast: Ivor Novello (Gaston), Madeleine Carroll (Anne), Kay Hammond, Laddie Cliff, Stanley Holloway, Claude Allister.

Autumn Crocus

Associated Talking Pictures 1934.

Dir: Basil Dean.

Scr: Dorothy Farnum, from the play by Dodie Smith.

Cast: Ivor Novello (Steiner), Fay Compton (Jenny), Esme Church, Frederick Ranalow, Jack Hawkins, Diana Beaumont, George Zucco, Muriel Aked.

The Rat (Talkie re-make)

RKO Radio 1938.

Dir: Jack Raymond.

Scr: Hans Gulder Rameau.

Cast: Anton Walbrook (Pierre Boucheron), Ruth Chatterton (Zélie de Chaumet), René Ray (Odile), Mary Clare, Beatrix Lehmann, Felix Aylmer, Hugh Miller.

Films of the Musicals:

Glamorous Night
Associated British 1937.
Dir: Brian Desmond Hurst.
Scr: Dudley Leslie, Hugh Brodie.
Cast: Mary Ellis (Militza), Barry McKay (Anthony), Otto Kruger (King Stefan), Victor Jory (Lyadeff), Maire O'Neil, Trefor Jones, Olive Gilbert, Charles Carson, Finlay Currie, Ernest Clarke, Anthony Holles.

The Dancing Years
Associated British 1950.
Dir: Harold French.

Scr: Warwick Ward and Jack Whittingham.
Cast: Dennis Price (Rudi), Gisèle Préville (Maria), Patricia Dainton (Grete), Anthony Nicholls (Prince Reinaldt), Gray Blake, Muriel George, Olive Gilbert, Martin Ross, Gerald Case, Carl Jaffé, Jeremy Spenser.

King's Rhapsody
British Lion 1955.
Dir: Herbert Wilcox.
Scr: Pamela Bower and Christopher Hassall, with additional dialogue by A. P. Herbert.
Cast: Errol Flynn (King Richard), Anna Neagle (Marta), Patrice Wymore (Cristiane), Martita Hunt (Queen Mother), Finlay Currie, Francis de Wolfe, Joan Benham, Reginald Tate, Miles Malleson, Lionel Blair.

Plays

Deburau
by Sacha Guitry, tr. Harley Granville-Barker.
Presented by H. M. Harwood at the Ambassadors, November 23rd 1921.
Dir: Harley Granville-Barker.
Cast: Robert Loraine (Deburau), Madge Titheradge (Marie Duplessis), Michael Sherbrooke, John Howell, Leslie Banks, J. Henry Twyford, Gladys Gaynor, Colette O'Niel, Jeanne Casalis, Bruce Winston, Cherry Carver, Bobbie Andrews and Ivor Novello (A Young Man).

The Yellow Jacket
by George C. Hazelton and Benrimo.
Presented and directed by Benrimo at the Kingsway, March 7th 1922.
Cast: Ivor Novello (Wu Hoo Git), Holman Clark (Property Man), John Tresakar (Chorus), Jevan Brandon-Thomas (Wu Sin Yiu), Ann Trevor, Doris Lloyd, Malcolm Morley, Hugh Williams, Ethel Ross, Cecil Cameron, Julia Keane.

Spanish Lovers
by J. Feliu Y Cordona.
Adapted from the French of Carlos de Battle and Antonin Lavergne by Christopher StJohn.
Presented and directed by Benrimo at the Kingsway, June 21st 1922.
Cast: Ivor Novello (Javier), Doris Lloyd (Maria Carmen), Malcolm Morley (Pencho), Dickson-Kenwin, Geoffrey Dunlop, Herbert Lugg, Hugh Williams, John Tresakar, Seton Blackden, Julia Keane, Ethel Ross, Los Caritos.

Enter Kiki
by André Picard, adpt. Sidney Blow and Douglas Hoare.
Presented by Gladys Cooper in conjunction with Frank Curzon and Gilbert Miller at the Playhouse, August 2nd 1923.
Cast: Gladys Cooper (Kiki), Ivor Novello (Victor Leroux), Paul Arthur, Henry Wenman, Jack Raine, Geoffrey Hammon,

Drelincourt Odlum, Frank Verner, Hannah Jones, Madeline Seymour.

The Rat
by 'David L'Estrange' (Ivor Novello & Constance Collier).
Presented by Julian Frank at the Prince of Wales, June 9th 1924.
Dir: Constance Collier.
Incidental music by Ivor Novello.
Cast: Ivor Novello (Pierre Boucheron), Isabel Jeans (Zélie de Chaumet), Dorothy Batley (Odile), W. Cronin Wilson (Stetz), Hannah Jones (Mère Colline), Dorothy St John, Jean Webster-Brough, James Lindsay, Nancy Pawley, Maurice Braddell.

Old Heidelberg
by Wilhelm Meyer-Forster, adapt. Rudolph Bleichmann.
Presented by Julian Frank at the Garrick, February 2nd 1925.
Dir: Ernest Benham.
Cast: Ivor Novello (Karl Heinrich), Kathie (Dorothy Batley), Ernest Benham (Lutz), E. W. Thomas, Ashton Pearce, Hannah Jones, Betty Sturgess, William Kendall, Alexander Onslow, Tatten Hall, Basil Howes.

Iris
by A. W. Pinero.
Presented by Gladys Cooper and Henry Ainley at the Adelphi, March 3rd 1925.
Cast: Gladys Cooper (Iris), Henry Ainley (Freddy Maldanado), Anew McMaster (Lawrence Trenwith), Joan Maude, Winifred Griffiths, Newman Forbes.
Ivor Novello replaced Anew McMaster on April 7th.

The Firebrand
by Edwin Justus Mayer.
Presented by Gilbert Miller, Frank Curzon and Ivor Novello at Wyndhams, February 8th 1926.
Dir: Lawrence Schwab.
Cast: Ivor Novello (Benvenuto Cellini), Ursula Jeans (Angela), Constance Collier (Duchess of Florence), Hugh Wakefield (Alessandro de Medici), D. A. Clarke-Smith, Campbell Gullan,

Elsie French, George Howe, Lawrence Ireland, Dorothy Debenham.

Downhill

by 'David L'Estrange' (Ivor Novello & Constance Collier).
Presented by Frank Curzon and Ivor Novello at the Queen's, June 16th 1926.
Dir: Constance Collier.
Cast: Ivor Novello (Roddy Berwick), Phyllis Monkman (Julia Blue), Glen Byam Shaw (Tim Walker), Frances Doble (Vivian Dexter), D. A. Clarke-Smith, Kathleen Grace, Betty Sturgess, Evelyn Roberts, Hannah Jones, J. Smith-Weight.

Liliom

by Ferenc Molnar.
Presented by Philip Ridgeway at the Duke of York's, December 23rd 1926.
Dir: Theodor Komisarjevsky.
Cast: Ivor Novello (Liliom), Fay Compton (Julie), Charles Laughton (Fiecesur), William Kendall, Violet Farebrother, Margaret Watson, Marjorie Mars.

Sirocco

by Noël Coward.
Presented and directed by Basil Dean at Daly's, November 24th 1927.
Cast: Ivor Novello (Sirio Marson), Frances Doble (Lucy Griffin), David Hawthorne, Helen Ferrers, Aubrey Mather, Blyth Daly, Margaret Watson, Ada King, Doris Garrick, Tony de Lungo, George Colouris.

The Truth Game

by 'H. E. S. Davidson' (Ivor Novello).
Presented by Ivor Novello and Barry O'Brien at the Globe, October 5th 1928.
Dir: W. Graham Browne.
Cast: Ivor Novello (Max Clement), Lily Elsie (Rosine Browne), Lilian Braithwaite (Evelyn Brandon), Viola Tree (Lady Joan Culver), Eric Copley, Frederic Oxley, Moya Mackintosh, Frederick Volpé, Glen Byam Shaw.

[The Truth Game (New York)

Presented by Lee Shubert at the Ethel Barrymore, December 27th 1930.
Dir: Rollo Wayne.
Cast: Ivor Novello (Max Clement), Billie Burke (Evelyn Brandon), Phoebe Foster (Rosine Browne), Viola Tree, Gerald McCarthy, Gwen Day Burroughs, Burton McEvilly, Albert Garcia Andrews, Forbes Dawson, Dorothy Bigelow.]

Symphony in Two Flats

by Ivor Novello.
Presented by Ivor Novello at the New, October 14th 1929.
Dir: Raymond Massey.
Cast: Ivor Novello (David Kennard), Benita Hume (Lesley), George Relph (Leo Chavasse), Lilian Braithwaite (Mrs Plaintiff), Viola Tree (Salmon), Minnie Rayner, Netta Westcott, Maidie Andrews, Ann Trevor, Ben Webster, Gwendolen Floyd, Anthony Hankey, Frederic Oxley.

[Symphony in Two Flats (New York)

Presented by Messrs Shubert at the Sam S. Shubert Theater, September 16th 1930.
Dir: Raymond Massey.
Cast: Ivor Novello, Benita Hume, Ivan Samson, Lilian Braithwaite, Ethel Baird, Minnie Rayner, Netta Westcott, Maidie Andrews, Ann Trevor, Una Venning, Frederic Oxley, Anthony Hankey.]

I Lived With You

by Ivor Novello.
Presented by Richard D. Rose at the Prince of Wales, March 2nd 1932.
Dir: Auriol Lee.
Cast: Ivor Novello (Felix Lenieff), Ursula Jeans (Glad Wallis), Minnie Rayner (Mrs. Wallis), Eliot Makeham (Mr Wallis), Cicely Oates (Aunt Flossie), Thea Holme (Ada), Robert Newton, Davina Craig, Hannah Jones, Jean Webster-Brough, Isabel Olmead, Gwen Floyd, Maud Buchanan, Beryl Harrison.

Party

by Ivor Novello.
Presented by Leslie Henson & Firth Shephard at the Strand, May 23rd 1932.
(Three performances were given at the Arts on May 19th, 20th and 21st.)
Dir: Athole Stewart.
Cast: Benita Hume (Miranda Clayfoot), Lilian Braithwaite (Mrs MacDonald), Agnes Imlay, Joan Swinstead, Roy Findlay, Sebastian Shaw, Gwladys Evan Morris, Nancy Pawley, Margaret Watson, Margaret Vines, Norah Howard, Gravely Edwards, Terrance Clibburn, Victor Boggetti, Pamela Willins and Namara, Elizabeth Pollock, Douglas Byng.
(Ivor Novello took over Sebastian Shaw's rôle on July 30th.)

Fresh Fields

by Ivor Novello.
Presented by Richard D. Rose at the Criterion, January 5th 1933.
Dir: Athole Stewart.
Cast: Lilian Braithwaite (Lady Lilian Bedworthy), Ellis Jeffreys (Lady Mary Crabbe), Robert Andrews (Tim Crabbe), Minnie Rayner (Mrs Pidgeon), Eileen Peel (Una Pidgeon), Martita Hunt (Lady Strawholme), Fred Groves (Tom Larcomb), Gwen Floyd, Martin Sands.

Fresh Fields (New York)

Presented by Aldrich & de Liagre at the Empire, February 10th 1936.
Dir: Alfred de Liagre.
Cast: Margaret Anglin, Mary Sargent, Derek Fariman, Elwyn Harvey, Agnes Doyle, Boyd Davis, Lilian Talbot, Audrey Ridgewell, Philip Tonge.]

Flies in the Sun

by Ivor Novello.
Presented by Richard D. Rose at the Playhouse, January 13th 1933.
Dir: Gladys Cooper.
Cast: Ivor Novello (Seraphine), Gladys Cooper (Jane Marquis), Dorothy Hyson (Dina), Anthony Bushell (Bob Mitchell), Joan Swinstead, Jevan Brandon-Thomas, Denys Blakelock, Thea Holme, Beryl Harrison, May Hallett, Agnes Imlay, Tom Macaulay, Tony de Lungo.

Proscenium

by Ivor Novello.
Presented by Moss Empires and Howard & Wyndham Tours at the Globe, January 14th 1933.
Dir: Athole Stewart.
Cast: Ivor Novello (Sir Geoffrey Bethel/Gray Raynor), Fay Compton (Norma Matthews), Zena Dare (Lady Raynor), Joan Barry (Eunice Manners), Keneth Kent (Hyman), Lena Maitland, Margaret Watson, Margot Sieveking, Henry Crocker, Madge Snell, Dorothy Boyd.

The Sunshine Sisters

by Ivor Novello.

> Presented by Ivor Novello and Richard D. Rose at the Queen's, November 8th 1933.
> Dir: Athole Stewart.
> Cast: Dorothy Dickson (Pearl), Phyllis Monkman (Ruby), Joan Clarkson (Emerald), Irene Browne (Duchess of Frynne), Jack Hawkins, Veronica Brady, Maidie Andrews, Sebastian Shaw, Joan Swinstead, Nora Nicholson, Victor Boggetti.

Murder in Mayfair

by Ivor Novello.

> Presented by Richard D. Rose at the Globe, September 5th 1934.
> Dir: Leontine Sagan.
> Cast: Ivor Novello (Jacques Clavel), Fay Compton (Mary Ventyre), Edna Best (Auriol Crannock), Zena Dare (Fania Sherry), Robert Andrews (Bill Sherry), Gwen Floyd, Linden Travers, Jean Webster-Brough, Hilda Anthony, Constance Travers, Olwen Brookes, Norman Pierce, Ireland Wood, Dorothy Batley, Christopher Hassall.

Full House

by Ivor Novello.

> Presented by Ivor Novello and Richard D. Rose at the Haymarket, August 25th 1935.
> Dir: Leslie Henson.
> Cast: Lilian Braithwaite (Frynne Rodney), Isabel Jeans (Lola Leadenhall), Heather Thatcher (Lady April Harrington), Robert Andrews (John Rodney), John Williams (Archie Leadenhall), Frank Cochrane, Maidie Andrews, Walter Lindsay, George Burn.

The Happy Hypocrite

by Clemence Dane and Richard Addinsell, from the story by Max Beerbohm.

> Presented by Ivor Novello and Richard D. Rose at His Majesty's Theatre, April 8th 1936.
> Dir: Maurice Colbourne.
> Cast: Ivor Novello (Lord George Hell), Vivien Leigh (Jenny Mere), Isabel Jeans (La Gambogi), Marius Goring (Amor), Carl Harbord (Mercury), Stafford Hilliard, Viola Tree, Joan Swinstead, Philip Desborough, Godfrey Kenton, Peter Graves, Charles Lefeaux, Philip Pearman, Geoffrey Gunn, Clive Donald, Kenneth Buckley, Malcolm Russell, Dorothy Batley.

Comedienne

by Ivor Novello.

> Presented by Ivor Novello at the Haymarket, June 16th 1938.

> Dir: Murray MacDonald.
> Cast: Lilian Braithwaite (Donna Lovelace), Barry Jones (Lord Bayfield), Cecily Byrne (Lady Mary Sambrook), Ralph Michael (Owen Sands), Kathleen Harrison (Winkie), Betty Marsden, Alan Webb, Fabia Drake, Edgar Norfolk, Ivan Samson, Mervyn Johns, Gwen Floyd, Jenny Laird.

Henry the Fifth

by William Shakespeare.

> Presented by Tom Arnold at the Theatre Royal, Drury Lane, on September 16th 1938.
> Dir: Lewis Casson.
> Cast: Ivor Novello (Henry V), Dorothy Dickson (Princess Katherine), Gwen Ffrangcon-Davies (Chorus), Frederick Bennett (Fluellen), Lawrence Baskcomb (Pistol), Sydney Bromley (Nym), Bert Evremonde (Bardolph), Peter Graves (The Dauphin), David Burney, George Skillan, Mario Francelli, Arthur Rees, Rayner Burton, Patrick Ross, Neil Porter, John Moore, Joan Swinstead, Veronica Brady, Stanley Vine, Eugene Leahy, Alex McCrindle, Leonard Thorne, Charles Doran, Stephen Jack, Alexander Sarner, Leonard Shepherd.

Ladies into Action (Second Helping)

by Ivor Novello.

> Presented by Ivor Novello at the Lyric, April 10th 1940.
> Dir: Harold French.
> Cast: Ivor Novello (Justin), Isabel Jeans (Susan Venables), Lilli Palmer (Felicity van der Loo), Martin Walker (Raymond Venables), Finlay Currie, Maidie Andrews, Peter Graves, Marjorie Tomlin, Kenneth Carten, Gwen Floyd.

Love from a Stranger

by Frank Vosper, from a story by Agatha Christie.

> ENSA Tour, Summer 1944.
> Dir: Daphne Rye.
> Cast: Ivor Novello (Bruce Lovell), Diana Wynyard (Cecily Harrington), Margaret Rutherford (Louise Garrard), Robert Andrews, Esma Cannon, Joan Benham.

We Proudly Present

by Ivor Novello.

> Presented by Peter Daubeny at the Duke of York's, May 2nd 1947.
> Dir: Max Adrian.
> Cast: Peter Graves (Bill Whittaker), Anthony Forwood (John Pearson), Phyllis Monkman (Phyl Perriman), Irene Handl (Franzi Mahler), Ena Burrill (Sandra Mars), Mary Jerrold, Anna Turner, Leo de Pokorny, Derek Hart, Edward Sinclair, Malcolm Russell, Peter Mitchell, John Downes, Norman Rutherford, Pauline Loring.

Musicals

Glamorous Night

> Presented at the Theatre Royal, Drury Lane, May 2nd 1935.
> Book by Ivor Novello.
> Lyrics by Christopher Hassall.

Music by Ivor Novello.
Dir: Leontine Sagan.
Designed by Oliver Messel.
Dances by Ralph Reader.

Musical Director: Charles Prentice.
Cast: Ivor Novello (Anthony Allan), Mary Ellis (Militza Hajos),
  Barry Jones (King Stefan), Lyn Harding (Baron Lydyeff),
  Minnie Rayner (Phoebe), Elisabeth Welch (Cleo Wellington),
  Olive Gilbert, Trefor Jones, Peter Graves, Victor Boggetti,
  Rudolph Brant, John Gatrell.
Numbers:
*Suburbia**
Her Majesty Militza
† *Fold Your Wings*
† *Glamorous Night*
  Operetta, incorporating
† *Shine Through My Dreams*
† *When the Gypsy Played*
  Rumba
  Skating Waltz
† *Shanty Town*
  The Gypsy Wedding
  March of the Gypsies
  Krasnian National Anthem
  *The Girl I Knew**
  Singing Waltz (*Waltz of June*)
  *The Royal Wedding**

Careless Rapture
Presented at the Theatre Royal, Dury Lane, September 11th
  1936.
Book by Ivor Novello.
Lyrics by Christopher Hassall.
Music by Ivor Novello.
Dir: Leontine Sagan.
Sets by Alick Johnstone.
Costumes by René Hubert.
Dances by Joan Davis.
Temple Ballet by Antony Tudor.
Musical Director: Charles Prentice.
Cast: Ivor Novello (Michael), Dorothy Dickson (Penelope Lee),
  Zena Dare (Phyllida Frame), Minnie Rayner (Mrs Ripple),
  Ivan Samson (Sir Rodney Alderney), Olive Gilbert (Mme
  Simonetti), Sybil Crawley, Eric Starling, Peter Graves, Nancy
  Pawley, Frederick Peisley, Olwen Brookes, Walter Crisham,
  Philip Friend, Gwen Floyd, Kenneth Howell, Enid Settle.
Numbers:
Thanks to Phyllida Frame
Singing Lesson
† *Music in May*
† *Why Is There Ever Good-bye?*
Studio Duet
Wait for Me
Rose Ballet
Hampstead Scene, incorporating:
  Hi-Ti-Tiddly-Eye
  Winnie, Get Off the Colonel's Knee
  Take a Trip to Hampstead
We Are the Wives
† *The Manchuko*
† *Love Made the Song I Sing to You*
Chinese Procession
Temple Ballet
The Bridge of Lovers

Crest of the Wave
Presented by Tom Arnold at the Theatre Royal, Drury Lane,
  September 1st 1937.
Book by Ivor Novello.

Lyrics by Christopher Hassall.
Music by Ivor Novello.
Dir: Leontine Sagan.
Sets by Alick Johnstone.
Costumes by René Hubert.
Dances by Ralph Reader.
Ballets arranged by Lydia Sokolova and Antony Tudor.
Musical Director: Charles Prentice.
Cast: Ivor Novello (Don Gantry/Otto Fresch), Dorothy Dickson
  (Honey Wortle), Marie Lohr (Duchess of Cheviot), Ena Burrill
  (Leonora Hayden), Minnie Rayner (Mrs Wortle), Peter Graves
  (Lord William Gantry), Walter Crisham (Freddie), Finlay
  Currie, Olive Gilbert, Reg Smith, Fred Hearne, Dorothy Batley,
  Renée Stocker, Jack Glyn, Aubrey Rouse.
Numbers:
† *Rose of England*
Versailles in Tinsel, incorporating:
  † *Haven of My Heart*
  Sarabande
  Mazurka
  Turbillon
† *Why Isn't it You?*
  Nautical
† *If You Only Knew*
  Café Scene, incorporating:
  Spring Duet
  The Venezuela
  Tango
March of the Ancestors
Oh, Clementine (*Lazy Old Mule*)
When Hollywood Plays
Christmas Carol
† *Used to You* (not used)

The Dancing Years
Presented by Tom Arnold at the Theatre Royal, Drury Lane,
  March 23rd 1939.
Book by Ivor Novello.
Lyrics by Christopher Hassall.
Music by Ivor Novello.
Dir: Leontine Sagan.
Designed by Joseph Carl.
Dances by Freddie Carpenter.
Musical Director: Charles Prentice.
Cast: Ivor Novello (Rudi Kleber), Mary Ellis (Maria Ziegler),
  Roma Beaumont (Grete), Olive Gilbert (Cäcilie Kurt), Anthony
  Nicholls (Prince Charles Metterling), Minnie Rayner (Hattie),
  Dunstan Hart (Ceruti), Peter Graves (Franzl), Frances Clare,
  Muriel Barron, Hilary Allen, Fred Hearne, Harry Ferguson,
  Hilton Porter, Roger Parker, Edgar Elmes, John Palmer, Maria
  Rita, Patrick Ross, Hilary de Charville, Victor Raymond, Fred
  Nye.
Numbers:
Dawn Prelude
Uniform (Graves)
† *Waltz of My Heart*
  Masque of Vienna 1911
† *The Wings of Sleep*
  Lorelei, incorporating:
  † *My Life Belongs to You*
† *I Can Give You the Starlight*
† *My Dearest Dear*
  Masque of Vienna 1914
Primrose
† *In Praise of Love*
† *The Leap Year Waltz*
  Masque of Vienna 1927

* Omitted from the published score and only performed in the
original production.

Supplementary Numbers:

† *Memory Is My Happiness* (Novello)

† *When It's Spring in Vienna*

Arc de Triomphe

Presented by Tom Arnold and Ivor Novello at the Phoenix, November 9th 1943.

Book by Ivor Novello.

Lyrics by Christopher Hassall.

Music by Ivor Novello.

Dir: Leontine Sagan.

Designed by Joseph Carl.

Mary Ellis's costumes by Cecil Beaton.

Dances by Keith Lester.

Paris Reminds Me of You staged by Cyril Ritchard.

Musical Director: Harry Acres.

Cast: Mary Ellis (Marie Forêt), Peter Graves (Pierre Bachelet), Raymond Lovell (Adhémar de Jonzé), Elisabeth Welch (Josephine), Harcourt Williams, Gwen Floyd, Netta Westcott, Hilary Allen, Nesta Ross, Edgar Elmes, Harry Fergusson, Renée Crewe (Olive Gilbert sang the rôle of Agnes Sorel in the opera sequence for part of the run). ·

Numbers:

Prelude

Shepherd Song

† *Man of My Heart*

† *Easy to Live With*

I Wonder Why

Apache Ballet

Josephine

† *Waking or Sleeping*

Royal France

† *Paris Reminds Me of You*

† *Dark Music* (Novello)

The Phantom Court

Vision Duet

Jeanne d'Arc, Opera Sequence, incorporating:

France Will Rise Again

Perchance to Dream

Presented by Tom Arnold at the Hippodrome, April 21st 1945.

Book, Lyrics and Music by Ivor Novello.

Dir: Jack Minster.

Designed by Joseph Carl.

Dances by Frank Staff.

Musical Director: Harry Acres.

Cast: Ivor Novello (Sir Graham Rodney/Valentine Fayre/Bay), Roma Beaumont (Melinda/Melanie/Melody), Muriel Barron (Lydia/Veronica/Iris), Robert Andrews (William/Bill), Margaret Rutherford (Lady Charlotte Fayre), Olive Gilbert (Ernestine/Mrs Bridport), Victor Boggetti, Anne Pinder, Dunstan Hart, Harry Fergusson, Lawrence Drew, Beryl Mariner, Roy Gunson, Gordon Duttson.

Numbers:

When the Gentlemen Get Together

† *Love is My Reason*

† *The Meeting*

† *The Path My Lady Walks*

A Lady Went to Market Fair

When I Curtsied to the King

† *Highwayman Love*

The Triumph of Spring (Ballet)

† *Autumn Lullaby*

† *A Woman's Heart*

† *We'll Gather Lilacs*

The Victorian Wedding

The Glo-Glo

The Elopement

Ghost Finale

King's Rhapsody

Presented by Tom Arnold at the Palace, September 15th 1949.

Book by Ivor Novello.

Lyrics by Christopher Hassall.

Music by Ivor Novello.

Dir: Murray MacDonald.

Designed by Edward Delaney and Frederick Dawson.

Dances by Pauline Grant.

Musical Director: Harry Acres.

Cast: Ivor Novello (Nikki), Vanessa Lee (Princess Cristiane), Zena Dare (Queen Elena), Phyllis Dare (Marta Karillos), Robert Andrews (Vanescu), Olive Gilbert (Countess Vera), Denis Martin, Michael Anthony, Victor Boggetti, Anne Pinder, John Palmer, Pamela Harrington, Wendy Warren, Eric Sutherland, Irene Claire, Ted Lane, Gordon Duttson.

Numbers:

The Dancing Lesson

Birthday Greetings

† *Someday My Heart Will Awake*

National Anthem

† *Fly Home, Little Heart*

Mountain Dove

† *If This Were Love*

The Mayor of Perpignan

† *The Gates of Paradise*

† *Take Your Girl*

† *The Violin Began to Play* (Novello)

Muranian Rhapsody (Ballet)

Coronation Hymn

† *The Years Together*, theme from the score, used as a number in the film version.

Gay's the Word

Presented by Tom Arnold at the Saville, February 16th 1951.

Book by Ivor Novello.

Lyrics by Alan Melville.

Music by Ivor Novello.

Dir: Jack Hulbert.

Designed by Edward Delaney and Berkeley Sutcliffe.

Dances by Irving Davies and Eunice Crowther.

Musical Director: Harry Acres.

Cast: Cicely Courtneidge (Gay Daventry), Lizbeth Webb (Linda), Thorley Walters (Peter Lynton), Carl Jaffé, Dunstan Hart, Denis Val Norton, May Tomlin, John Wynyard, Maidie Andrews, Beryl Harrison, Molly Lumley, June Laverick, Susan Swinford, Hilary de Charville.

Numbers:

Ruritania

Everything Reminds Me of You

It's Bound to be Right on the Night

Father Thames

Teachers' Ballet

† *Finder, Please Return*

An Englishman in Love

† *If Only He'd Looked My Way*

Vitality

Teaching

Greek Dance

Sweet Thames

Gaiety Glad

† *A Matter of Minutes*

† *On Such a Night as This*

† *Bees Are Buzzin'*

Bibliography

The author wishes to thank the following for their kind permission to reproduce quotations from the following books:

Peter Noble, *Ivor Novello, Man of the Theatre*, Falcon Press 1951.

W. Macqueen Pope, *Ivor, the Story of an Achievement*, W. H. Allen 1951.

Clara Novello Davies, *The Life I Have Loved*, Heinemann 1940.

Edward Marsh (in correspondence with Christopher Hassall), *Ambrosia and Small Beer*, Longmans 1964.

Adrian Brunel, *Nice Work*, Forbes Roberston 1949.

Michael Balcon, *A Lifetime of Films*, Hutchinson 1969.

Phyllis Bottome, *From the Life*, Faber and Faber 1944.

Noël Coward, *Present Indicative*, Heinemann 1937.

Basil Dean, *Seven Ages*, Hutchinson 1970.

Basil Dean, *Mind's Eye*, Hutchinson 1973.

Rhys Davies, *The Painted King*, Heinemann 1954.

François Truffaut, *Hitchcock*, Secker and Warburg 1968.

And Her Mother Came Too from the Musical Play *A to Z*. Lyrics by Dion Titheradge. Copyright © 1921 by Ascherberg, Hopwood & Crew Ltd.

We'll Remember (Grin, Grin, Grin, Win, Win, Win). Lyrics by Collie Knox & Ivor Novello. Copyright © 1939 by Ascherberg, Hopwood & Crew Ltd., & Chappell & Co. Ltd. Used by permission.

The Violin Began to Play from the Musical Production *King's Rhapsody*. Lyrics by Ivor Novello. Copyright © 1949 by Chappell & Co. Ltd. Used by permission.

Discography

Compiled by Adrian Edwards

Record numbers: All records listed are United Kingdom catalogue numbers, except VICTOR (American 78's) and ROCOCO (Canadian LP's). ROCOCO LP's are available from specialist dealers in U.K., including Collector's Corner, 62 New Oxford Street and 63 Monmouth Street, London, and Woodbridge Record Shop, Woodbridge, Suffolk.

Popular Novello songs: only the original artists, and artists associated with Ivor Novello, are listed.

MISCELLANEOUS SONGS to 1925 (acoustic recordings)

Megan—Hubert Eisdell	HMV 4 2531 or HMV B 740
Page's Road Song—Clara Butt	COLUMBIA X 316 or LP: ROCOCO 5306
Bless You—Frances Alda	HMV B 135, VICTOR 66027 or VICTOR 524
Laddie in Khaki—Francis Alda	VICTOR 64781
Thoughts of You—Francis Alda	VICTOR 526 or VICTOR 64781
Every Bit of Loving—Frances Alda	VICTOR 526 or VICTOR 66056
Every Bit of Loving—Jose Collins	COLUMBIA F 1041
I Want the Sun and the Moon—Jose Collins, Claude Flemming	COLUMBIA F 1054

NB: Jose Collins's songs featured in the musical *A Southern Maid*, 1920, reissued on Jose Collins's LP *The Maid of the Mountains and other successes* — WORLD RECORDS SH 169

Song	Record number
I Want the Sun and the Moon—Violet Essex, Peter Dawson	HMV B 1114
Up There (A Little Girl's Show)—Bessie Jones	HMV B 1357
Slumber Tree/Up There—Renee Mayer (child artist)	HMV B 608
Keep The Home Fires Burning—Renee Mayer	HMV 2 3159

NB: Reissued on LP *Oh What a Lovely War* — WORLD RECORDS SH 130

Song	Record number
Keep The Home Fires Burning—John McCormack	VICTOR 766 or VITOR 64696

Fairy Laughter—Rosina Buckman

COLUMBIA 2604 AND HMV E 257

The Rat Step (fox trot)—Romaine Orchestra

HMV B 1893

The Rat Step (fox trot)—Savoy Havana Band

COLUMBIA 3533

NB: Apache dance performed by Ivor Novello and Dorothy St John in *The Rat*.

Any Little Thing (featured in revue *Tails Up*, 1918)—Phyllis Monkman, Jack Buchanan (original artists)

COLUMBIA L 1254

Any Little Thing—Davy Burnaby, Louise Leigh (Bessie Jones)

HMV B 965

Not Really—Doris Cowan

HMV B 301

The Little Damozel—Lucrezia Bori

VICTOR 1162

The Radiance of Your Eyes—Reinald Werrenrath

VICTOR 45155

The Radiance of Your Eyes—Ruby Heyl

HMV B 1012

When the Great Day Comes—Coldstream Guards Band

HMV B 826

In the Clouds—Pathe Military Band

PATHE 5527

If—Jamison Dodds

PATHE 5249

The Home Bells are Ringing—Ernest Pike

ZONOPHONE 1640

Land of Might Have Been (from *Our Nell*, 1924)—Colin O'More

VOCALION X 9651

Friend (music by Clara Novello Davies; words by Algernon Sassin)—Peter Dawson

ZONOPHONE T 1294

Comfort (music by Clara Novello Davies)—Alice Lakin

HMV 03378 or HMV C 455

ELECTRIC RECORDINGS OF ABOVE

Bless You—Derek Oldham (*c.* 1935)

HMV B 8239

Keep The Home Fires Burning—Olive Gilbert (1939)

HMV B 8981

Thoughts of You—Gracie Fields (*c.* 1930)

HMV B 3176

Friend—Mostyn Thomas (*c.* 1931)

COLUMBIA DX 234

THEODORE AND CO, 1916

Overture
Any Old Where—Henry Leoni

HMV C 749

Every Little Girl Can Teach Me Something New—George Grossmith and chorus

HMV 02692

I'll Make Myself at Home, Dear—Julia James and Fred Leslie
Valse Saracenne—orchestra

HMV B 754

My Friend John—Leslie Henson

HMV 02691

Oh, How I Want to Marry All the Little Candy Girls—Henry Leoni and chorus
What a Duke Should Be—Dave Burnaby and chorus

HMV B 753

Isn't There a Crowd Everywhere; *You Better Not Wait for Me* (From *Theodore and Co. vocal gems*)—Light Opera
   Company

HMV C 765

Every Little Girl . . . (from *Ivor Novello—vocal gems—see **COLLECTIONS**)—Peter Graves, 1946

HMV C 3521 or C 4080

Music also by Jerome Kern and Paul Rubens, not listed above.

SEE-SAW, *1916*

Orchestral Selection (Novello and Philip Braham): *See-Saw*; *The Nowhere Walk*; *The Ghost of Cleopatra*; *I Can't Find a Place for That*; *The Automatic Wedding*; *Dream Boat*; *They Call it London Town*; *The Sandwichette*; *Jenny Johnson*; *Come and Risk It*—The Mayfair Orchestra　　　　　　　　　　HMV C 773

Dream Boat—Louise Leigh (Bessie Jones), Eric Courtland, Walter Jeffries　　　　HMV B 853

Dream Boat (from *My Earlier Songs* recorded *c*. 1935—see **COLLECTIONS**)—Olive Gilbert, Olive Groves and Edgar Elmes　　　　　　　　　　　　　　　　　　　　　　　　HMV C 2965

ARLETTE, *1917*

Ivor Novello's lyrics by Clifford Grey.

The People's King (*His Country First of All*)—Leonard McKay
Cousinly Love—Adrah Fair, Johnnie Fields and Leonard McKay　　　　　　　　HMV C 830

Didn't Know the Way To—Winifred Barnes and Joseph Coyne　　　　　　　　HMV 04213

It's Just a Memory—Winifred Barnes　　　　　　　　　　　　　　　　　　HMV 03594

On the Staff—Stanley Lupino and chorus　　　　　　　　　　　　HMV 02773 or D 413

Hail, All Hail (*Entrance of the Prince*) (from an orchestral medley of tunes from *Arlette*)—New Mayfair Orchestra　　　　　　　　　　　　　　　　　　　　　　　　　　HMV C 831

NB: Music also by Guy Le Feuvre (lyrics by Adrian Ross), not listed above.

TABS, *1918*

Mr Pau Puk Keewis—Harry Glen and chorus　　　　　　　　　　COLUMBIA L 1260

I Said Goodbye—Beatrice Lillie and trio　　　　　　　　　　　COLUMBIA L 1256

Something Doing Over There—Ethel Baird　　　　　　　　　　COLUMBIA L 1258

My River Girl—Beatrice Lillie and Alfred Austin　　　　　　　COLUMBIA L 1258

I Hate to Give Trouble—Beatrice Lillie and Margaret Campbell　　COLUMBIA L 1257

Goblin Golliwog Trees—Margaret Campbell and quartet　　　　COLUMBIA L 1259

I Said Goodbye—Gertrude Lawrence, 1932　　　DECCA K 689 or LP: ACE OF CLUBS ACL 1171

WHO'S HOOPER, *1919*

The Wedding Jazz—Cicely Debenham and chorus
Wonderful Love—Cicely Debenham and Fred Winn　　　　　　COLUMBIA F 1001

There's an Angel Watching Over Me—Cicely Debenham and Paul Plunket
My London Town—Paul Plunket and chorus　　　　　　　　　COLUMBIA F 1002

When No-one's Looking—Marjorie Gordon and Robert Michaelis
Each Day in Passing—Marjorie Gordon　　　　　　　　　　　COLUMBIA F 1004

Garden of Our Dreams—Marjorie Gordon and Robert Michaelis
A Ladies' Man—Robert Michaelis　　　　　　　　　　　　　COLUMBIA F 1005

Come Landlord, Fill the Flowing Bowl—Fred Winn and Alfred Beers　　COLUMBIA F 1007

Come Landlord, Fill the Flowing Bowl—W. H. Berry (original cast) and Ernest Pike　　HMV 04269 or D 444

There's an Angel Watching Over Me—Violet Loraine　　　　　　HMV 2 3419

Wedding Jazz—Violet Loraine   HMV 03708 or D 444

Wonderful Love—W. H. Berry (original cast) and Violet Loraine   HMV D 443

Orchestral selections—Adelphi Theatre Orchestra, conductor Howard Talbot   COLUMBIA 725

Orchestral selections—New Mayfair Orchestra   HMV C 932

NB: Music also by Howard Talbot, not listed above.

GOLDEN MOTH, *1921*

Dear Eyes That Shine—De Groot and the Piccadilly Orchestra   HMV B 1323

Orchestral selection: *Lonely Soldier*; *Dartmoor Days*; *If I Ever Lost You*; *Nuts in May*; *My Girl*; *One Step*; *Dear Eyes That Shine*; *Fairy Prince*; *Dance*—Herman Finck and his Orchestra   COLUMBIA 888

Orchestral selection—The Mayfair Orchestra   HMV C 1053

A TO Z, *1921*

And Her Mother Came Too—Jack Buchanan (1922)   HMV B 1319
NB: Reissued on LP *The Debonair Jack Buchanan*   MUSIC FOR PLEASURE MFP 1160

And Her Mother Came Too—Jack Buchanan (from *Jack Buchanan Medley*, *c.* 1933)   HMV C 2630
NB: Reissued on LP *Jack Buchanan*   WORLD RECORDS SH 283

There Are Times (LP *An Evening with Beatrice Lillie*)—Beatrice Lillie, *c.* 1955   DECCA LK 4129

Night May Have Its Sadness (from *My Earlier Songs*—see *COLLECTIONS*)—Patrick Waddington, 1935 HMV C 2965

Orchestral selection: *When I'm Dressed in Blue*; *I've Never Been Kept Waiting*; *The Oldest Game in the World*; *Too Much Mother* (*And Her Mother Came Too*); *Smile*; *There Are Times*; *My Kind of Boy*; *I Hate That Tune*; *Night May Have Its Sadness*—Mayfair Orchestra, conductor Philip Braham   HMV C 1058

PUPPETS, *1924*

And That's Not All—Jack Hylton Orchestra   HMV B 1830

April's Lady—The Romaine Orchestra   HMV B 1787

Same Old Moon (from *My Earlier Songs*—see *COLLECTIONS*)—Olive Groves, *c.* 1935   HMV C 2965

SYMPHONY IN TWO FLATS, *play 1929*

Give Me Back My Heart—Peggy Wood   HMV B 3282
NB: 1929 Peggy Wood in Nöel Coward's *Bitter Sweet*.

THE HOUSE THAT JACK BUILT, *1929*

The Thought Never Entered My Head—Winnie Melville and Derek Oldham   HMV B 3276

Orchestral selection: *The House I'd Build*; *The Thought Never Entered My Head*; *Topsy, the Queen of the Fairies*; *My Heart is Saying* (Vivian Ellis); *I've Fallen in Love* (Vivian Ellis); *Teardrops from her Eyes*; *She's Such a Comfort* (Arthur Schwartz); *Finale*—New Mayfair Orchestra   HMV C 1791
NB: Only Novello credited on record label.

MURDER IN MAYFAIR, *play 1934*

Two scenes from the play—Ivor Novello and Edna Best/Ivor Novello and Fay Compton   HMV C 2697

MISCELLANEOUS SONGS

We'll Remember (1940)—Olive Gilbert   HMV B 8981

Among the Hills of Wales (1950)—Denis Martin   PARLOPHONE R 3280

Pray For Me (last song)—Olive Gilbert   COLUMBIA DB 2964

Odile—De Groot and the Piccadilly Orchestra (1926)   HMV B 2389

Who Shall Say That Heaven (from *Cochran's 1930 Revue vocal gems*)—Light Opera Company   HMV C 1920

Clara Novello Davies (conducting)

The Ash Grove/The Bells of Aberdovey (in Welsh)—Royal Welsh Ladies Choir (c. 1928)   COLUMBIA 9437

Victory (music by Clara Novello Davies; words by John Morava; soloist Dunstan Hart)/*Kentucky Babe*(Adam Geibel)—Victory Singers, conductor Clara Novello Davies   HMV B 9082

GLAMOROUS NIGHT

Lyrics by Christopher Hassell

Far Away in Shanty Town—Elisabeth Welch
The Girl I Knew—Elisabeth Welch   HMV C 2741

Glamorous Night—Mary Ellis
When the Gypsy Played—Mary Ellis   HMV C 2742

Fold Your Wings—Mary Ellis and Trefor Jones
Shine Through My Dreams—Trefor Jones, Drury Lane Orchestra, conductor Charles Prentice   HMV C 2743
NB: Reissued on LP *Ivor Novello—The Great Shows*, double album   WORLD RECORDS SHB 23

Orchestral selection: *Her Majesty Militza*; *Shine Through My Dreams*; *Fold Your Wings*; *When the Gypsy Played*; *Far Away in Shanty Town*; *Glamorous Night*; *Royal Wedding*—Drury Lane Orchestra, conductor Charles Prentice   HMV C 2756

Glamorous Night vocal gems: *Shine Through My Dreams*; *Her Majesty Militza*; *Fold Your Wings*; *Glamorous Night*—Muriel Barron, Webster Booth, chorus and orchestra   COLUMBIA DX 691
NB: Muriel Barron played Militza on tour and at the London Coliseum in 1936.
NB: Stereo LP version (contains music not recorded by original cast)—BBC Concert Orchestra, conductor Marcus Dods, with Rae Woodland, Robert Thomas and Monica Sinclair   COLUMBIA TWO 243

NB: See also **COLLECTIONS**.

CARELESS RAPTURE

Lyrics by Christopher Hassell

Love Made the Song—Sybil Crawley and Eric Starling
Music in May—Dorothy Dickson   HMV B 8495

Studio scene—Dorothy Dickson, Olive Gilbert and Ivor Novello
Why Is There Ever Goodbye—Olive Gilbert   HMV C 2858

The Bridge of Lovers (finale)—Olive Gilbert
The Miracle of Nichaow (Temple Ballet music)—Olive Gilbert, Drury Lane Theatre Orchestra, conductor Charles Prentice   HMV C 2862/3
NB: Reissued on LP *Ivor Novello—The Great Shows* double album   WORLD RECORD SHB 23

Orchestral selection: **Why Is There Ever Goodbye**; **Music in May**; **Rose Ballet**; **Wait for Me**; **Manchuko**; **Love Made the Song**; **Finale**—Drury Lane Theatre Orchestra, conductor Charles Prentice   HMV C 2860

NB: Stereo LP version (contains music not recorded by original cast)—BBC Concert Orchestra, conductor Marcus Dods, with Elaine Blighton, Ann Howard, Veronica Lucas, Leslie Fry and Jon Lawrenson   COLUMBIA TWO 260

CREST OF THE WAVE

Lyrics by Christopher Hassell

The Haven of Your Heart—Olive Gilbert
Rose of England—Edgar Elmes and chorus   HMV B 8624

If You Only Knew—Dorothy Dickson and chorus
Why Isn't It You—Dorothy Dickson and Walter Crisham   HMV B 8623
NB: Reissued on LP   WORLD RECORDS SH 216

Used to You—Dorothy Dickson and Ivor Novello   78rpm unpublished
NB: Issued on LP **40 Years of English Musical Comedy**   ROCOCO 4007

Rose of England (from **Ivor Novello**—vocal gems—see **COLLECTIONS**)—Olive Gilbert   HMV C 3521 or C 4080

Orchestral selection: **Rose of England**; **Mazurka**; **If You Only Knew**; **Clementina**; **The Haven of Your Heart**; **Why Isn't it You**; **Nautical Tango**; **If You Only Knew**—Drury Lane Theatre Orchestra, conductor Charles Prentice   HMV C 2921

THE DANCING YEARS

Lyrics by Christopher Hassell

I Can Give You the Starlight—Mary Ellis
Waltz of my Heart—Mary Ellis   HMV B 8890

My Dearest Dear—Mary Ellis and Ivor Novello
My Life Belongs to You—Mary Ellis and Dunstan Hart   HMV B 8891

Primrose—Roma Beaumont
Wings of Sleep—Mary Ellis and Olive Gilbert   HMV B 8892

Leap Year Waltz—Drury Lane Theatre Orchestra, conductor Charles Prentice
Three ballet tunes—conductor Ivor Novello   HMV B 8897
NB: Reissued on LP **Ivor Novello—The Great Shows**, double album   WORLD RECORDS SHB 23

Orchestral selection: **Uniform**; **My Life Belongs to You**; **Waltz of My Heart**; **Primrose**; **The Wings of Sleep**; **I Can Give You the Starlight**; **My Dearest Dear**; **Finale**—Drury Lane Theatre Orchestra, conductor Charles Prentice   HMV C 3097

LP of 1968 London revival (contains music not recorded by original cast of 1939)—June Bronhill as Maria Ziegler   RCA SF/RD 7958 or INTS 1049

* **Memory is My Happiness**—Richard Tauber   PARLOPHONE RO 20523

* **Memory is My Happiness**—John McHugh   COLUMBIA FB 2964

* **When It's Spring in Vienna**—Ann Howard   COLUMBIA TWO 188
NB: This is a studio recording of **The Dancing Years**, with Anne Rogers as Maria.

My Dearest Dear—Vanessa Lee   HMV 7EG 8353

The Dancing Years (soundtrack of film version) contains **Waltz of My Heart**; **I Can Give You the Starlight**—Vanessa Lee (uncredited on record label)   HMV B 9966

Wings of Sleep—Mary Ellis, Olive Gilbert and Ivor Novello   Private recording
NB: Issued on LP **40 Years of English Musical Comedy**—recorded in performance   ROCOCO 4007

NB: See also **COLLECTIONS**.

* Supplementary numbers

ARC DE TRIOMPHE

Lyrics by Christopher Hassell

Man of My Heart—Mary Ellis
Waking or Sleeping—Mary Ellis

HMV B 9356

Easy to Live With—Mary Ellis and Peter Graves/*Dark Music* (lyric by Ivor Novello)—Elisabeth Welch—Phoenix Theatre
    Orchestra, conductor Tom Lewis
NB: Reissued on LP

HMV B 9357
WORLD RECORDS SH 216

France Will Rise Again (not original cast: from *Ivor Novello—Vocal Gems*—see **COLLECTIONS**)—Webster Booth and
    Helen Hill

HMV C 3522 or C 4081

Orchestral selection: *Paris Reminds Me of You*; *Dark Music*; *Easy to Live With*; *Shepherd's Song*; *Waking or
    Sleeping*; *Man of My Heart*; *France Will Rise Again*—Phoenix Theatre Orchestra, conductor Harry
    Acres

HMV C 3377

PERCHANCE TO DREAM

Lyrics by Ivor Novello

Curtsy to the King—Roma Beaumont, dialogue with Ivor Novello
A Woman's Heart—Muriel Barron, dialogue with Ivor Novello (piano)

DECCA F 8532

Love Is My Reason—Muriel Barron, dialogue with Ivor Novello
This Is My Wedding Day—Muriel Barron

DECCA F 8531

Highwayman Love—Olive Gilbert and chorus
We'll Gather Lilacs—Muriel Barron and Olive Gilbert
NB: Reissued on LP
NB: Stereo LP version (contains music not recorded by original cast)—BBC Concert Orchestra, conductor Marcus Dods, with Elisabeth
    Robinson, Ann Howard, Patricia Lambert and Robert Bowman

DECCA K 1132
DECCA LF 1309 or ACE OF CLUBS ACL 1112
COLUMBIA TWO 250

We'll Gather Lilacs—Vanessa Lee

HMV 7EG 8353

We'll Gather Lilacs—Olive Gilbert

COLUMBIA DB 2964

Orchestral selection: *Love Is My Reason*; *When the Gentlemen Get Together*; *Highwayman Love*; *We'll Gather
    Lilacs*; *A Woman's Heart*; *The Glo Glo*; *My Wedding Day*; *Curtsy to the King*; *The Meeting*—Harry Acres and his
    Orchestra

DECCA K 1133

NB: See also **COLLECTIONS**.

KING'S RHAPSODY

Lyrics by Christopher Hassell

Someday My Heart Will Awake—Vanessa Lee
Take Your Girl—Olive Gilbert and chorus
Fly Home Little Heart—Olive Gilbert
The Mayor of Perpignan—Phyllis Dare
The Gates of Paradise—Vanessa Lee, Olive Gilbert and Denis Martin

HMV C 3916

Mountain Dove; *If This Were Love*—Vanessa Lee
The Violin Began to Play—Dennis Martin and Larry Mandon
The Violin Began to Play—Vanessa Lee

HMV C 3917

Someday My Heart Will Awake—Vanessa Lee
Coronation scene and Finale—Olive Gilbert, Vanessa Lee and chorus

HMV C 3918

The Gates of Paradise—Denis Martin, Olive Gilbert and Vanessa Lee
Muranian Rhapsody (ballet)—Harry Acres and his Orchestra, narrator Ivor Novello HMV C 3977/8
NB: Reissued on LP *Ivor Novello—The Great Shows*, double album WORLD RECORDS SHB 23
NB: Stereo LP version (contains music not recorded by original cast)—BBC Concert Orchestra, conductor Vilem Tausky, with Cynthia Glover, Patricia Kern, Marjorie Westbury and Robert Bowman COLUMBIA TWO 270

Orchestral selection: *Take Your Girl*; *The Gates of Paradise*; *Mountain Dove*; *If This Were Love*; *Someday My Heart Will Awake*; *The Mayor of Perpignan*; *The Night You Were Mine* (not in vocal score); *Mother of Heaven*; *Someday My Heart Will Awake*—London Theatre Orchestra, conductor Roy Robertson DECCA F 9278

Soundtrack of *King's Rhapsody* film version:
Main title—orchestra
A Violin Began to Play—Patrice Wymore and Edmund Hockridge
The Years Together—Anna Neagle
If This Were Love—Patrice Wymore and Edmund Hockridge
Someday My Heart Will Awake—Patrice Wymore PARLOPHONE R 4079/80 or GEP 8553
NB: See also **COLLECTIONS**.

GAY'S THE WORD

Lyrics by Alan Melville

Bees are Buzzin'—Cicely Courtneidge
Gaiety Glad—Cicely Courtneidge and chorus
It's Bound to be Right on the Night—Cicely Courtneidge and chorus COLUMBIA DB 2805

If Only He'd Looked My Way—Cicely Courtneidge
Vitality—Cicely Courtneidge and chorus COLUMBIA DB 2806

Finder Please Return—Lizbeth Webb
On Such a Night as This—Lizbeth Webb and chorus COLUMBIA DB 2807

A Matter of Minutes—Thorley Walters
Sweet Thames; *Guards on Parade*; *Ruritania*—Lizbeth Webb, Cicely Courtneidge and male chorus
COLUMBIA DB 2808
NB: Reissued on LP—orchestra conducted by Bob Probst WORLD RECORDS SH 216

Finder Please Return/On Such a Night as This—Vanessa Lee HMV B 10032

Finder Please Return/If Only She'd Looked My Way—Denis Martin PARLOPHONE R 3360

Orchestral selection: *Bees Are Buzzin'*; *If Only She'd Looked My Way*; *A Matter of Minutes*; *Finder Please Return*; *Gaiety Glad*; *On Such a Night as This*; *Vitality*—The Melachrino Orchestra, conductor George Melachrino conductor George Melachrino HMV C 4079

VALLEY OF SONG

Music edited by Ronald Hanmer
Lyrics by Christopher Hassell

Rainbow in the Fountain (featured by June Bronhill in the 1968 revival of *The Dancing Years*, Saville Theatre)—June Bronhill RCA SF/RD 7958 or INTS 1049

COLLECTIONS

My Earlier Songs—by Ivor Novello HMV C 2965
Spoken introduction—Ivor Novello
Keep The Home Fires Burning—Edgar Elmes
The Little Damosel (lyric by Frederick E. Weatherly)—Olive Groves

Bless You—Olive Gilbert
And Her Mother Came Too (from *A to Z*)—Patrick Waddington
Dream Boat (from *See-Saw*)—Olive Groves, Olive Gilbert, Edgar Elmes
Land of Might-Have-Been (lyric by Edward Marsh, featured in *Our Nell*)—Olive Groves, Olive Gilbert
Same Old Moon (from *Puppets*)—Olive Groves
Night May Have Its Sadness (from *A to Z*)—Patrick Waddington

Ivor Novello Vocal Gems   HMV C 3521/2 or C 4080/1
Soloists with orchestra, conductor Harry Acres
Keep The Home Fires Burning—orchestra
Bless You—Olive Gilbert
Every Little Girl (from *Theodore and Co.*)—Peter Graves
Didn't Know the Way To (from *Arlette*)—orchestra
And Her Mother Came Too (from *A to Z*)—Peter Graves
Thoughts of You—Olive Gilbert
Glamorous Night—Helen Hill
Shine Through My Dreams—Webster Booth
Rose of England—Olive Gilbert
Waltz of My Heart—Helen Hill
My Live Belongs to You—Webster Booth
France Will Rise Again (from *Arc de Triomphe*)—Helen Hill and Webster Booth
April's Lady (from *Puppets*)—orchestra
I Can Give You the Starlight—Helen Hill
Love is My Reason—Webster Booth
We'll Gather Lilacs—Olive Gilbert

Ivor Novello—His Greatest Songs   HMV CLP 1258 mono or CSD 1263 stereo
Soloists, chorus (The Williams Singers), Michael Collins Orchestra
Glamorous Night—Vanessa Lee
Fold Your Wings—Julie Bryan and Ivor Immanuel
Someday My Heart Will Awake—Williams Singers
We'll Gather Lilacs—Marion Grimaldi and Williams Singers
I Can Give You the Starlight—Vanessa Lee
Rose of England—Ivor Immanuel and Williams Singers
Waltz of My Heart—Vanessa Lee
Love Is My Reason—Julie Bryan and Ivor Immanuel
Shine Through My Dreams—Marion Grimaldi and Williams Singers
Music in May—Williams Singers
Fly Home Little Heart—Vanessa Lee
My Dearest Dear—Ivor Novello, Julie Bryan and Ivor Immanuel

Ivor Novello Highlights   WORLD RECORD CLUB R 17 and SC 23
Coward and Novello   MUSIC FOR PLEASURE 1036
Orchestra conducted by John Gregory
Love Is My Reason—Vanessa Lee and Bruce Trent
I Can Give You the Starlight—Vanessa Lee
Rose of England—Bruce Trent
Glamorous Night—Vanessa Lee
Shine Through My Dreams—Bruce Trent
Someday My Heart Will Awake—Vanessa Lee
We'll Gather Lilacs—Vanessa Lee and Bruce Trent
My Life Belongs to You (W.R.C. pressings only)—Bruce Trent

Ivor Novello—The Great Shows, double album   WORLD RECORDS SHB 23
Original cast recordings from *Glamorous Night, Careless Rapture, The Dancing Years* and *King's Rhapsody*.

Ivor Novello   WORLD RECORDS SH 216
Original cast recordings from *Gay's The Word, Arc de Triomphe* and *Crest of the Wave*.

INDEX

Photographic Credits

Photo Anderson, Rome, 55 (above)

Sir Felix Aylmer, 13 (left), 108 (right)

Dorothy Batley, 118 (below), 126 (left), 126 (right), 178 (above)

British Library, 26, 29, 30

British Library Newspaper Library, 238 (left), 238 (right), 239

British Film Institute, 11 (right), 48, 49, 52 (below), 55 (below), 66 (The Rank Organisation Ltd), 68 (above), 68 (below) (The Rank Organisation Ltd), 69 (The Rank Organisation Ltd), 70 (above) (The Rank Organisation Ltd), 73 (The Rank Organisation Ltd), 74 (The Rank Organisation Ltd), 75 (The Rank Organisation Ltd), 76 (right) (The Rank Organisation Ltd), 77 (The Rank Organisation Ltd), 78 (The Rank Organisation Ltd), 79 (The Rank Organisation Ltd), 80 (above) (The Rank Organisation Ltd), 80 (below) (The Rank Organisation Ltd), 90 (below) (The Rank Organisation Ltd), 93 (The Rank Organisation Ltd), 94 (The Rank Organisation Ltd), 97 (above) (The Rank Organisation Ltd), 97 (below) (The Rank Organisation Ltd), 100 (Paramount Pictures), 101 (below) (The Rank Organisation Ltd), 102 (The Rank Organisation Ltd), 103 (The Rank Organisation Ltd), 104 (The Rank Organisation Ltd), 105 (EMI Film Distributors), 148 (Universal Films), 149 (above), 149 (below) (Universal Films), 230 (left) (EMI Film Distributors), 259 (British Lion Films Ltd)

Christopher Brunel, 51 (Photo George Maillard Kesslere, B.P.), 55 (above), 58 (right), 80 (centre) (The Rank Organisation Ltd), 81 (The Rank Organisation Ltd), 83 (below) (The Rank Organisation Ltd), 85 (The Rank Organisation)

Camera Press Ltd, 21 (centre)

John Counsell, 182, 183 (above)

Zena Dare, 10, 164 (left), 166 (above), 172, 173 (right), 183 (below), 206 (below), 246 (above), 246 (below), 247 (above)

Gordon Duttson, 9, 15 (left), 17 (left), 19 (left), 19 (right), 21 (left), 221 (above), 230 (right), 240 (left), 241, 244 (below), 260 (above), 261, 263

Mary Ellis, 7, 189, 190–191, 191 (above), 192, 193, 195 (above), 196, 197 (above), 197 (below), 198–199, 200, 201 (above), 201 (below), 202 (above), 202 (below), 224, 229, 232, 233 (left), 233 (right), 234 (above), 235 (above), 237

EMI Records, 250, 256 (Photograph Angus McBean, Courtesy Harvard Theatre Collection), 257 (Photograph Angus McBean, Courtesy Harvard Theatre Collection), 258 (Photograph Angus McBean, Courtesy Harvard Theatre Collection)

Olive Gilbert, 164 (right)

Peter Graves, 212 (Photograph Angus McBean, Courtesy Harvard Theatre Collection)

Mander and Mitchenson Theatre Collection, 11 (left), 15 (right), 18 (left), 24, 25, 31, 32, 34, 35, 37, 38 (above), 39, 40, 41 (left), 41 (right), 43, 44, 45, 47, 50, 58 (left), 61 (below), 64 (United Artists), 65 (below), 70 (below right) (The Rank Organisation Ltd), 72, 82, 83 (above), 84 (above) (The Rank Organisation Ltd), 88–89, 108 (left), 110, 111, 112 (left), 112 (right), 116, 118 (above), 119 (below), 124, 127 (below), 129, 131, 132 (left), 132 (right), 133, 134 (above), 134 (below), 140 (left), 140 (right), 152, 153, 155 (above), 155 (below), 156, 165, 167 (left), 167 (right), 168 (Photo Anthony Buckley Ltd), 170 (right), 174, 176–177, 179 (above), 181, 184–185, 194, 203, 208, 222–223, 231, 255 (below), 262, 264

Phyllis Monkman, 169 (above), 169 (below), 260 (below)

The New York Public Library, 146, 147

Anne Pinder, 245, 251

Paul Popper Ltd, 18 (right)

Mabel Poulton, 84 (below) (The Rank Organisation Ltd), 90 (above) (The Rank Organisation Ltd), 91 (The Rank Organisation Ltd), 92 (The Rank Organisation Ltd)

Winifred Newman-Bruce, 249, 252

Radio Times Hulton Picture Library, 23, 60 (above), 86 (above), 107, 125, 128, 139 (above), 139 (below), 159, 160 (below), 161 (left), 161 (right), 187, 226, 242 (right), 243 (below), 244 (above)

Barry Sinclair, verso of title page, 33, 36, 42, 247 (below), 254, 255 (above)

Syndication International, 236

Theatre Museum of the Victoria and Albert Museum, endpapers, 13 (left), 13 (right), 17 (right) (Photo Photopress), 21 (right), 28, 38 (below), 52 (above), 53, 54, 56, 57 (above), 57 (below), 59, 60 (below), 61 (above), 62 (United Artists), 63 (United Artists), 65 (above) (United Artists), 67 (The Rank Organisation Ltd), 70 (below left) (The Rank Organisation Ltd), 71 (The Rank Organisation), 76 (left) (The Rank Organisation Ltd), 86 (below) (Photo Rolf Mahier, Berlin), 87 (The Rank Organisation Ltd), 95 (above) (The Rank Organisation Ltd), 95 (below) (The Rank Organisation Ltd), 96 (above) (The Rank Organisation Ltd), 96 (below) (The Rank Organisation Ltd), 98 (The Rank Organisation Ltd), 101 (above), 108 (right), 109, 114, 115, 117, 119 (above), 120, 122 (left), 122 (right), 123, 127 (above), 135, 136 (above) (Courtesy *Punch*), 136 (below left), 136 (below right), 137, 138 (above), 138 (below), 141, 142, 143, 145 (below), 150, 151 (above), 151 (below), 154, 157, 158, 160 (above), 163, 166 (below), 170 (left), 173 (left), 175 (left) (Courtesy *The Sketch*), 175 (right) (Courtesy *The Tatler*), 178 (below), 179 (below), 180 (left) (Photograph Angus McBean, Courtesy Harvard Theatre Collection), 180 (right) (Photograph Angus McBean, Courtesy Harvard Theatre Collection), 188, 204, 205, 206 (above), 207 (above), 207 (below), 210–211, 213, 214, 215 (above), 215 (centre), 215 (below), 216–217, 218 (above) (Photograph Angus McBean, Courtesy Harvard Theatre Collection), 218 (below), 219 (above) (Courtesy *Punch*), 220 (left), 220 (right) (Photograph Angus McBean, Courtesy Harvard Theatre Collection), 221 (below), 222 (left), 227 (Courtesy *The Bystander*), 234–235 (Photograph John Vickers), 240 (right), 242 (left) (Photo Cecil Beaton), 243 (above), 248 (Courtesy *The Tatler*), 253

Paul Tanqueray, frontispiece

United Press International, 144, 219 (below)

Sandy Wilson, 145 (above), 162 (above), 162 (below)

First night of " Symphony in

Frances Doble
? (Frank Lewis) - ?
Anthony Lindsay - Hogg

Gertrude Jennings
Bobbie Andrews

Mary Whitty

Leslie Henson
Benita Hume

Anthony Hankey.